职业院校专业课程改革系列教材

U0743853

外贸制单

WAIMAO ZHIDAN

主　编◎吴燕萍　张建红
　　　　徐　燕
副主编◎李　倩　于银萍
　　　　陈秋霞

浙江工商大学出版社
ZHEJIANG GONGSHANG UNIVERSITY PRESS
·杭州·

图书在版编目(CIP)数据

外贸制单 / 吴燕萍,张建红,徐燕主编. —杭州:浙江工
商大学出版社,2020.11
ISBN 978-7-5178-4133-3

Ⅰ. ①外… Ⅱ. ①吴… ②张… ③徐… Ⅲ. ①对外贸易—
原始凭证—高等职业教育—教材 Ⅳ. ①F740.44

中国版本图书馆 CIP 数据核字(2020)第190736号

外贸制单
WAIMAO ZHIDAN
主编 吴燕萍　张建红　徐　燕

责任编辑 柳　河
封面设计 雪　青
责任印制 包建辉
出版发行 浙江工商大学出版社
　　　　　　(杭州市教工路198号　邮政编码310012)
　　　　　　(E-mail:zjgsupress@163.com)
　　　　　　(网址:http://www.zjgsupress.com)
　　　　　　电话:0571-89995993,89991806(传真)
排　版 杭州朝曦图文设计有限公司
印　刷 浙江全能工艺美术印刷有限公司
开　本 880mm×1230mm　1/16
印　张 14.5
字　数 373千
版印次 2020年11月第1版　2020年11月第1次印刷
书　号 ISBN 978-7-5178-4133-3
定　价 72.00元

编 委 会

陈秋霞　戴　飞　季国平　李　倩
吴燕萍　于银萍　徐　燕　张建红　徐晓燕
（按姓氏首字母排列）

总顾问：陆梦青　郑可立

（教材编写组合影）

主编简介

吴燕萍,女,获柯桥区教坛新秀、柯桥区学科带头人、柯桥区学科三星级教师、最美教学能手等称号。多篇论文在国家级、省级期刊上发表,获浙江省教师教学能力大赛二等奖,绍兴市教师教学能力大赛一等奖。辅导学生参加全国跨境电商比赛获团体一等奖。

张建红,女,多次参加各级教师比赛获奖,多篇论文在全国期刊上发表,2014年辅导学生参加全国技能大赛获省一等奖、全国三等奖,多次被评为"局级先进工作者""区优秀青年教师""局级优秀共产党员"。

徐燕,女,外贸专业教师,从教十三年,任外贸高三班专业课高考课程十年,主要为外贸业务协调、外贸商函、外贸制单等。曾编著由安徽师范大学出版社出版的《外贸高职考淘宝攻略同步检测双卷训练》。

前　言

一、开设本课程的目标

中职外贸专业学生高考除了语文和数学两门文化课之外,还有理论专业高考和技能专业高考。外贸技能高考采用的是在一小时内闭卷手工填制合同和国际贸易单据的形式,满分为120分。考试分值为出口合同填制40分,信用证分析及国际贸易单证制作80分。填制合同、填制信用证分析表以及制作国际贸易单证旨在考查学生掌握订立合同、分析信用证、制作国际贸易单据等基本技能。

对于外贸高考班,本校采用的是各外贸专业教师轮流任课的制度,其优势在于每位外贸教师都可以得到同等的高考班任教历练,从而提升其专业水平。同时,轮流任课对外贸教师来说是一种减负。当然,这也有一些弊端:一方面,外贸制单教师的教学经验不能很好地积累并得到充分应用,而且,每一位外贸技能任课教师都要大量地查找可用的资料,同时还要对每一张单据做一些简单的知识点梳理和归纳;另一方面,从近几年的技能高考情况看,外贸技能高考题目的深度和广度都有所提高,但每一位教师的力量和智慧都是有限的,无法最大化地发挥每位教师手头上的资源。

因此,本次校本教材开发,一方面是为了节约每一位任教外贸制单课教师的时间和精力,为教师减轻教学负担;另一方面,这样做可以精炼外贸制单知识点,提高学生的学习效率,更好地服务外贸专业学生,让他们以更好的姿态迎接外贸技能高考。

二、教材设计基本思路

外贸技能高考主要涉及六张单据,即:合同、信用证分析表、商业发票、装箱单、汇票及订舱委托书。因此,外贸技能高考校本教材设计的基本思路如下:

首先,确定本教材的大致内容,为本校本教材列提纲(目录)。由于本校本教材目的明确,主要是针对外贸技能高考开发的,所以大致将教材分为五大块内容:外贸技能高考概述及考纲、外贸技能高考的六张单据解析及练习、综合练习、参考答案及附录。其中,重点在第二块内容。

其次,确定每张单据内容,并根据学生的认知规律和教学规律,统一设置标准模板。各编写教师根据模板要求,梳理、归纳、列举单据知识点,并设计配套练习;确定每张单据内容,统一设置标准模板。每张单据主要通过以下几方面,让学生从了解到理解,再从理解到掌握。

1. 每张单据的意义。设计意图为一方面使学生理解缮制每一张不同单据的特殊意义,另一方面使学生在心理上对每一张单据引起重视。

2. 外贸实践中每类单据的多种格式。设计意图为拓展学生的视野。

3. 单据的概况。设计意图为使学生对每张单据的内容有大致的了解。

4. 单据内部知识点详解。设计意图为提升学生考试的应变能力。

5. 单据易错点集锦。设计意图为提醒学生在今后做题过程中要绕开或避免一些单据上的陷阱。

6. 专项单据的填制练习。设计意图为通过练习进一步巩固知识点，夯实基础。

7. 综合性单据练习。设计意图为通过高考仿真模拟练习，提高应试能力。

再次，教研组将每位教师上交的资料进行汇总，再将汇总好的整套单据资料发给每一位参编教师。在每一次教研会上，教研组依次对每张单据进行分析、纠错、改进，并由每位参编教师对所有单据知识点做进一步深度挖掘并加以补充。

最后，在本教材内容进行审核整理并装订成册。

三、同类教材的比较分析

市面上外贸制单的教材非常多，但是本校本教材与其他教材相比，有非常显著的优势。

本教材根据学生的认知规律和教学规律，结合外贸高职考的要求，有针对性地对外贸制单知识点进行梳理、归纳和总结，并结合练习加以巩固，从而通过学生的练习反馈掌握情况，查漏补缺。所以，本教材在设计上更合理，更符合学生的认知，更易于被学生接受，同时本教材在难度和深度上超过同类教材，是针对外贸高职技能考"量身打造"的，其应试性更强。

本书由吴燕萍设计全书结构、撰写提纲，并负责前言及合同的填制，陈秋霞负责信用证分析表的填制，张建红负责商业发票的填制，于银萍负责装箱单的填制，徐燕负责汇票的填制，李倩负责订舱委托书的填制。本书的出版得到了学校的大力支持，同时也得到了省特级教师陆梦青和宁波市名师郑可立极具价值的参考资料和意见。我们对他们提供的帮助表示感谢。我校外贸教研组的任课老师陈秋霞、李倩、吴燕萍、徐燕、于银萍、张建红(根据姓氏首字母排序，排名不分先后)为本书的编写投入了大量的精力，付出了辛勤的劳动，在此也对他们表示特别感谢!

由于编者水平有限，难免有疏漏之处，敬请读者惠予批评指正。

吴燕萍

2019 年 8 月 20 日

目录

CONTENTS

第一章 外贸技能高考概述及大纲

第一节 外贸技能高考概述

一、《外贸制单》课程地位

《外贸制单》是国际贸易专业的核心课程,也是一门动手操作的技能课程,它具有应用性、理论与实践联系密切的特点。在对外贸易中,正确制作单据是出口结汇顺利实现的一个关键,因此,外贸制单的重要性也就可见一斑。

外贸高考专业课总分300分,分两个模块进行考试:第一个模块是外贸技能,即《外贸制单》,占120分;第二个模块是外贸专业理论,分为《外贸业务协调》(100分)和《外贸商函》(80分),共180分。因此,从高考占分比重也可以看出《外贸制单》这门课的重要性。

二、外贸技能高考变化

1. 技能成绩分析

在2014年及之前的几年,学生技能高考分值差距不大,好的班级学生成绩基本上都处在110—120分,而从近几年的情况来看,成绩差距开始拉大。

2. 难度分析

技能高考考查范围和灵活度变得越来越大,对学生知识量储备的要求也越来越高,从格式的填写到对外贸实践操作的理解都从不同层次对学生的能力提出了更高要求。此外,特殊条款的设置更是拉开了学生成绩的差距。

3. 规范化分析

外贸实践的很多做法没有统一的章法,唯一可以作为标准的就是银行审单的要求,故在学生知识点的考查中,高职教师更注重单据的规范化。

因此,在这样的外贸高职考大背景下,唯有将外贸外延知识融合到《外贸制单》这门课中,加强对学生外贸制单的规范化要求,培养学生举一反三的能力,才能在外贸技能高考中拔得胜筹。

第二节　外贸技能高考考纲

一、考试形式

采用手工填制合同和国际贸易单据的形式,闭卷。

二、考试时间

60分钟。

三、分值分配

满分为120分。考试分值为出口合同填制40分,信用证分析及国际贸易单证制作80分。

四、考试题型

填制合同,填制信用证分析表以及制作国际贸易单证。

五、考试能力要求

掌握订立合同、分析信用证、制作国际贸易单证等基本技能。

六、参考教材

1.《外贸业务协调》(高等教育出版社,许宝良主编,2012年6月第1版)
2.《外贸商函》(高等教育出版社,许宝良主编,2012年12月第1版)
3.《外贸制单》(高等教育出版社,许宝良主编,2013年1月第1版)

第三节　考试内容及范围

•出口合同填制

一、填写合同的约首

1. 填写合同的名称、合同编号
2. 填写订约日期
3. 填写合同当事人的名称和地址

二、填写合同的基本条款

1. 填写出口商品名称及规格
2. 填写商品价格条款(货币符号、计价单位、成交金额、贸易术语)

3. 填写成交商品计量单位及成交总量

4. 填写商品成交金额及总金额（大、小写）

5. 填写商品包装方式及包装材料

6. 填写运输标志（唛头）

7. 填写出口装运条款

8. 填写保险条款

9. 填写支付条款

三、填写合同的约尾

1. 填写签约地点、生效时间

2. 双方当事人签字

●信用证分析及国际贸易单证制作

一、填制信用证分析表

1. 填写信用证基本信息

2. 填写信用证对运输的要求

3. 填写信用证付款信息

4. 填写信用证对单据的要求

5. 填写信用证中的其他相关交易信息

二、填制商业发票

1. 填写出票人

2. 填写出票日期

3. 填写发票抬头

4. 填写运输线路

5. 填写唛头

6. 填写货物描述

7. 填写货物的数量

8. 填写单价、总值

9. 签署

三、填制装箱单

1. 填写装箱单号码

2. 填写抬头

3. 填写唛头

4. 填写箱量

5. 填写货物描述

6. 填写毛重

7. 填写净重

8. 填写体积

9. 填写箱量大写数

10. 填写签单人

四、填制订舱委托书

1. 填写托运人

2. 填写收货人

3. 填写通知人

4. 填写起运港、目的港

5. 填写唛头

6. 填写货物描述

7. 填写包装件数

8. 填写毛重和总体积

9. 填写分批装运和转运

10. 填写预配箱量

五、填制汇票

1. 填写出票依据(开证行、信用证号码、信用证日期)

2. 填写汇票号码

3. 填写汇票金额(小写)

4. 填写出票地点及出票日期

5. 填写付款期限

6. 填写汇票金额(大写)

7. 填写收款人、付款人、出票人

(备注:根据信用证填制商业发票、装箱单、订舱委托书、汇票中的1—2张单据。)

第二章 外贸技能高考单据分析及练习

第一节 外贸合同的填制

一、国际贸易合同的概念及意义

国际贸易合同在国内又被称为外贸合同或进出口贸易合同,即营业地处于不同国家或地区的当事人就商品买卖所发生的权利和义务关系而达成的书面协议。国际贸易合同属于社会交往中比较正式的契约文体,具有准确性、直接性和法定效力性等特点。

国际贸易中,当一方的发盘为另一方有效接受时,双方的合同即告成立,双方交易磋商过程中的往来函电即可成为双方合同成立的书面证明。为了进一步明确双方关系,一般要签订书面合同或成交确认书,从而将双方的权利、义务及各项交易条件以书面形式确定下来。

二、国际贸易合同模板

SALES CONTRACT

TO:＿＿＿＿＿＿＿＿＿

S/C NO:＿＿＿＿＿＿＿＿＿

DATE:＿＿＿＿＿＿＿＿＿

We hereby confirm having sold to you the following goods on terms and conditions as stated below:

Commodity & Specifications	Quantity	Unit Price	Amount
Total:			
TOTAL CONTRACT VALUE:			

SHIPPING MARK：

PACKING：

PORT OF SHIPMENT：

PORT OF DESTINATION：

TIME OF SHIPMENT：

TRANSSHIPMENT：

PARTIAL SHIPMENT：

TERMS OF PAYMENT：

INSURANCE：

Signed by：

THE SELLER：   THE BUYER：

三、国际贸易合同条款概述

1. 约首包括名称、合同编号、签约日期、签约地点、双方名称、地址、联系电话。

2. 文本包括以下几个方面：

(1)交易商品名称。

(2)品质条款(确定品质的方法和标准、确认品质的时间和地点、品质公差条款等)。

(3)数量条款(确定的单位、交付约定数量的地点和时间、重量的计算、溢短装条款)。

(4)价格条款(价格术语、使用货币种、佣金、折扣等)。

(5)包装条款(内包装、外包装、填塞物、包装尺寸、重量、唛头等)。

(6)保险条款(投保人、险别、保险金额、理赔地点等)。

(7)交货条款(装运交货地点、时间、方式、装运通知等)。

(8)支付条款(支付时间、条件、币种、延期和拒付的规定)。

(9)检验条款(检验的地点、标准、机构等)。

(10)索赔条款(索赔期限、证明文件等)。

(11)仲裁条款(仲裁地点、适用仲裁程序规则、仲裁机构等)。

(12)不可抗力条款(不可抗力事故范围、通知的时间和方式、证明文件、报告、单据、负责条款等)。

(13)违约和取消合约条款(违约的处理、赔偿金额等)。

(14)适用法律。

(15)其他条款。

3. 约尾包括双方签字、生效日期。

四、合同详解之约首

1. 合同名称

合同的形式主要有合同(contract)、确认书(confirmation)、协议(agreement)、备忘录(memorandum)等。按合同制作人分类：卖方制作的，称为"销售合同"(Sales Contract)；买方制作的，称为"购货合同"(Purchase Contract)。按合同的内容繁简可分为销售合同(Sales Contract)和销售确认书(Sales Confirmation)。

2. 合同编号

给合同编号主要是为了方便管理与查找,各公司有各自的习惯,编法各不相同。

3. 签约日期及签约地点

根据《中华人民共和国合同法》,当事人采用合同书形式订立合同的,自双方当事人签字或者盖章时,合同成立;当事人采用信件、数据电文等形式订立合同的,可以在合同成立之前先签订确认书,签订确认书时,合同成立。

当事人采用数据电文形式订立合同的,收件人的主营业地为合同成立的地点;没有主营业地的,其经常居住地为合同成立的地点,但是如果当事人另有约定的,按照其约定。当事人采用合同书形式订立合同的,双方当事人签字或者盖章的地点为合同成立的地点。

4. 双方名称、地址、联系电话

名称、地址务必分行填写,地址应从小到大。如:

绍兴延安西路1882号绍兴大学186信箱(邮编:312000)。

Mailbox 186, 1882 West Yan'an Rd., Shaoxing University, Shaoxing 312000.

五、合同详解之文本

1. 唛头

(1)卖方缮制唛头

卖方自制、设计或由卖方决定按欧洲标准格式刷制。

该标准化运输标志包括:

①收货人或买方名称的英文缩写字母或简称;

②参考号,如运单号、订单号或发票号;

③目的地名称;

④货物件数。

(2)唛头的多种表达方式

①在信用证上给出 AS PER L/C;

②唛头(运输标志)由卖方(买方)决定/商定/选择或唛头的选择权归卖方(买方)

AT THE SELLER'S/BUYER'S OPTION OR OPTION BY THE SELLER/BUYER;

③卖方应用不褪色的油墨在每个包装上印上包装编号、毛重、尺码以及"防潮"和"小心轻放"的字样

THE SELLER SHALL MARK EACH PACKAGE WITH FADELESS PAINT THE PACKAGE NUMBER, GROSS WEIGHT,MEASUREMENT AND THE WORDING:"KEEP AWAY FROM MOISTURE" AND "HANDLE WITH CARE";

④无唛头 N/M;

⑤唛头包括买方缩写名称KU、销售合同号码、目的港和件号

INCLUDING KU,S/C NO.,PORT OF DESTINATION AND CARTON NO.。

2. 商品名称

按照有关的法律和惯例,交易标的物的描述是构成商品说明的一个主要组成部分,是买卖双方交换货物的一项基本依据。它关系到买卖双方的权利和义务。商品名称是指为了区别于其他商品而使用的商品

的称呼。商品名称可分为通用名称和特定名称。命名的方式可以从商品功能、商品形象、商品产地、商品的象征意义等方面着手,一般以文字形式表示。如:

65%棉35%人造丝女士外套。

65 PCT COTTON 35 PCT RAYON LADIES' COATS.

3. 品质条款

(1)品质的表达

看货成交 spot bargain

看样成交 sale by sample 或 sth as per the sample

凭规格买卖 sale by specification

凭标准买卖 sale by standard

凭商标或品牌买卖 sale by mark or brand

凭等级买卖 sale by grade

凭产地名称买卖 sale by name of origin

凭说明书和图样买卖 sale by description and illustration

(2)规格

①颜色

紫色 Purple　银色 Silver　绿色 Green　红色 Red　黄色 Yellow　蓝色 Blue

粉红 Pink　褐色 Brown　橙色 Orange　灰色 Gray　浅蓝色 Light blue　暗红色 Dark red

②尺码

长 Length　宽 Width　高 Height　厚 Thickness　深 Depth

③重量

毛重 Gross weight　净重 Net weight

4. 数量条款

(1)常用计量单位

米 Meter　匹 Bolt　公吨 Metric ton　立方英尺 Cubic foot　立方米 Cubic meter

盎司 Ounce　双 Pair　打 Dozen　件 Piece　英寸 Inch　套 Set　码 Yard　组/套 Series

(2)溢短装条款表达

①数量和金额允许5%的上下浮动。

5% MORE OR LESS IN QUANTITY AND AMOUNT IS ALLOWED/ACCEPTABLE/PERMITTED.

②2.25公吨,数量允许10%上下浮动。

25MTS, 10% MORE OR LESS ALLOWED.

③1000公吨,可以增减50公吨。

1,000 METRIC TONS WITH 50 METRIC TONS MORE OR LESS.

④1000公吨,由买方决定增减5%,增减部分的货物按装货时的市场价格计算。

1,000 METRIC TONS,5% MORE OR LESS AT BUYER'S OPTION WITH MORE OR LESS PORTION PRICED AT THE MARKET PRICE AT THE TIME OF SHIPMENT.

5. 价格条款

（1）价格术语表达（包括佣金、折扣等）

FOB + 装运港　　　　　　　　FCA + 出口地

CFR/CIF + 目的港　　　　　　CPT/CIP + 目的地

如果价格中含折扣或佣金，在价格术语中则要表示出来。

如：FOB上海，包含5%的佣金，则可以表示为FOBC5或FOBC5%.

（2）货币单位大小写

货币	缩写	大写
美元	USD	U.S. Dollars
港币	HKD	Hong Kong Dollars
英镑"镑（pound sterling）"	GBP	pounds sterling "镑"以下单位为"便士（penny）" 注意：单数penny，复数pence
举例：GBP1,234,567.89 Say pounds sterling one million two hundred thirty-four thousand five hundred sixty-seven and pence eighty-nine		
欧元	EUR	Euro(s)
加元	CAD	Canadian Dollars
澳元	AUD	Australian Dollars
日元	JPY	Japanese Yen

6. 包装条款

包装条款译法归纳

a. ...be packed in... 用……包装

The goods are to be packed in cartons.货物用纸箱包装。

b. be packed in... of...net each用……包装，每件净重……

Packed in cartons of about 50 kgs net each.

用纸箱包装，每箱净重约50千克。

c. ...be packed in..., each containing... 用……包装，每件内装……

Packed in cartons, each containing 4 boxes of 5 kgs each.

用纸箱包装，每箱4盒，每盒约5公斤。

d. ...be packed in..., lined with... 用……包装，内衬……

Packed in cartons, lined with waterproof paper.

用纸箱包装，内衬防水纸。

e. ...be packed...to..., ...to... 将若干……装入……，若干……装入……

Socks are packed 12 pairs to a box and 12 boxes to a carton.

袜子12双装入一个盒子，12盒装入一个纸箱。

【注意】

如果把数量12 pairs 放在句首，则句中第一个介词to应变为in。

如：12 pairs of socks are packed in a box...

7. 保险条款

保险条款译法归纳

a. INSURANCE：TO BE EFFECTED／COVERED（BY＋某人）（ON＋某物）（FOR＋金额）（AGAINST/COVERING＋险别）（WITH W/W CLAUSE）（AS PER＋保险条款）（UP TO＋地点）。

保险：（由某人）（为某物）（根据……条款）（按……金额）投保（……险别）（直至某地）。

b.（SUBJECT TO/OR）AS PER OMCC OF PICC（01/01/1981）

按中国人民保险公司1981年1月1日的海运货物保险条款办理

c. 额外保险费用由买方承担

THE EXTRA PREMIUM SHOULD BE FOR THE BUYER'S ACCOUNT

d. 由某人承担

AT THE BUYER'S EXPENSES／BORNE BY THE BUYER／COVERED BY THE BUYER

e. 如有索赔,在目的地用汇票货币支付。

CLAIMS, IF ANY, PAYABLE AT THE DESTINATION IN THE CURRENCY OF THE DRAFT.

f. 按110%的发票金额,三种表达:

FOR 110% OF THE INVOICE VALUE

FOR 10% ABOVE THE INVOICE VALUE

FOR THE INVOICE VALUE PLUS 10%

如:由卖方承担,通过中国人民保险公司按照发票金额的110%投保一切险及战争险,若有索赔,则在目的港以汇票货币赔付。

TO BE COVERED BY THE SELLER THROUGH PICC FOR 110% OF THE INVOICE VALUE AGAINST ALL RISKS AND WAR RISK, CLAIMS, IF ANY, PAYABLE AT THE DESTINATION IN THE CURRENCY OF THE DRAFT.

8. 交货条款

交货条款译法归纳

a. 最迟,不迟于:NOT LATER THAN

b. 允许分批装运和转运:TRANSSHIPMENT AND PARTIAL SHIPMENT ALLOWED

c. 在……月底:AT THE END OF…

d. 在……之前:BEFORE…

e. 收到信用证后……内完成:WITHIN…DAYS AFTER RECEIPT OF THE L/C

f. 在……日或之前:ON OR BEFORE…

g. 在……期间:DURING…

h. 每月平均装运:IN…EQUAL MONTHLY SHIPMENTS

i. 只允许在香港中转:TRANSSHIPMENT ALLOWED AND EFFECTED VIA HONGKONG ONLY

9. 支付条款

支付条款译法归纳

a. 信用证兑付方式：即期付款 SIGHT PAYMENT、延期付款 DEFERRED PAYMENT、承兑 ACCEPTANCE、议付 NEGOTIATION。

b. 信用证种类：跟单信用证（Documentary L/C）、光票信用证（Clean L/C）、不可撤销信用证（Irrevocable L/C）、可撤销信用证（Revocable L/C）、保兑信用证（Confirmed L/C）、不保兑信用证（Unconfirmed L/C）、即期付款信用证（Sight Payment L/C）、延期付款信用证（Deferred Payment L/C）、承兑信用证（Acceptance L/C）、议付信用证（Negotiation L/C）、即期信用证（Sight L/C）、远期信用证（Usance L/C）、假远期信用证（Usance L/C Payable at sight）、可转让信用证（Transferable Credit）、不可转让信用证（Non-transferable Credit）、循环信用证（Revolving Credit）、对开信用证（Reciprocal Credit）、对背信用证（Back to Back Credit）。

c. 装船日后15天内在议付有效：VALID FOR NEGOTIATION IN CHINA UNTIL THE 15TH DAY(WITHIN 15 DAYS) AFTER SHIPMENT

d. 在装运月前30天到达卖方：30 DAYS BEFORE THE MONTH OF SHIPMENT

e. 以卖方为受益人：IN FAVOR OF THE SELLER

f. 100%保兑不可撤销即期信用证：BY 100% IRREVOCABLE L/C TO BE AVAILABLE BY SIGHT DRAFT

g. 所有中国以外的银行费用由付款人承担：ALL BANKING CHARGES OUTSIDE CHINA ARE FOR ACCOUNT OF THE DRAWEE

h. 无追索权：WITHOUT RECOURSE

i. 在开证行指定的付款行：IN PAYING BANK DESIGNATED BY ISSUING BANK

j. 凭海运提单传真件：AGAINST THE FAX OF B/L

k. 支付余款：PAY THE BALANCE

例1：100%不可撤销即期信用证由买方开立并在2014年7月25日之前到达卖方，该信用证在装运日期后15天内在中国议付有效。如信用证迟到，卖方对迟延装运不承担任何责任，卖方有权撤销本合同和/或提出损害赔偿。

BY 100% IRREVOCABLE SIGHT LETTER OF CREDIT TO BE OPENED BY THE BUYER IN TIME TO REACH THE SELLER BEFORE JULY 25, 2014 AND TO BE AVAILABLE FOR NEGOTIATION IN CHINA UNTIL THE 15TH DAY AFTER THE DATE OF SHIPMENT. IN CASE OF LATE ARRIVAL OF THE L/C, THE SELLER SHALL NOT BE LIABLE FOR ANY DELAY IN SHIPMENT AND HAVE THE RIGHT TO RESCIND THE CONTRACT.

例2：不可撤销可转让信用证，在开证行指定的付款行处30天迟期付款。

TO BE EFFECTED BY AN IRREVOCABLE TRANSFERABLE L/C AVAILABLE BY DEFERRED PAYMENT AT 30 DAYS' SIGHT IN PAYING BANK DESIGNATED BY ISSUING BANK.

例3：30%前T/T，70%凭保兑的不可撤销即期信用证支付，在装运日期前的30天内到达卖方有效。

30% BY T/T IN ADVANCE, 70% BY CONFIRMED IRREVOCABLE SIGHT L/C TO REACH THE SELLER 30 DAYS BEFORE THE DATE OF SHIPMENT.

六、合同易错点集锦

1. 公司地址应在其名称下换行书写。

如：ABC CO.

123 ZHONGHUA ROAD，KEQIAO DISTRICT，SHAOXING CITY，ZHEJIANG，CHINA

2. 格式若有变化，则灵活应用。

如：有 MEN'S SUIT 两种，一种为棕色，一种为蓝色，货描处如何填写？在只给出两个空格的情况下，品名和规格要并到一起填写如下。

Commodity & Specifications	Quantity	Unit Price	Amount
MEN'S SUIT:BROWN			
MEN'S SUIT:BLUE			
TOTAL CONTRACT VALUE:			

3. 填空式的合同填写难度大，固定词组搭配要记牢。

如：(1) 由……承担：for one's account = at one's expenses = be borne by sb

(2) 定金与订金分清楚：

定金(down payment)是一种重要的担保方式，通常定金被视为解约金，即交付定金的一方当事人不履行约定的义务时，无权要求返还定金。

订金(deposit)有时也被称为认购金、诚意金，如果买方决定不购买，卖方应该将认购金退还。

4. 金额大小写要牢记，单复数要区分。

5. 单词拼错：大写金额(FORTY)、货币单位大小写、月份缩写(日期10以内，0补足，如：2018年10月1日，则应书写为OCT.01,2018或OCT.1st,2018)。

6. 合同条款翻译：包装条款、装运条款(每月分两批装等)、支付条款。

7. 计量单位用错：纸盒(BOX)。

8. 港口名称尽量具体化，后加国别。

9. 含佣金或折扣时，术语后加佣金率或折扣率再加地名，需要记清不同贸易术语后面地名的书写要求。如：FOB成交，从上海到纽约，含5%折扣，应表示为FOBC5% SHANGHAI。此处5%或5都可以，折扣则用D表示。

10. 计量单位(DOZEN用单数)。

11. 填制时，英文全部大写。

12. 买卖双方盖章签字，只要填买卖双方的名称，地址不要写，再对应打上法人代表签字。

13. 如果资料中单价没有计量单位(如：USD2.15)，则应自己加上。

规格	成交数量	单价
GBW32	2,000PCS	USD2.15/PC

七、专项练习

练习一

请根据下列资料填写销售合同。

我国 NANTONG VICTORY TRADING CO.,LTD.（地址：NO.234,GONGNONG ROAD,NANTONG,CHINA）与新加坡 THE GOLDEN LION TRADING CO.,LTD.（NO.250,QUEEN ROAD,SINGAPORE）互相建立贸易关系。新加坡方对南通的 LOTUS 牌 TICKING 系列产品很感兴趣。

货号	数量	包装方式	CIFC3 单价
GWAS01	1000 箱	24 件/纸箱	美元 88.00/件
GWAS02	800 箱	16 件/纸箱	美元 92.50/件

经过双方磋商,达成协议如下：

装运：2018 年 12 月,卖方须将货物运至所在地的集装箱堆场,交给多式联运的经营人,由其按通常方式、惯常路线运至目的地。

付款：即期信用证,2018 年 10 月中旬前开到。

保险：加成 10% 投保协会货物 A 险。

合同号码：NTSL4445。

日期：2018 年 9 月 23 日。

SALES CONTRACT

TO：_____　　　　　　　　　　　　　　S/C NO._____

　　　　　　　　　　　　　　　　　　　　　　　　　　DATE：_____

We hereby confirm having sold to you the following goods on terms and conditions as stated below：

Commodity & Specifications	Quantity	Unit Price	Amount
TOTAL：			
TOTAL CONTRACT VALUE：			

SHIPPING MARK：

PACKING：

SHIPMENT：

TERMS OF PAYMENT：

INSURANCE：

Signed by：

THE SELLER：　　　　　　　　　　　THE BUYER：

练习二

请根据下列资料填写销售合同。

2018年9月,加拿大某公司(CANADIAN K. & LIFDON DISTRIBUTORS RM.1008-1011,OFFICE TOWER, CONVENTION PLAZA,1 HARBOUR ROAD,VANCOUVER CANADA)与天津晨星有限公司(TIANJIN MORNING STAR CORPORATION, 16TH FLOOR, DRAGON MANSION, 1008 LIYANG ROAD, TIANJIN, CHINA)就排球(VOLLEYBALL)经过几个回合的交易磋商,达成如下交易条件:

规格	成交数量	单价
GBW32	2,000PCS	USD2.15
GBW322	2,000PCS	USD2.60
ERVS	3,000PCS	USD1.45

成交价格条件:CIF VANCOUVER

包装条件:每纸箱装50个,共140纸箱

装货/装运条件:2018年11月发运,自中国天津港经海运至加拿大温哥华港,允许分批和转船。

保险条件:由卖方按CIF成交金额的120%投保协会货物条款(A)和协会战争险。

付款条件:80%的发票金额凭即期不可撤销信用证结算,20%的发票金额采用电汇方式预付。

检验:由生产方出具质量检验证明。

唛头:在信用证中指出。

合同号:TJCHX050212

合同日期:2018年9月2日

SALES CONTRACT

TO:_____   S/C NO._____

                              DATE:_____

We hereby confirm having sold to you the following goods on terms and conditions as stated below:

Commodity & Specifications	Quantity	Unit Price	Amount
TOTAL:			

TOTAL CONTRACT VALUE:

SHIPPING MARK:

PACKING:

PORT OF SHIPMENT:

PORT OF DESTINATION:

TIME OF SHIPMENT：

TRANSSHIPMENT：

PARTIAL SHIPMENT：

TERMS OF PAYMENT：

INSURANCE：

INSPECTION：

Signed by：

THE SELLER：　　　　　　　　　　THE BUYER：

练习三

请根据下列资料填写销售合同。

合同号码：TJ101211

签订日期地点：2018年9月11日于天津

卖方：泰佛贸易有限公司（TIFERT TRADING CO.,LTD.）

买方：日本通用贸易公司（GENERAL TRADING COMPANY,JAPAN）

商品名称："鸽牌"印花细布（"DOVE" BRAND PRINTED SHIRTING）

规格：30s×36s 72×69 35/6"×42码

数量：67200码

单价：CIF大阪每码3.00日元

总值：210600.00日元

装运期：2018年12月4日前自中国港口至大阪，允许分批装运和转船。

付款条件：凭不可撤销即期信用证付款，于装运期前1个月开到卖方，并于上述装运期后15天内在中国议付有效。

保险：由卖方根据中国人民保险公司1981年1月1日中国保险条款按发票金额的110%投保一切和战争险。

SALES CONTRACT

TO：＿＿＿＿＿＿＿　　　　　　　　　　　　S/C NO.＿＿＿＿＿＿＿

DATE：＿＿＿＿＿＿＿

We hereby confirm having sold to you the following goods on terms and conditions as stated below：

Commodity & Specifications	Quantity	Unit Price	Amount
TOTAL：			
TOTAL CONTRACT VALUE：			

SHIPPING MARK:

PACKING:

PORT OF SHIPMENT:

PORT OF DESTINATION:

TIME OF SHIPMENT:

TRANSSHIPMENT:

PARTIAL SHIPMENT:

TERMS OF PAYMENT:

INSURANCE:

Signed by:

THE SELLER: THE BUYER:

练习四

请根据下列资料填写销售合同。

THE SELLER:BEIJING LIGHT INDUSTRIAL PRODUCTS IMP. & EXP. CORP.

THE BUYER:BOSTON TRADE CO.,LTD.

(1)PLEASE QUOTE YOUR LOWEST PRICE FOR 1000 DOZEN FOUNTAIN PENS MODEL NO. LC001 CFR BOSTON.

(2)AS REQUESTED,WE ARE MAKING YOU A FIRM OFFER AS FOLLOWS:

1000 DOZEN FOUNTAIN PENS,MODEL NO. LC001,PACKED IN BOXES OF ONE DOZEN EACH, AND 20 BOXES TO A CARTON,AT USD20 PER DOZEN CFR BOSTON FOR SHIPMENT DURING MARCH/APRIL 2009. PAYMENT IS TO BE MADE BY CONFIRMED,IRREVOCABLE L/C PAYABLE BY DRAFT AT SIGHT.

(3)WHILE WE THANK YOU FOR THE ABOVE OFFER,WE REGRET TO SAY THAT YOUR PRICE IS NOT TO BE ACCEPTABLE. THERE IS NO POSSIBILITY OF THIS DEAL UNLESS YOU REDUCE YOUR PRICE BY 5%.

(4)IN VIEW OF OUR LONG BUSINESS RELATIONS,WE ACCEPT YOUR COUNTER OFFER. PLEASE SEND US YOUR ORDER WITH SHIPPING MARK "N/M" BY RETURN.

(5)WE ARE PLEASED TO CONFIRM HAVING ORDERED 1000 DOZEN FOUNTAIN PENS ON THE TERMS AND CONDITIONS STATED IN OUR COUNTER OFFER. PLEASE SEND US RELEVANT S/C.

(6)ENCLOSED IS OUR S/C NO. 5454 SIGNED IN BEIJING ON 18TH JANUARY,2009.

SALES CONTRACT

TO:_____   S/C NO._____

                                       DATE:_____

We hereby confirm having sold to you the following goods on terms and conditions as stated below:

Commodity & Specifications	Quantity	Unit Price	Amount
TOTAL:			
TOTAL CONTRACT VALUE:			

SHIPPING MARK：

PACKING：

PORT OF SHIPMENT：

PORT OF DESTINATION：

TIME OF SHIPMENT：

TRANSSHIPMENT：

PARTIAL SHIPMENT：

TERMS OF PAYMENT：

INSURANCE：

Signed by：

THE SELLER：   THE BUYER：

练习五

请根据下列资料填写销售合同。

合同号码：08CAN-1108

签订日期地点：2018年11月8日于南京

卖方：JIANGSU INTERNATIONAL IMP. & EXP. CORP.,LTD.

　　80 ZHONGSHAN ROAD,NANJING,CHINA

　　FAX：86-025-12345678　TEL：86-025-1234567

买方：SHEMSY NEGOCE ID CORP.

　　75 ROUTE 96570 DARDILLY,FRANCE

　　FAX：33-56-34567891　TEL：33-56-123456789

商品名称：皮包 货物根据买方FE022G号订单

ITEM NO. SL100   1000PCS   2美元每件

ITEM NO. SG120   2000PCS   1.5美元每件

ITEM NO. SF200   3000PCS   3美元每件

单价:FOB上海包括5%佣金

包装条款:根据买方的要求

唛头:根据买方的要求

装运条件:收到电汇的30%定金后45天内海运发货,从中国港到买方要求的港口,允许分批装运和转运。

付款条件:电汇30%作为定金,70%采用见票后30天的付款交单方式。

保险:由买方投保。

SALES CONTRACT

TO:_____   S/C NO._____

                                             DATE:_____

We hereby confirm having sold to you the following goods on terms and conditions as stated below:

Commodity & Specifications	Quantity	Unit Price	Amount
TOTAL:			
TOTAL CONTRACT VALUE:			

SHIPPING MARK:

PACKING:

PORT OF SHIPMENT:

PORT OF DESTINATION:

TIME OF SHIPMENT:

TRANSSHIPMENT:

PARTIAL SHIPMENT:

TERMS OF PAYMENT:

INSURANCE:

Signed by:

THE SELLER: THE BUYER:

练习六

请根据下列资料填写销售合同。

合同号码:TJ101211

签订日期:2018年11月8日

卖方:泰佛贸易有限公司(TIFERT TRADING CO.,LTD. / 86,ZHUJIANG ROAD,TIANJIN,CHINA)

买方:ASTAK FOOD,INC. / 5-18 ISUKI-CHOHAKI,TOKYO,JAPAN

商品名称:中国大米,2018年良好平均品质

规格:BROKEN GRAINS（MAX.）20%,ADMIXTURE（MAX.）0.2%, MOISTURE(MAX.) 10%

数量:2000公吨

单价:CIF大阪每公吨360美元

包装:50公斤一麻袋,总共40000袋

装运:在2018年12月份,从天津到日本东京,允许分批装运和转运。

付款条件:由买方开立即期信用证,在2018年11月25日前开到,并于装运期后15天内在中国议付有效。

保险:根据中国人民保险公司1981年1月1日中国海运货物保险条款按发票金额的110%投保一切。

备注:数量和金额允许5%溢短装,由卖方决定。

TIFERT TRADING CO.,LTD.

86,ZHUJIANG ROAD,TIANJIN,CHINA

SALES CONTRACT

TO:ASTAK FOOD,INC.   S/C NO._____

　　5-18 ISUKI-CHOHAKI,TOKYO,JAPAN   DATE:_____

We hereby confirm having sold to you the following goods on terms and conditions as stated below:

Commodity & Specifications	Quantity	Unit Price	Amount
TOTAL:			
TOTAL CONTRACT VALUE:			

REMARKS:

SHIPPING MARK:

PACKING:

PORT OF SHIPMENT:

PORT OF DESTINATION:

TIME OF SHIPMENT:

TRANSSHIPMENT:

PARTIAL SHIPMENT:

TERMS OF PAYMENT:

INSURANCE:

Signed by:

THE SELLER: THE BUYER:

第二节 信用证分析表的填制

一、信用证分析表的作用是把复杂的内容归类，从而提高后续制单的完整性和准确性。

二、信用证分析表的模板视具体情况可稍做改动，主要体现在"单据名称"栏中(见下表)。

信用证号		合约号			受益人				
开证银行				开证申请人					
开证日期		兑付方式		起运口岸			目的地		
金额				可否转运			成交方式		
汇票付款人				可否分批					
汇票期限		见票_____天期		装运期限			唛头		
				有效期					
				有效地点					
				提单日_____天内议付		_____天内寄单			

单证名称	提单	副本提单	商业发票	海关发票	装箱单	重量数量单	尺码单	保险单	产地证	普惠制产地证	贸促会产地证	出口许可证	装船通知书	投保通知	寄投保通知邮据	寄单证明	寄样证明	品质证明书
提交银行																		
提交客户																		

注：在"提交银行"或"提交客户"对应的栏目中填写应提交的单据份数，信用证要求提交的单据没有注明份数，默认为1份。

提单	抬头			保险	险种			
	通知							
运费支付方式(预付或到付)					投保加成率		赔款地点	

注：如果提供的信用证的内容没有涉及信用证分析表的某些栏目，该栏目为空。

三、《浙江省高校招生职业技能考试大纲》外贸类理论知识中对信用证分析表填制的考试内容及范围

1. 填写信用证基本信息

2. 填写信用证对运输的要求

3. 填写信用证付款信息

4. 填写信用证对单据的要求

5. 填写信用证中的其他相关交易信息

四、MT700格式信用证（见下表）

Tag代号	Field Name栏目名称	Content/Options 内容
*27	Sequence of Total(报文页次)	1n/1n 一个数字/一个数字
*40A	Form of Documentary Credit(跟单信用证类别)	24x 24个字
*20	Documentary Credit Number(信用证编号)	16x 16个字
23	Reference to pre-advice(预告的编号)	16x 16个字
31C	Date of Issue(开证日期)	6n 6个数字
*40E	Applicable Rules(适用的惯例)【一般写UCP LATEST VERSION】	4*35x 4行×35个字
*31D	Date and Place of Expiry(信用证的到期日及到期地点)	6n/29x 6个数字/29个字
51A	Applicant Bank(开证申请人的银行)	A or D A或D
*50	Applicant(开证申请人)	4*35x 4行×35个字
52A	Issuing Bank(开证行)	
57A	Advising through...Bank(通过……银行通知)	A,B or D A,B或D
*59	Beneficiary(受益人)	4*35x 4行×35个字
*32B	Currency Code，Amount(信用证的币种代码与金额)	3a/15n 3个字母/15个数字
39A	Percentage Credit Amount(信用证金额允许浮动的范围)	2n/2n 2个数字/2个数字
39B	Maximum Credit Amount Tolerance(最高信用证金额)	13x 13个字
39C	Additional Amounts Covered(可附加金额)	4*35x 4行×35个字
*41A	Available with...(指定的有关银行及信用证的付款方式)	A or D A或D
42C	Drafts at...(汇票付款日期)	3*35x 3行×35个字
42A	Drawee—BIC(汇票付款人——银行代码,用于限制议付信用证)	A or D A或D
42D	Drawee(汇票付款人,用于自由议付信用证)	
42M	Mixed Payment Details(混合付款指示)	4*35x 4行×35个字
42P	Deferred Payment Details(延迟付款指示)	4*35x 4行×35个字
43P	Partial Shipments(分批装运)	1*35x 1行×35个字

Tag代号	Field Name栏目名称	Content/Options内容	
43T	Transshipment(转船)	1*35x	1行×35个字
44A	Loading on Board / Dispatch / Taking in Charge(装船 / 发运 / 接受监管地点)[非海运和空运]	1*65x	1行×65个字
44B	Place of Final Destination / For Transportation to... / Place of Delivery(最终目的地 / 运往……/交货地)[非海运和空运]	1*65x	1行×65个字
44C	Latest Date of Shipment(最迟装运日)	6n	6个数字
44D	Shipment Period(装运期)	6*65x	6行×65个字
44E	Port of Loading / Airport of Departure(装运港 / 出发机场)[海运和空运]	1*65x	1行×65个字
44F	Port of Discharge / Airport of Destination(卸货港 / 目的地机场)[海运和空运]	1*65x	1行×65个字
45A	Description of Goods and/or Services(货物描述)	50*65x	50行×65个字
46A	Documents Required(单据要求)	50*65x	50行×65个字
47A	Additional Conditions(附加条款)	50*65x	50行×65个字
71B	Charges(费用负担)	6*35x	6行×35个字
48	Period for Presentation(交单期限)	4*35x	4行×35个字
*49	Confirmation Instructions(保兑指示)	7x	7个字
53A	Reimbursing Bank(偿付行)	A or D	A 或 D
78	Instructions to Paying/Accepting/Negotiating Bank(银行间指示)	12*65x	12行×65个字
72	Sender to Receiver Information(附言)	6*35x	6行×35个字

五、根据考纲要求具体的填制方法

1. 填写信用证基本信息

（1）信用证编号　DOCUMENTARY CREDIT NUMBER

可在信用证20栏目中找，照抄，要求区分数字和英文大写字母。

（2）合约号　S/C NO.

①可在信用证45A（货物描述）、46A（单据要求）、47A（附加条款）中的唛头信息中去找；

②若信用证中找不到S/C NO.，可以找P/I（PROFORMA INVOICE形式发票）；

③若信用证和P/I中都有，则只能写S/C NO.；

④若信用证和P/I都没有，则此栏空白。

（3）受益人　BENEFICIARY

一般为出口商，在信用证59栏目中找。注意信息填写要完整规范，名称、地址分行填写，如有传真号码、邮政编码等也需要填写。

（4）开证行　ISSUING BANK / OPENIGN BANK

若信用证中没有写明ISSUING BANK或OPENING BANK，则可在APPLICATION HEADER（应用报头）中找，或者在FROM，SENDER，RECEIVED FROM后面找。

注:FROM 开证行　TO 通知行

区分:51A　APPLICANT BANK　开证申请人的银行

APPLICANT BANK是指开证申请人的资金账户所在的银行,如果申请人不在其开户银行开证,必须在信用证中列出其开户行,以便其付款赎单时扣款;如果申请人通过其开户行开证,则信用证中就不会出现51A这个代码。如果ISSUING BANK和APPLICANT BANK两个银行同时出现而且不一样,一定要填开证行。

(5)开证申请人　APPLICANT

一般为进口商,在信用证50栏目中找。注意信息填写要完整规范,名称、地址分栏填写。

(6)开证日期　DATE OF ISSUE

在信用证31C栏目中找, 一般以6位数字表示(年—月—日),填入信用证分析表中的格式要求为"月—日—年",与合同签订日期格式一样。

(7)兑付方式　AVAILABLE WITH...

在信用证*41A中找。

①若为ANY BANK BY NEGOTIATION,则写L/C BY NEGOTIATION;　　议付信用证

②若为ANY BANK BY PAYMENT,则写L/C BY PAYMENT;　　付款信用证

③若为ANY BANK BY ACCEPTANCE,则写L/C BY ACCEPTANCE.　　承兑信用证

(8)金额　AMOUNT

币种+金额,比如USD25,406.00。

若金额中出现允许上下浮动的范围,则也要体现。它可能出现在39A栏目中,也有可能出现在47A栏目中。

如03/03,则USD25,406.00　+/-3%

如03/05,则USD25,406.00　+3%/-5%

如5 PCT MORE OR LESS BOTH IN CREDIT AMOUNT AND QUANTITY ARE ACCEPTABLE.

(9)有效期、有效地点　DATE AND PLACE OF EXPIRY

在信用证31D栏目中找,一般以6位数字表示(年-月-日),填入信用证分析表中的格式要求为"月-日-年",与合同签订日期格式一样。

有效地点:①若已知具体国别,照抄;②若"PLACE"后面写着"AT YOUR COUNTRY"或者BENEFICIARY'S COUNTRY,则用"CHINA"替代。

(10)交单期限　PERIOD FOR PRESENTATION

在信用证48栏目中找,如DOCUMENTS TO BE PRESENTED WITHIN 10 DAYS AFTER THE DATE OF SHIPMENT,BUT WITHIN THE VALIDITY OF THE CREDIT,则填写10天。

若信用证中没有写明,则默认为21天。

2. 填写信用证对运输的要求

(1)起运口岸/目的地

在信用证44A,44B,44E或44F栏目中找,地点照抄。

若出现"CHINESE MAIN PORT"此类短语,也照抄。

若出现"SHIPMENT FROM SHANGHAI PORT,CHINA",则写成"SHANGHAI PORT,CHINA"。

（2）可否转运/可否分批

在信用证43P与43T中找,照抄。

（3）装运期限

在信用证44C中找,注意日期的书写格式为"月—日—年"。

若信用证中未写明装运期限,则与信用证的有效期为同一天,此为"双到期"信用证。

3. 填写信用证付款信息

（1）汇票付款人　DRAWEE

在信用证42D中找,汇票的付款人一般为银行,不能是开证申请人或者受益人。

①若条款中出现银行的地址,也需照抄,名称、地址分栏填写;

②若条款后为ISSUING BANK,则填写开证行的信息(如有地址也须照抄);

③若条款后为OURSELVES,则也填写开证行的信息(如有地址也须照抄)。

（2）汇票付款期限　DRAFTS AT...

在信用证42C中找。

①若条款中出现的为即期(SIGHT),则填***,如"见票___***___天";

②若条款中出现见票后若干天(AT 30 DAYS AFTER SIGHT / AT 30 DAYS' SIGHT),则填具体的天数,"如见票_30_天";

③若条款中出现提单日后若干天(AT 30 DAYS AFTER B/L DATE),则照抄,如"见票_30 DAYS AFTER B/L DATE_天"。

4. 填写信用证其他信息

（1）成交方式

填写价格术语,在信用证45A(货物描述)中找,一般出现在单价条款中,如"CIF NEWYORK"。

注:如45A中出现"DESCRIPTION OF GOODS AND/OR SERVICES: SANITARY WARE FOB SHENZHEN PORT, INCOTERM 2010 DETAILS ACCORDING TO P/O NO.ERN386",则填写时必须加上版本FOB SHENZHEN PORT, INCOTERM 2010.

（2）唛头　SHIPPING MARK

①若信用证45A中指定了唛头,则必须参照信用证缮制;

②若信用证中没有唛头,此栏留空;

③若信用证中没有唛头,补充资料中有,此栏也留空。

5. 填写信用证对单据的要求

在"提交银行"或"提交客户"对应的栏目中填写应提交的单据份数,信用证要求提交的单据没有注明份数,则默认为1份。

（1）提单　BILL OF LADING

例1:FULL SET OF CLEAN ON BOARD OCEAN BILL OF LADING MADE OUT TO ORDER AND BLANK ENDORSED, MARKED FREIGHT TO COLLECT NOTIFYING THE APPLICANT.

（全套提单,提单份数为3份,副本提单不需要填写,留空）

全套提单的表示方式:COMPLETE SET B/L, 3/3 FULL SET OF...

例2:2/3 SET OF CLEAN ON BOARD OCEAN BILL OF LADING MADE OUT TO ORDER AND

BLANK ENDORSED, MARKED FREIGHT PREPAID AND NOTIFY APPLICANT.

（提单份数为2份）

例3：FULL SET OF CLEAN ON BOARD OCEAN BILL OF LADING MADE OUT TO ORDER OF KRUNGTHAI BANK PUBLIC COMPANY LIMITED MARKED FREIGHT PREPAID PLUS TWO NON-NEGOTIABLE COPIES, NOTIFY APPLICANT.

（全套提单，加两份不可议付副本提单。提单份数为3份，副本提单为2份）

例4：FULL SET OF CLEAN ON BOARD OCEAN BILL OF LADING IN TRIPLICATE WITH TWO NON-NEGOTIABLE COPIES MADE OUT TO THE ORDER OF FIRST BANGKOK CITY BANK LTD. BANGKOK, NOTIFY APPLICANT AND MARKED FREIGHT PREPAID.

（提单份数为3份，副本提单为2份）

例5：2/3 SET OF CLEAN ON BOARD OCEAN BILL OF LADING, SET OF 1/3 SHOULD BE SENT DIRECTLY TO APPLICANT, MADE OUT TO ORDER AND BLANK ENDORSED, MARKED FREIGHT PREPAID NOTIFY APPLICANT.

（提单份数为2份，交客户1份）

（2）商业发票　COMMERCIAL INVOICE

例1：MANUALLY SIGNED COMMERCIAL INVOICE IN 3 COPIES SHOWING S/C NO. AND L/C NO. AS WELL AS ISSUING BANK'S NAME.

（手签的商业发票一式三份，要求显示合同号码、信用证号码和开证行名称。）

例2：SIGNED COMMERCIAL INVOICE IN 10 COPIES SHOWING SEPARATELY FOB VALUE, FREIGHT CHARGE, INSURANCE PREMIUM, CIF VALUE AND COUNTRY OF ORIGIN.

（签字的商业发票10份，要求分别显示FOB价、运费、保险费、CIF价和原产国。）

（3）海关发票　CUSTOMS INVOICE

例1：CUSTOMS INVOICE 3 COPIES

（海关发票3份）

例2：CUSTOMS INVOICE AND 3 COPIES

（海关发票1份正本+3份副本，则海关发票共4份）

（4）装箱单　PACKING LIST

例1：PACKING LIST IN TRIPLICATE

（装箱单3份）

例2：PACKING LIST

（装箱单默认为1份）

例3：PACKING LIST IN QUADRUPLICATE, ONE OF WHICH SHOULD BE SENT DIRECTLY TO APPLICANT.

（装箱单一式四份，其中一份寄给开证申请人。装箱单3份交银行，1份交客户）

例4：PACKING LIST DETAILING THE COMPLETE INNER PACKING SPECIFICATION AND CONTENTS OF EACH PACKAGE.

（载明每件货物内部包装的规格和内容的装箱单）

份数的表示：

一式两份 IN DUPLICATE

一式三份 IN TRIPLICATE

一式四份 IN QUADRUPLICATE

一式五份 IN QUINTUPLICATE

一式六份 IN SEXTUPLICATE

一式七份 IN SEPTUPLICATE

一式八份 IN OCTUPLICATE

一式九份 IN NONUPLICATE

一式十份 IN DECUPLICATE

（5）重量单 WEIGHT LIST / WEIGHT NOTE

例1：WEIGHT LIST IN 5 COPIES.（重量单5份。）

（6）尺码单 MEASUREMENT LIST

例1：MEASUREMENT LIST 3 FOLDS.（尺码单3份。）

（7）保险单 INSURANCE POLICY OR CERTIFICATE

①46A栏目中有保险单信息（CIF/CIP）

例1：INSURANCE POLICY IN DUPLICATE FOR 120 PCT OF THE INVOICE VALUE COVERING F.P.A. AS PER O.M.C.C. OF PICC DATE 01 / 01 / 2010 WAREHOUSE TO WAREHOUSE CLAUSES INCLUDED IN THE SAME CURRENCY OF THE DRAFTS CLAIMS PAYABLE IN SINGAPORE.

（保险单2份）

例2：INSURANCE POLICY OR CERTIFICATE IN NEGOTIABLE FORM COVERING GOODS FOR THE INVOICE VALUE PLUS 10 PCT AGAINST ALL RISKS AND WAR RISK.

（保险单1份）

②46A栏目中没有保险单信息（FOB/CFR/FCA/CPT）或保险由买方安排（INSURANCE IS BEING ARRANGED BY THE BUYER）

（8）产地证 CERTIFICATE OF ORIGIN

例1：CERTIFICATE OF ORIGIN IN 2 COPIES（产地证2份）

例2：CERTIFICATE OF ORIGIN CERTIFYING GOODS OF ORIGIN IN CHINA ISSUED BY COMPETENT AUTHORITIES（由主管当局签发的产地证1份）

例3：CERTIFICATE OF ORIGIN IN TRIPLICATE SHOWING THE NAME OF THE MANUFACTURER （显示工厂名称的产地证3份）

例4：ASEAN-CHINA FREE TRADE AREA PREFERENTIAL TARIFF CERTIFICATE OF ORIGIN FORM E IN DUPLICATE.（产地证2份）

产地证除了CERTIFICATE OF ORIGIN,还包括：

《中国—东盟自由贸易区》优惠原产地证明书   FORM E

《〈亚太贸易协定〉原产地证明书》   FORM B

《"中国与巴基斯坦自由贸易区"优惠原产地证明书》   FORM P

《"中国—智利自由贸易区"优惠原产地证书》　　　　　　FORM F

(9)普惠制产地证　FORM A

例1:CERTIFICATE OF ORIGIN GSP FORM A(普惠制产地证1份)

例2:G.S.P. CERTIFICATE OF ORIGIN FORM A IN 3 COPIES(普惠制产地证3份)

例3:G.S.P. CERTIFICATE OF ORIGIN FORM A ISSUED BY COMPETENT AUTHORITIES (由主管当局签发的普惠制产地证1份)

(10)贸促会产地证　贸促会　CCPIT

例1:CERTIFICATE OF ORIGIN OF THE GOODS,1 ORIGINAL+1 COPY ISSUED BY CCPIT OR RELATIVE COMPETENT ORGANIZATION.

(由中国国际贸易促进委员会或相关职能机构签发的货物原产地证明,1份正本+1份副本)

例2:CERTIFICATE OF ORIGIN ISSUED AND SIGNED BY THE CHINA COUNCIL FOR THE PROMOTION OF INTERNATIONAL TRADE.(贸促会产地证1份)

(11)出口许可证　EXPORT LICENSE

根据一国出口商品管制的法令规定,由有关当局签发准许出口的证件。

例1:EXPORT LICENSE IN DUPLICATE ARE REQUIRED(出口许可证2份)

(12)装船通知书　SHIPPING ADVICE（又称DECLARATION OF SHIPMENT或NOTICE OF SHIPMENT）

《2000通则》规定:"卖方必须给予买方已装船的及时通知……"以便买方有充分的时间办理投保,否则由此而产生的损失和危险应由卖方承担。

在信用证业务中,要求出现装船通知的表示条款并不统一,可能出现要求:

①提供"SHIPMENT ADVICE"(装船通知);

②告知"SHIPMENT DETAILS"(装运详情)。

例1:COPY OF FAX MESSAGE SENT TO THE APPLICANT ADVISING SHIPPING DETAILS INCLUDING NAME OF VESSEL AND NUMBER OF BILL OF LADING.(装船通知1份)

例2:SHIPPING ADVICE TO THE APPLICANT SHOWING ALL SHIPPING DETAILS.（装船通知1份）

(13)投保通知

例1:SHIPPING ADVICE TO THE CYPRUS INSURANCE COMPANY ON THE FAX NO.29125312 SHOWING THE OPEN POLICY NO.13-3614 AND ALL SHIPPING DETAILS.(投保通知1份)

(14)受益人证明　BENEFICIARY'S CERTIFICATE

受益人证明是一种由受益人自己出具的证明,以便证明自己履行了信用证规定的任务或证明自己按信用证要求办事,如证明所交货物的品质、运输包装的处理、按要求寄单等。

①寄单证明

寄单证明通常是受益人根据规定,在货物装运前后一定时期内,邮寄、传真、快递给规定的收受人全套或部分副本单据,并将证明随其他单据交银行议付。

例1:A CERTIFICATE OF BENEFICIARY STATING THAT ONE COPY OF INVOICE, ONE COPY OF MEASUREMENT LIST AND ONE ORIGINAL OF INSURANCE POLICY HAVE BEEN SENT TO APPLICANT BY COURIER.(寄单证明交银行1份　　商业发票、尺码单、保险单寄客户各一份)

②寄样证明

例1:CERTIFICATE TO SHOW THAT THE REQUIRED SHIPMENT SAMPLES HAVE BEEN SENT BY DHL TO THE APPLICANT ON JULY 10,2005.(寄样证明寄银行1份)

（15）品质证明书 CERTIFICATE OF QUALITY

例1:CERTIFICATE OF QUALITY IN 3 COPIES ISSUED BY CIQ.(品质证明书3份)

例2:INSPECTION CERTIFICATE OF QUALITY IN DUPLICATE.(品质证明书2份)

6. 填写信用证对提单的要求

例1:FULL SET OF CLEAN ON BOARD OCEAN BILL OF LADING MADE OUT TO ORDER AND BLANK ENDORSED,MARKED FREIGHT COLLECT NOTIFYING THE APPLICANT.

抬头填写:TO ORDER

通知填写:开证申请人名称、地址

运费支付方式:FREIGHT COLLECT

例2:3/3 FULL SET OF CLEAN ON BOARD OCEAN BILL OF LADING SHOWING FREIGHT PREPAID MADE OUT TO ORDER OF SHIPPER,BLANK ENDORSED,MARKED FREIGHT PREPAID,NOTIFYING APPLICANT WITH FULL ADDRESS.

抬头填写:TO ORDER OF SHIPPER(+受益人名称、地址）

通知填写:开证申请人名称、地址

运费支付方式:FREIGHT PREPAID

例3:3/3 FULL SET OF CLEAN ON BOARD OCEAN BILL OF LADING SHOWING FREIGHT PREPAID MADE OUT TO OUR ORDER,BLANK ENDORSED,NOTIFYING APPLICANT WITH FULL ADDRESS.

抬头填写:TO ORDER OF+开证行名称、地址

通知填写:开证申请人名称、地址

运费支付方式:FREIGHT PREPAID

7. 填写信用证对保险的要求

例1:INSURANCE POLICY COVERING ALL RISKS AND WAR RISK FOR 110 PCT OF THE INVOICE VALUE WAREHOUSE TO WAREHOUSE CLAUSE INCLUDED UP TO FINAL DESTINATION AT SCHORNDORF, CLAIM IF ANY PAYABLE IN GERMANY.

险种:ALL RISKS AND WAR RISK,WAREHOUSE TO WAREHOUSE CLAUSE INCLUDED UP TO FINAL DESTINATION AT SCHORNDORF

投保加成率:10%/投保加成:110%

赔款地点:GERMANY

例2:INSURANCE POLICY IN DUPLICATE FOR 120 PCT OF THE INVOICE VALUE COVERING FPA AS PER CIC OF PICC DATED 01/01/2010 WAREHOUSE TO WAREHOUSE CLAUSE INCLUDED IN THE SAME CURRENCY OF THE DRAFTS CLAIM PAYABLE IN SINGAPORE.

险种:FPA AS PER CIC OF PICC DATED 01/01/2010 WAREHOUSE TO WAREHOUSE CLAUSE

投保加成率:20% / 投保加成:120%

赔款地点:SINGAPORE

六、易错点集锦

1. 开证申请人、受益人、开证行名称和其地址填写时必须分行。

2. 填写金额时,要求三位一分。

3. 日期填写格式"月—日—年",特别注意九月的简写(SEPT.)。

4. 投保加成:110%,投保加成率:10%。

5. 单据要求

46A SHIPPING ADVICE TO APPLICANT 装船通知给银行和客户

47A SHIPPING ADVICE TO APPLICANT 装船通知给客户

47A SHIPMENT SAMPLES SHOULD BE SENT TO THE BUYER 样品给客户

46A 或 47A SHIPMENT SAMPLES SHOULD BE SENT TO THE BUYER AND A CERTIFICATE FOR THIS EFFECT IS REQUIRED 样品给客户,寄样证明给银行

46A 或 47A SHIPMENT SAMPLES SHOULD BE SENT TO THE BUYER AND A CERTIFICATE AND RELATIVE POST RECEIPT FOR THIS EFFECT IS REQUIRED 样品给客户,寄样证明和寄样证明邮寄收据给银行(若表格后面有空白列,则需把寄样证明邮寄收据补上;若没有,则不需要写寄样证明邮寄收据。注:寄样证明邮寄收据不等于寄投保通知邮据)

47A FIVE SHIPPING SAMPLES TO APPLICANT 5个样品给客户

47A FIVE SHIPPING SAMPLES TO APPLICANT AND A CERTIFICATE FOR THIS EFFECT IS REQUIRED 5个样品给客户,寄样证明给银行

46A BENEFICIARY'S CERTIFICATE CERTIFY THAT ONE COPY OF INVOICE,ONE COPY OF PACKING LIST AND ONE COPY OF B/L SHOULD BE SENT TO THE APPLICANT 寄单证明给银行,发票、装箱单和副本提单给客户

46A 或 47A ONE COPY OF INVOICE,ONE COPY OF PACKING LIST AND ONE COPY OF B/L SHOULD BE SENT TO THE APPLICANT AND A CERTIFICATE AND RELATIVE POST RECEIPT FOR THIS EFFECT IS REQUIRED. 寄单证明和寄单邮寄收据给银行,发票、装箱单和副本提单给客户

47A ALL DOCUMENTS MUST BE PRESENTED THROUGH BENEFICIARY'S BANKER AND EXTRA COPY OF INVOICE AND TRANSPORT DOCUMENT FOR L/C ISSUING BANK'S FILE REQUIRED 额外的一份发票和副本提单给银行

46A BENEFICIARY'S CERTIFICATE CERTIFY THAT ONE SET OF NON-NEGOTIABLE SHIPPING DOCUMENTS HAVE BEEN SENT BY DHL TO THE APPLICANT WITHIN 05 WORKING DAYS AFTER THE DATE OF B/L 寄单证明给银行,除汇票、寄单证明外,该L/C要求的所有单据副本给客户。

注:

①如果有寄单证明,一定要看后面写的寄给谁,如果不是客户,就没有提交客户的单据;

②在"提交银行"或"提交客户"对应的栏目中填写应提交的单据份数,信用证要求提交的单据没有注明份数,默认为1份;

③注意COPY OF TRANSPORT DOCUMENT 与 NON-NEGOTIABLE SHIPPING DOCUMENTS 的区别;

④如果出现SIGNED COMMERCIAL INVOICE IN 01/03 (ORIGINAL/COPIES),指的是1份正本和三份

副本；

⑤如果46A栏目中出现SIGNED COMMERCIAL INVOICE IN ONE ORIGINAL AND TWO COPIES, ONE OF WHICH SHOULD BE SENT TO APPLICANT,指的是商业发票提交银行2份,客户1份；

⑥如果46A栏目中出现SIGNED COMMERCIAL INVOICE IN ONE ORIGINAL AND TWO COPIES WHICH SHOULD BE SENT TO APPLICANT,指的是商业发票提交银行1份正本,客户2份副本。

七、专项练习

练习一

根据以下业务背景资料,填写信用证分析表。

DOCUMENTARY CREDIT

RECEIVED FROM:BANK OF CHINA,SYDNEY,AUSTRALIA

DESTINATION:BANK OF CHINA,NINGBO BRANCH

SEQUENCE OF TOTAL　　　　*27:1/1

FORM OF DOC. CREDIT　　　*40A:IRREVOCABLE

DOC. CREDIT NUMBER　　　*20:R027-20160416

DATE OF ISSUE　　　　　*31C:20160623

EXPIRY　　　　　　　　*31D:DATED 20161005　　　PLACE:COUNTERS OF NEGOTIATING
　　　　　　　　　　　　　　　　BANK

APPLICANT　　　　　　*50:SYDNEY INTERNATIONAL TRADE CO.
　　　　　　　　　　　　155/6 WEST STREET,SYDNEY,AUSTRALIA

BENEFICIARY　　　　　*59:NINGBO DONGSHAN VEGETABLES CO., LTD.,
　　　　　　　　　　　　NO.221 ZHONGSHAN ROAD,NINGBO,CHINA 315228

AMOUNT　　　　　　　*32B:CURRENCY USD AMOUNT 19,600.00

AVAILABLE WITH　　　*41D:ANY BANK ON SIGHT BASIS BY NEGOTIATION

DRAFTS AT　　　　　42C:DRAFTS AT SIGHT FOR FULL INVOICE VALUE

DRAWEE　　　　　　*42D:BANK OF CHINA,SYDNEY,AUSTRALIA

PARTIAL SHIPMENT　*43P:PROHIBITED

TRANSSHIPMENT　　*43T:ALLOWED

LOADING IN CHARGE　*44A:NINGBO,CHINA

FOR TRANSPORTATION TO...　*44B:SYDNEY,AUSTRALIA

LATEST DATE OF SHIP.　*44C:20160920

DESCRIPT. OF GOODS　*45A:20M/T FROZEN SOYABEANS CIF SYDNEY AS PER S/C NO.
　　　　　　　　　　　　DF2016022 DATED 20160416
　　　　　　　　　　　　SHIPPING MARK:SYDNEY NO.1-1000

DOCUMENTS REQUIRED　*46A:
　　　　　　　　　　　　+SIGNED COMMERCIAL INVOICE IN TRIPLICATE

+3/3 SET OF CLEAN ON BOARD OCEAN BILLS OF LADING MADE OUT TO ORDER AND BLANK ENDORSED, MARKED FREIGHT PREPAID NOTIFY APPLICANT.

+PACKING LIST IN TRIPLICATE

+ INSURANCE POLICY OR CERTIFICATE IN DUPLICATE ENDORSED IN BLANK, COVERING ALL RISKS AND WAR RISK AS PER C.I.C. DATED 01/01/1981 FOR 110% OF INVOICE VALUE. CLAIM PAYABLE AT SYDNEY, AUSTRALIA IN THE CURRENCY OF DRAFTS

+CERTIFICATE OF ORIGIN GSP FORM A IN DUPLICATE

+ SHIPPING ADVICE AND 1 ORIGINAL CERTIFICATE OF ORIGIN GSP FORM A HAVE BEEN SENT TO APPLICANT AFTER SHIPMENT BY COURIER

ADDITIONAL CONDITIONS   *47A:WITHOUT

DETAILS OF CHARGES   *71B:ALL BANKING CHARGES OUTSIDE AUSTRALIA ARE FOR ACCOUNT OF THE BENEFICIARY.

PRESENTATION PERIOD   *48:DOCUMENTS MUST BE PRESENTED WITHIN 15 DAYS AFTER THE DATE OF SHIPMENT, BUT WITHIN THE VALIDITY OF THE CREDIT.

CONFIRMATION   *49:WITHOUT

INSTRUCTIONS   *78:REIMBURSEMENT BY TELECOMMUNICATION IS PROHIBITED. NEGOTIATING BANK MUST SEND ALL DOCUMENTS TO US, I. E. BANK OF CHINA, SYDNEY, AUSTRALIA IN ONE LOT BY COURIER SERVICE AND REIMBURSE YOURSELVES FROM REIMBURSING BANK FOR EACH PRESENTATION OF DISCREPANT DOCUMENTS UNDER THIS CREDIT. THIS CREDIT IS ISSUED SUBJECT UNIFORM CUSTOMS AND PRACTICE FOR DOCUMENTARY CREDITS(1993 REVISION)ICC PUBL. 500.

信用证分析表练习一

信用证号		合约号		受益人			
开证银行				开证申请人			
开证日期		兑付方式		起运口岸		目的地	

续表

金额		可否转运		成交方式	
汇票付款人		可否分批			
汇票期限	见票＿＿＿天期	装运期限		唛头	
		有效期			
		有效地点			
		提单日＿＿＿天内议付	＿＿＿天内寄单		

单证名称	提单	副本提单	商业发票	海关发票	装箱单	重量数量单	尺码单	保险单	产地证	普惠制产地证	贸促会产地证	出口许可证	装船通知书	投保通知	寄投保通知邮据	寄单证明	寄样证明	品质证明书
提交银行																		
提交客户																		

注：在"提交银行"或"提交客户"对应的栏目中填写应提交的单据份数，信用证要求提交的单据没有注明份数，默认为1份。

提单	抬头		保险	险种	
	通知				
运费支付方式（预付或到付）				投保加成率	赔款地点

注：如果提供的信用证的内容没有涉及信用证分析表的某些栏目，该栏目为空。

练习二

根据以下业务背景资料，填写信用证分析表。

DOCUMENTARY CREDIT

FORM OF DOC. CREDIT　　　　*40A：IRREVOCABLE

DOC. CREDIT　NUMBER　　　*20：DOC-812-353

DATE　OF　ISSUE　　　　　　31C：20171223

EXPIRY　　　　　　　　　　*31D：DATED 20180315　　PLACE：CHINA

APPLICANT　　　　　　　　*50：RAM PLASTICS CO.，LTD.，

　　　　　　　　　　　　　　201 HAUK ROAD，MALVIYA NAGAR NEW DELHI，INDIA

APPLICANT BANK	51A:STATE BANK OF INDIA,NEW DELHI
BENEFICIARY	*59:SHANGHAI LUCKY PLASTIC IMP. AND EXP. CO.,LTD.,
	22/F JINMAO TOWER SHANGHAI,CHINA
AMOUNT	*32B:CURRENCY USD AMOUNT 18,600.00
AVAILABLE WITH	*41D:ANY BANK BY NEGOTIATION
DRAFTS AT	42C:DRAFTS AT SIGHT FOR FULL INVOICE VALUE
DRAWEE	42A:STATE BANK OF INDIA,NEW DELHI
PARTIAL SHIPMENT	43P:ALLOWED
TRANSSHIPMENT	43T:ALLOWED
PORT OF LOADING	44E:SHANGHAI,CHINA
PORT OF DISCHARGE	44F:NHAVA SHEVA,INDIA
LATEST DATE OF SHIP.	44C:20180228
DESCRIPT. OF GOODS	45A:PVC STRIPS CIF NHAVA SHEVA AS PER S/C
	NO. SL08121
DOCUMENTS REQUIRED	46A:+MANUALLY SIGNED INVOICE IN TRIPLICATE SHOWING FOB VALUE FREIGHT CHARGE AND INSURANCE PREMIUM SEPARATELY
	+DETAILED PACKING LIST IN DUPLICATE
	+CERTIFICATE OF ORIGIN IN DUPLICATE SHOWING THE NAME OF THE MANUFACTURER
	+FULL SET OF CLEAN ON BOARD BILL OF LADING MADE OUT TO ORDER OF SHIPPER AND BLANK ENDORSED AND MARKED FREIGHT PREPAID NOTIFY APPLICANT AND ALSO SHOWING THE NAME, ADDRESS,TEL. NO. OF THE CARRIER'S AGENT AT THE PORT OF DISCHARGE
	+INSURANCE POLICY IN DUPLICATE FOR AT LEAST 110 PCT OF THE INVOICE VALUE COVERING INSTITUTE CARGO CLAUSE(A) AS PER I.C.C. DATED 01/01/1982 AND SHOW THE ACTUAL PREMIUM CHARGE
	+ONE SET OF NON-NEGOTIABLE SHIPPING DOCUMENTS SHOULD BE SENT DIRECTLY TO THE APPLICANT AND A CERTIFICATE AND RELATIVE POST RECEIPT FOR THIS EFFECT IS REQUIRED
ADDITIONAL CONDITIONS	47A:1.ALL DOCUMENTS MUST SHOW THE CREDIT NUMBER
	2.A DISCREPANCY HANDING FEE OF USD80.00 SHOULD BE DEDUCTED AND INDICATED ON THE BILL SCHEDULE

FOR EACH PRESENTATION OF DISCREPANT DOCUMENTS

UNDER THIS CREDIT

3.THIS DOCUMENTARY CREDIT IS SUBJECT TO UCP600

4.SHIPPING MARKS:RAM/SL081218/N. SHEVA/NO. 1-100

PRESENTATION PERIOD 48:DOCUMENTS MUST BE PRESENTED WITHIN 15 DAYS AFTER THE DATE OF SHIPMENT,BUT WITHIN THE VALIDITY OF THE CREDIT.

ADVISE THROUGH 57A:BANK OF COMMUNICATIONS SHANGHAI BRANCH

DETAILS OF CHARGES 71B:ALL BANKING CHARGES OUTSIDE INDIA ARE FOR A/C OF THE BENEFICIARY.

INSTRUCTION 78:WE SHALL ARRANGE REMITTANCE OF THE PROCEEDS TO YOU ON RECEIPT OF DOCUMENTS COMPLYING WITH THE TERMS OF THIS L/C CONFIRMING THAT THE DRAFT AMOUNT HAS BEEN ENDORSED ON THIS LETTER OF CREDIT.

信用证分析表练习二

信用证号		合约号			受益人			
开证银行				开证申请人				
开证日期		兑付方式		起运口岸			目的地	
金额				可否转运			成交方式	
汇票付款人				可否分批				
汇票期限	见票____天期			装运期限			唛头	
				有效期				
				有效地点				
				提单日____天内议付		____天内寄单		

单证名称	提单	副本提单	商业发票	海关发票	装箱单	重量数量单	尺码单	保险单	产地证	普惠制产地证	贸促会产地证	出口许可证	装船通知书	投保通知	寄投保通知邮据	寄单证明	寄样证明	品质证明书
提交银行																		

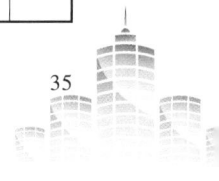

续表

提交客户																		

注:在"提交银行"或"提交客户"对应的栏目中填写应提交的单据份数,信用证要求提交的单据没有注明份数,默认为1份。

提单	抬头		保险	险种			
	通知						
运费支付方式(预付或到付)				投保加成		赔款地点	

注:如果提供的信用证的内容没有涉及信用证分析表的某些栏目,该栏目为空。

练习三

根据以下业务背景资料,填写信用证分析表。

DOCUMENTARY CREDIT

RECEIVED FROM:BANK OF CHINA,BARCELONA BRANCH

TO:BANK OF CHINA,ZHEJIANG BRANCH

SEQUENCE OF TOTAL	*27:1/1
FORM OF DOC. CREDIT	*40A:IRREVOCABLE
DOC. CREDIT NUMBER	*20:211LC200116
DATE OF ISSUE	*31C:170218
EXPIRY	*31D:DATED 170415　PLACE:IN THE BENEFICIARY'S COUNTRY
APPLICANT	*50:HOP TONG HAI(PIE) LTD.,
	BLK 15,NORTH BRIPDE ROAD
	#04-9370 BARCELONA SPAIN
	100032,
	FAX:2953397
BENEFICIARY	*59:ZHEJIANG BAIMEI GARMENTS
	IMP. & EXP. CO.,LTD.,
	JINAN MANSION 306 HONGDA ROAD,
	XIAOSHAN DISTRICT,HANGZHOU,
	ZHEJIANG,CHINA
AMOUNT	*32B:CURRENCY USD AMOUNT 37,850.00
AVAILABLE WITH	*41D:ANY BANK IN CHINA BY NEGOTIATION
DRAFTS AT	42C:120 DAYS AFTER SIGHT
DRAWEE	42D:BANK OF CHINA,NEW YORK BRANCH
PARTIAL SHIPMENT	43P:ALLOWED
TRANSSHIPMENT	43T:ALLOWED
PORT OF LOADING	44A:CHINA MAIN PORT,CHINA

PORT OF DISCHARGE   44B:BARCELONA PORT,SPAIN

           WITH TRANSSHIPMENT AT SINGAPORE

LATEST SHIPMENT   44C:170405

GOODS DISCRIPT   45A:1,300 DOZEN 100% COTTON OVERALLS,

           SHIRTS AND SINGLETS AS PER S/C

           NO. 02EC301302 DATED 26-01-2017 AS DETAILS

           BELOW:

1)600 DOZEN(7,200PCS) 100% COTTON OVERALLS AT USD45.00 PER DOZEN;

2)600 DOZEN(7,200PCS) 100% COTTON SHIRTS AT USD16.50 PER DOZEN;

3)100 DOZEN(1,200PCS) 100% COTTON SINGLETS AT USD9.50 PER DOZEN;

TRADE TERMS:CFRC3 BARCELONA AS PER INCOTERMS 2010

PACKING:TO BE PACKED IN CARTONS,100% COTTON OVERALLS:30PCS/CTN;

    100% COTTON SHIRTS:120PCS/CTN;100% COTTON SINGLETS:300PCS/CTN

DOCUMENTS REQUIRED *46A:+COMMERCIAL INVOICE MANUALLY SIGNED IN INK IN

            TRIPLICATE SHOWING FREIGHT CHARGES,INSURANCE

            COST AND FOB VALUE,AND THE COUNTRY OF ORIGIN

            IS P.R. CHINA AND THE GOODS SHIPPED ARE NEITHER

            ISRAELI ORIGIN NOR DO THEY CONTAIN ISRAELI

            MATERIALS NOR ARE THEY EXPORTED FROM ISRAELI

           +SIGNED PACKING LIST

           +CERTIFICATE OF ORIGIN

           +INSURANCE POLICY/CERTIFICATE IN DUPLICATE ENDORSED

            IN BLANK FOR 110% OF CIF VALUE,COVERING ALL RISKS

            AND WAR RISK OF C.I.C. OF PICC(1/1/1981),WAREHOUSE

            TO WAREHOUSE AND SHOWING THE CLAIMING CURRENCY

            IS THE SAME AS CURRENCY OF CREDIT

           +FULL SET OF CLEAN ON BOARD OCEAN BILLS OF LADING

            MADE OUT TO ORDER MARKED FREIGHT PREPAID

            AND NOTIFY APPLICANT

           +SHIPMENT ADVICE SHOWING THE NAME OF THE CARRYING

            VESSEL,DATED OF SHIPMENT,MARKS,AMOUNT AND

            THE NUMBER OF THIS DOCUMENTARY CREDIT TO

            APPLICANT WITHIN 10 DAYS AFTER THE DATE OF

            BILL OF LADING

ADDITIONAL CONDITIONS 47A:+MORE OR LESS 10PCT OF QUANTITY OF GOODS AND

            CREDIT AMOUNT IS ALLOWED

           +THE NUMBER AND THE DATE OF THIS CREDIT AND

THE NAME OF ISSUING BANK MUST BE QUOTED ON ALL DOCUMENTS

+SHIPMENT MUST BE EFFECTED BY 1×20' FCL CONTAINER LOAD B/L TO SHOW EVIDENCE OF THIS EFFECT IS REQUIRED

+ONE SET OF NON-NEGOTIABLE SHIPPING DOCUMENTS TO BE FAXED TO APPLICANT WITHIN TWO DAYS AFTER SHIPMENT BENEFICIARY'S CERTIFICATE TO THIS EFFECT IS REQUIRED

+SHIPPING MARKS:C.T.H./BARCELONA/NO.:1-UP

DETAILS OF CHARGES 　71B:ALL CHARGES AND COMMISSIONS OUTSIDE ARE FOR BENEFICIARY ACCOUNT

PRESENTATION PERIOD 　48:WITHIN 10 DAYS AFTER THE DATE OF SHIPMENT, BUT WITHIN THE VALIDITY OF EXPIRY DATE OF THIS CREDIT

CONFIRMATION 　*49:WITHOUT

INSTRUCTION TO THE PAYING BANK 　78:DOCUMENTS TO BE DESPATCHED IN ONE LOT BY COURIER TO BANK OF CHINA,BARCELONA BRANCH

信用证分析表练习三

信用证号		合约号			受益人			
开证银行				开证申请人				
开证日期		兑付方式		起运口岸			目的地	
金额				可否转运			成交方式	
汇票付款人				可否分批				
汇票期限	见票____天期			装运期限			唛头	
				有效期				
				有效地点				
				提单日____天内议付		____天内寄单		

单证名称	提单	副本提单	商业发票	海关发票	装箱单	重量数量单	尺码单	保险单	产地证	普惠制产地证	贸促会产地证	出口许可证	装船通知书	投保通知	寄投保通知邮据	寄单证明	寄样证明	品质证明书

提交银行															
提交客户															

注:在"提交银行"或"提交客户"对应的栏目中填写应提交的单据份数,信用证要求提交的单据没有注明份数,默认为1份。

提单	抬头		保险	险种	
	通知				
运费支付方式(预付或到付)				投保加成率	赔款地点

注:如果提供的信用证的内容没有涉及信用证分析表的某些栏目,该栏目为空。

练习四

根据以下业务背景资料,填写信用证分析表。

DOCUMENTARY CREDIT

FROM:HABIB BANK LTD.,DUBAI

TO:BANK OF CHINA,SHANGHAI BRANCH

SEQUENCE OF TOTAL　　　　27:1/1

FORM OF DOC. CREDIT　　　*40A:IRREVOCABLE

DATE OF ISSUE　　　　　　*31C:20170401

DOC. CREDIT NUMBER　　　*20:17-LC-205

EXPIRY　　　　　　　　　*31D:DATED 20170517

　　　　　　　　　　　　PLACE:IN COUNTRY OF BENEFICIARY

APPLICANT　　　　　　　*50:EASTERN CITY TRADING INC.,

　　　　　　　　　　　　P.O.BOX NO.8901,DUBAI,U.A.E.

BENEFICIARY　　　　　　*59:SHANGHAI SHENGYANG GROUP,

　　　　　　　　　　　　NO. 1150 SHAOXING ROAD,SHANGHAI,

　　　　　　　　　　　　CHINA

AMOUNT　　　　　　　　*32B:CURRENCY USD AMOUNT 24,800.00

POS./NEG. TOL.(%)　　　*39A:05/05

AVAILABLE WITH　　　　*41D:FREELY NEGOTIABLE AT ANY BANK BY NEGOTIATION

DRAFTS AT　　　　　　　*42C:45 DAYS' SIGHT

DRAWEE　　　　　　　　42A:ISSUING BANK

PARTIAL SHIPMENT　　　43P:ALLOWED

TRANSSHIPMENT　　　　43T:NOT ALLOWED

PORT OF LOADING　　　　44E:ANY CHINESE PORT

PORT OF DISCHARGE　　　44F:DUBAI,U.A.E.

LATEST DATE OF SHIP.   44C:20170502

DESCRIPTION OF GOODS   45A:100% WOOL CARPETS CIF DUBAI,U.A.E.AS PER S/C NO. SSYG17086 200PCS USD124.00/PC

DOCUMENTS REQUIRED   46A:+2/3 SET OF CLEAN ON BOARD BILL OF LADING MADE OUT TO THE ORDER OF SHIPPER,BLANK ENDORSED AND MARKED FREIGHT PREPAID AND NOTIFY APPLICANT AND US

+COMMERCIAL INVOICE IN 6 COPIES,ONE OF WHICH SHOULD BE SENT DIRECTLY TO APPLICANT,STATING THAT GOODS ARE MADE IN CHINA

+PACKING LIST IN QUADRUPLICATE

+CERTIFICATE OF ORIGIN IN TRIPLICATE

+INSPECTION CERTIFICATE OF QUALITY IN QUADRUPLICATE

+INSURANCE POLICY IN DUPLICATE FOR 120 PCT OF THE INVOICE VALUE,COVERING ALL RISKS AND WAR RISK,CLAIM TO BE PAYABLE IN DUBAI

+BENEFICIARY'S CERTIFICATE STATING THAT ONE COPY OF SIGNED INVOICE AND ONE ORIGINAL OF BILL OF LADING MUST BE SENT TO THE ACCOUNTEE BY COURIER SERVICE AFTER SHIPMENT

ADDITIONAL CONDITION   47A:+DOCUMENTS NEGOTIATED WITH ANY DISCREPANCY WILL ATTRACT A HANDLING FEE OF USD40.00. THIS FEE WILL BE DEDUCTED FROM PROCEEDS REMITTED BY OURSELVES

+ALL DOCUMENTS MUST INDICATE ISSUING BANK AND L/C NO.

+SHIPPING MARKS:EASTERN/NO. 01TH/DUBAI,U.A.E./NO.1-UP

DETAILS OF CHARGES   71B:ALL BANKING COMMISSIONS CHARGES OUTSIDE DUBAI, PLUS ADVISING AND REIMBURSING COMMISSIONS, ARE FOR THE ACCOUNT OF BENEFICIARY

PRESENTATION PERIOD   48:DOCUMENTS TO BE PRESENTED WTHIN 15 DAYS AFTER THE DATE OF SHIPMENT INDICATED ON TRANSPORT DOCUMENT,BUT WITHIN THE CREDIT VALIDITY

CONFIRMATION   *49:WITHOUT

INSTRUCTION TO THE PAYING BANK   78:ALL DOCUMENTS MUST BE FORWARDED TO US BY COURIER SERVICE IN ONE LOT

ADVISE THROUGH BANK   57A:BANK OF CHINA,SHANGHAI BRANCH

信用证分析表练习四

信用证号		合约号		受益人				
开证银行				开证申请人				
开证日期		兑付方式		起运口岸			目的地	
金额				可否转运			成交方式	
汇票付款人				可否分批				
汇票期限		见票____天期		装运期限			唛头	
				有效期				
				有效地点				
				提单日____天内议付		____天内寄单		

单证名称	提单	副本提单	商业发票	海关发票	装箱单	重量数量单	尺码单	保险单	产地证	普惠制产地证	贸促会产地证	出口许可证	装船通知书	投保通知	寄投保通知邮据	寄单证明	寄样证明	品质证明书
提交银行																		
提交客户																		

注:在"提交银行"或"提交客户"对应的栏目中填写应提交的单据份数,信用证要求提交的单据没有注明份数,默认为1份。

提单	抬头		保险	险种	
	通知				
运费支付方式(预付或到付)				投保加成率	赔款地点

注:如果提供的信用证的内容没有涉及信用证分析表的某些栏目,该栏目为空。

练习五

根据以下业务背景资料,填写信用证分析表。

DOCUMENTARY CREDIT

APPL. HEADER:SUMITOMO BANK LTD.,OSAKA

SEQUENCE OF TOTAL	27:1/1
FORM OF DOCUMENTARY CREDIT	40A:IRREVOCABLE
DOCUMENTARY CREDIT NUMBER	20:G/FO-7752807
DATE OF ISSUE	31C:170223
EXPIRY	31D:DATED 170610 PLACE:NINGBO,CHINA
APPLICANT	50:TOSHU CORPORATION OSALM
	12-36,KYUTARO-MACHI 4-CHOME
	CHUO-KU,OSAKA 561-8177,JAPAN
BENEFICIARY	59:DONGYUE KNITWEARS AND HOME
	TEXTILES IMPORT AND EXPORT
	CORPORATION
	197 ZHONGSHAN ROAD,NINGBO,
	CHINA
CURRENCY CODE. AMOUNT	32B:USD201,780.00
AVAILABLE WITH	41D:ANY BANK BY NEGOTIATION
DRAFTS AT	42C:AT SIGHT FOR 100 PCT OF INVOICE
	VALUE
DRAWEE	42D:THE SUMITOMO BANK,LTD.,YOKOHAMA
PARTIAL SHIPMENT	43P:ALLOWED
TRANSSHIPMENT	43T:PROHIBITED
LOADING/DISPATCH/TAKING/FROM	44A:NINGBO,CHINA
FOR TRANSPORTATION TO	44B:YOKOHAMA,OSAKA
DESCRPT. OF GOODS/SERVICES	45A:CIF YOKOHAMA,OSAKA

WOMEN'S SHIRT(CONTRACT NO. 99JA7031KL)

ST/NO.	QUANTITY	UNIT PRICE
11-100	67,200PCS	USD1.43/PC
11-101	48,000PCS	USD1.46/PC
11-102	27,600PCS	USD1.29/PC

DOCUMENTS REQUIRED   46A:+COMMERCIAL INVOICE IN QUINTUPLICATE

+PACKING LIST IN 3 COPIES

+FULL SET LESS ONE ORIGINAL (2/3)CLEAN ON

BOARD OCEAN BILLS OF LADING MADE OUT TO

ORDER, BLANK ENDORSED MARKED FREIGHT PREPAID NOTIFY APPLICANT AND US

+CERTIFICATE OF ORIGIN FORM A IN DUPLICATE

+INSURANCE POLICY OR CERTIFICATE IN DUPLICATE ENDORSED IN BLANK WITH CLAIM PAYABLE IN JAPAN IN THE CURRENCY OF THE DRAFT COVERING 120 PCT OF INVOICE VALUE INCLUDING INSTITUTE WAR CLAUSE, INSTITUTE CARGO CLAUSES (ALL RISKS), INSTITUTE S.R.C.C. CLAUSES

+BENEFICIARY'S CERTIFICATE STATING THAT ONE ORIGINAL B/L AND CERTIFICATE OF ORIGIN FORM A DIRECTLY TO THE APPLICANT (ATTN. OSALM SECTION) WITHIN 2 DAYS AFTER SHIPMENT BY AIR COURIER

ADDITIONAL COND.　　47A:+T.T IS ACCEPTABLE

+THE GOODS SHOULD BE CONTAINERIZED

+BENEFICIARY'S SHIPPING ADVICE TO THE ACCOUNTEE WITHIN 2 DAYS AFTER SHIPMENT

CONFIRMATION　　*49:WITHOUT

DETAILS OF CHARGES　　71B:ALL BANK CHARGES OUTSIDE AND COMMISIONS INCLUDING REIMBURSEMENT AS PER A/C OF BENEFICIARY

PRESENTATION PERIOD　　48:WITHIN 10 DAYS AFTER DATE OF SHIPMENT BUT WITHIN THE VALIDITY OF THE CREDIT

INSTRUCTION　　78:ALL SHIPPING DOCUMENTS TO BE SENT DIRECTLY TO THE OPENING OFFICE UPON RECEIPT OF THE PROCEEDS IN ONE LOT

信用证分析表练习五

信用证号		合约号			受益人			
开证银行				开证申请人				
开证日期		兑付方式		起运口岸			目的地	
金额				可否转运			成交方式	
汇票付款人				可否分批				

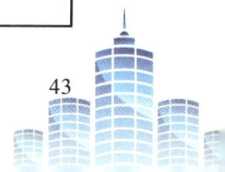

汇票期限	见票____天期		装运期限		唛头	
			有效期			
			有效地点			
			提单日____天内议付	____天内寄单		

单证名称	提单	副本提单	商业发票	海关发票	装箱单	重量数量单	尺码单	保险单	产地证	普惠制产地证	贸促会产地证	出口许可证	装船通知书	投保通知	寄投保通知邮据	寄单证明	寄样证明	品质证明书
提交银行																		
提交客户																		

注:在"提交银行"或"提交客户"对应的栏目中填写应提交的单据份数,信用证要求提交的单据没有注明份数,默认为1份。

提单	抬头		保险	险种			
	通知						
运费支付方式(预付或到付)				投保加成		赔款地点	

注:如果提供的信用证的内容没有涉及信用证分析表的某些栏目,该栏目为空。

第三节 商业发票的填制

一、商业发票的定义

商业发票(Commercial Invoice)简称发票(Invoice),它是卖方(出口方)向买方(进口方)开具的载有交易货物名称、数量、价格等内容的总清单,是装运货物的总说明。

注:它是信用证下的中心单据,是全套出口单据的中心。

二、商业发票的作用

(一)交易的证明文件(履约)

发票全面阐述了所装运货物及交货条件,例如卖的什么货物,卖了多少,总价是多少……这样进口方可以一目了然地看出所购货物的相关信息,确保出口方按规定装运。

(二)记账的凭证

发票是销售货物的凭证。出口商依据发票的内容逐笔登记入账,以此核算业务盈亏。进口商则依据出口商提供的发票,核对签订合同的项目,了解和掌握合同的履约情况,进行验收,按时结算货款。

(三)报关征税的依据

出口商在货物装运前需要向海关递交商业发票,作为报关发票;进口商在清关时需要向当地海关当局递交出口商发票。海关凭商业发票核算税金,并作为验关放行和统计的凭证之一。

(四)替代汇票

在即期付款不出具汇票的情况下,发票可作为买方支付货款的根据,替代汇票进行核算。光票付款的方式下,因为没有货运单据跟随,也经常跟随发票。所以商业发票起着证实装运货物和交易情况的作用。

另外,一旦发生保险索赔时,发票可以作为货物价值的证明。

三、发票的种类

除商业发票以外,发票还包括形式发票、海关发票、领事发票等。

1. 形式发票(PROFORMA INVOICE),也称预开发票或估价发票,是进口商为向其本国当局申请进口许可证或请求核批外汇,在未成交之前,要求出口商将拟出售成交的商品名称、单价、规格等条件开立的一份参考性发票。

2. 海关发票(CUSTOMS INVOICE)是某些国家规定在进口货物时,必须提供其海关规定的一种固定格式和内容的发票。

3. 领事发票(CONSULAR INVOICE),又称签证发票,是按某些国家法令规定,出口商对其国家输入货物时必须取得进口国在出口国或其邻近地区的领事签证的、作为装运单据一部分和货物进口报关的前提条件之一的特殊发票。

下面,列举几种发票模板供大家参考。

1. 高考指定商业发票模板

SELLER	商业发票 COMMERCIAL INVOICE			
BUYER	INVOICE NO.		INVOICE DATE	
	L/C NO.		S/C DATE	
	S/C NO.		PRICE TERM	
	FROM		TO	
MARKS	DESCRIPTION OF GOODS	QUANTITY	UNIT PRICE	AMOUNT
	TOTAL:			
TOTAL AMOUNT IN WORDS:				

2. 其他格式的商业发票

COMMERCIAL INVOICE

Messers：

INVOICE NO.:＿＿＿＿＿＿＿＿

INVOICE DATE:＿＿＿＿＿＿＿＿

L/C NO.:＿＿＿＿＿＿＿＿

L/C DATE:＿＿＿＿＿＿＿

Exporter：

Transport details：

Terms of payment：

MARKS AND NUMBERS	DESCRIPTION OF GOODS	QUANTITY	UNIT PRICE （USD/CASE）	AMOUNT （USD）

Signature

3. 形式发票

公司抬头

PROFORMA INVOICE

形式发票

TO:买方公司名称

DATE/日期：

P/I NO.：

P/O NO.：

ISSUER：

S/M 唛头	COMMODITIES AND SPECIFICATIONS 货名及规格	QTY 数量	UNIT PRICE 单价	TOTAL AMOUNT 总价
			贸易术语	
TOTAL	金额大写			

CONDITIONS：

1. Payment Terms：

2. Port of Loading：

3. Port of destination：

4. Delivery time：

5. Country of Origin：

6. Price terms：

7. PI Validity：

9. Beneficiary：

BENEFICIARY'S BANK：

BUYER：   SELLER：

DATE：   DATE：

4. 海关发票(以加拿大海关发票为例)

<table>
<tr><td colspan="4" align="center">CANADA CUSTOMS INVOICE</td></tr>
<tr>
<td colspan="2">1. Vendor(Name and Address) Vendeur(Nom et adresse)</td>
<td colspan="2">2. Date of Direct Shipment to Canada / Date d' expedition directe vers ie Canade</td>
</tr>
<tr>
<td colspan="2" rowspan="2"></td>
<td colspan="2">3. Other References(include Purchaser's Order No.) Autres reterences(inclure ie n de commande de Í acheteur)</td>
</tr>
<tr>
<td colspan="2"></td>
</tr>
<tr>
<td colspan="2">4. Consignee
(Name and Address)
Destinataire(Nom et adresse)</td>
<td colspan="2">5. Purchaser's Name and Address(if other than Consignee)
Nom et adresse de Í acheteur
(S'll differe du destinataire)</td>
</tr>
<tr>
<td colspan="2" rowspan="3"></td>
<td colspan="2">6. Country of Transshipment / Pays de transbordement</td>
</tr>
<tr>
<td>7. Country of Origin of Goods(pays d' origine des marchandises)</td>
<td>IF SHIPMENT INCLUDES GOODS OF DIFFERENT ORIGINS ENTER ORIGINS AGAINST ITEMA IN12 SIL' EXPEDON COMPREND DES MARCHANDISES D' ORIGINES</td>
</tr>
<tr>
<td></td>
<td></td>
</tr>
<tr>
<td colspan="2">8. Transportation Give Mode and Place of Direct Shipment to Canada</td>
<td colspan="2">9. Conditrions of Sale and Terms of Payment</td>
</tr>
<tr>
<td colspan="2" rowspan="2"></td>
<td colspan="2">10. Currency of Settlement / Devises du paiement</td>
</tr>
<tr>
<td colspan="2"></td>
</tr>
<tr>
<td rowspan="2">11.
No. of
Pkgs</td>
<td rowspan="2">12. Specification of Commodities</td>
<td rowspan="2">13.
Quantity</td>
<td colspan="2" align="center">Selling Price / Prix de vente</td>
</tr>
<tr>
<td>14.
Unit Price</td>
<td>15. Total</td>
</tr>
<tr>
<td></td>
<td></td>
<td></td>
<td></td>
<td></td>
</tr>
<tr>
<td colspan="2" rowspan="2">18. if any Of fields 1 to 17 are included on an attached commercial invoice, check this box si tout renseignement relatlvement aux zones 1 e 17 ligure sur une ou des tactures</td>
<td rowspan="2">☐</td>
<td>16. Total Weight / Poids Total</td>
<td rowspan="2">17.
Invoice
Total</td>
</tr>
<tr>
<td>Net   Gross/Brut</td>
</tr>
<tr>
<td colspan="2">19. Exporter's Name and Address(if other than Vendor)
Nom et adresse de Í exportateur(s'll differe du vendeur)</td>
<td colspan="2">20. Originator(Name and Address)/Expediteur d' origine
(Nom et adresse)</td>
</tr>
<tr>
<td colspan="2"></td>
<td colspan="2"></td>
</tr>
</table>

CANADA CUSTOMS INVOICE		
21. Departmental Rulikg(if applicable)/Decision du Ministere (S' lly a lieu) N/A	22. If fields 23 to 25 are not applicable, check this box	☐

23. if included in field 17 indicate amount Si compris dans ie total a ia zone 17, preciser （Ⅰ）Transportation charges, expense and insurance from the place of direct shipment to Canada Les frais de transport, depenses et assurances a partir du point of expedition directe vers is Canada.	24. If not included in field 17 indicate amount Si non compris dans le total a ie zone 17, Dreciser （Ⅰ）Transportation charges, expense and insurance to the place of direct shipment to Canada Les frais de transport, depenses et assurances Iusqu' au point d' of expedition directd vers ie Canada	25. Check （if applicable） Cochet （s'lly a liso） （Ⅱ）Royalty payments or subsequent proceede are paid or payable by the purchaser Des redevances ou prodults ont ete ou seront Verses par Í acheteur
	N/A	☐
（Ⅱ）Costs for const: action, erection and assembly incurred atter importation into Canada Les couts de construction, d' erection et d' assemblage,, pres imporaation au.Canada	（Ⅱ）Amounts for commissions other than buying commissions Les commissions autres que celles versees Pour Í achat	（Ⅱ）The purchaser has supplied goods or services for use in the production of these goods L'acheteur a fouml des merchandises ou des Services pour ia production des merchandises
N/A	N/A	
	（Ⅲ）Export packing Le cout de Í emballage d' exportation	
（Ⅲ）Export packing Le cout de Í emballage d' exportation	N/A	☐
N/A		
		.

5. 领事发票（以巴西领事发票为例）

THE GOVERNMENT OF BRAZIL	
Date: Invoice NO.: Issued At:	Port of Loading: Port of Discharge: Date of Departure: Carrier:
EXPORTER	CONSIGNEE

续表

Marks and Numbers	Quantity	Description of Goods	Value of Shipment
Total:			

Other Charges:	Amount of Charges:
	Total:
Certified Correct By: Witnessed By: Fee Paid:	

四、发票条款概述

1. 出票人的名称和地址(NAME AND ADDRESS OF DRAWER)

2. 发票名称(NAME OF INVOICE)

一般在此栏已经预先印制"商业发票"(COMMERCIAL INVOICE)或"发票"(INVOICE)字样。如果 L/C 要求提供 COMMERCIAL INVOICE,我们可以用 INVOICE 替代。

3. 发票抬头人(TO...)

除非信用证指定发票抬头人,一般情况下,此栏填制进口人即开证申请人(APPLICANT)的名称和地址。

4. 发票日期(DATE OF INVOICE)

发票日期是所有单据日期中最早的,甚至可以早于信用证的开证日期。

5. 发票编号(INVOICE NO.)

此栏填制由出口公司自己所定的发票编号。

6. 合约号码(CONTRACT NO.)

注意发票的货物涉及不止一个合同的,此栏应显示全部合同号。

7. 起运地(FROM)

应明确具体,不能笼统。如果 L/C 中规定起运地为 ANY CHINESE PORT,则在填写此栏时应填写具体的港口。

8. 目的地(TO)及使用的运输方式(MODE OF TRANSPORT)

目的地填写方法同上,后面再加实际的运输方式,比如运输方式为海运,则在目的地后加上 BY SEA。

9. 信用证的号码(L/C NO.)

如果非信用证结算,则此栏空白。

10. 开证银行(ISSUING BANK)

如果非信用证结算,则此栏空白。

11. 唛头及件号(MARKS ＆ NUMBERS)

(1)按 L/C 或合同规定填写。

(2)如果无唛头,则可以用 NO MARKS 或 N/M 来表示。

(3)L/C 规定的唛头其中有 NO.1-UP,那么在单据填写过程中应该把 UP 改为实际的最大包装数,而不应该照抄。

12. 数量和商品描述(QUANTITIES AND DESCRIPTIONS)

(1)信用证支付方式下的发票对货物描述应严格按照信用证的规定,如托收,则根据实际所装货物的情况填制。

(2)信用证规定的货名并非英文,发票也应照原文显示,必要时可在旁加注英文解释。

(3)除 L/C 所规定的货物外,发票不能再显示其他货物或免费样品。

13. 单价(UNIT PRICE)

单价由四个组成部分:价格术语、计价货币、单位数额和计量单位。

14. 总价和累计总金额(AMOUNT)

总价应为发票上列明的单价与数量的乘积,而且不能超过信用证的金额。

15. 签名(SIGNATURE)

此栏填制出口公司的名称及负责人签字或盖章。但根据 UCP600 的规定,除非另有规定,商业发票无须签署。

16. 特殊条款(SPECIAL TERMS/CONDITIONS)

一般有以下几种:

(1)注明特定号码;

(2)注明货物的原产地及包装细节;

(3)注明运费、保险费;

(4)缮打证明文句。

17. 加注"ORIGINAL"字样

通常的做法是在其中一张发票上加注"ORIGINAL"字样,加注位置在本栏目或在发票的右上角空白处。

五、商业发票的详解

1. 出口商名称和详细地址(EXPORTER'S NAME AND ADDRESS)

此栏填制出口公司名称和详细地址,应与信用证中受益人相一致。多数情况下,此栏出口公司已预先印制。

2. 商业发票须载明"发票"或"商业发票"(INVOICE OR COMMERCIAL INVOICE)字样

3. 发票抬头人(TO/BUYER/MESSERS):

(1)支付方式——L/C:收货人(一般为买方/开证申请人)名称和详细地址。

(2)支付方式——汇款/托收:买方(进口方)。

(3)如果发票条款或附加条款中出现 IN THE NAME OF / MADE OUT IN THE NAME OF / MADE IN THE NAME OF / MADE IN THE TITLE OF / CONSIGNED TO 等,则后面跟的名称都是发票的抬头,填在发票的 TO / BUYER/MESSERS 一栏。

例:信用证

APPLICANT:ABC CO. LTD.,PARIS,

又规定:"INVOICE TO BE MADE OUT IN THE NAME OF DEF CO. LTD.,PARIS",

则填制发票时,TO/BUYER/MESSERS一栏填写 DEF CO. LTD.,PARIS.。

(说明开证人仅为中间商,非真实买主)

4. 发票编号和签发日期(NUMBER AND DATE)

信用证和合同号码(L/C NO. AND CONTRACT NUMBER)。

5. 运输方式及起讫地点(FROM……TO……PER……)

(1)填写时要写上具体港名,港口出现重名的还应注明国别或地区;

(2)如实际有转运,则转运地点也应在TO后面明确标出。

例:货物从广州经由香港转船至德国的法兰克福,则填写:FROM GUANGZHOU TO FRANKFURT W/T AT HONG KONG 或 FROM GUANGZHOU TO FRANKFURT VIA HONG KONG.

6. 唛头(SHIPPING MARKS)

(1)有唛头,则照抄,但是如果能计算出箱数,要把UP改成具体的箱数;如果无法计算箱数,则还是写UP;

(2)无唛头:N/M(NO MARK);

(3)自制,一般制作标准唛头包括收货人或买方名称的缩写、参考号码、目的港、件号(具体参看资料要求)。

7. 数量及货物描述(QUANTITIES AND DESCRIPTIONS)

(1)这栏中所填的内容应与信用证货描内容严格一致;

(2)货物描述内容一般包括合同的四个主要条款:数量条款、品质规格条款、包装条款、详见合同。

例:<u>1000KGS CHINESE WHITE ANGORA RABBIT HAIR</u>

      ①数量

<u>SUPER GRADE</u>   <u>PACKED IN 10 BALES</u>

 ②品质   ③包装

<u>AS PER CONTRACT NO. 01ZAO1IA7007</u>

    ④详见合同

注:L/C数量条款中若有"约、大概、大约"时,可理解成有关数量不超过10%的增减幅度。

8. 如果信用证没有具体货描,但是补充资料中出现如型号、规格等货物描述的内容,则都要写在发票货描一栏中。

9. 如出现分批装运的描述,则写实际出口的货物描述时,把分批装运的描述也一起写上。

10. 单价、总值及价格条件(UNIT PRICE,AMOUNT AND PRICE TERM)

单价(Unit Price)由四个部分组成:计价货币(USD)、单位金额(28.00)、PER PC(计量单位)、价格术语(CIF NEW YORK)。

注:有的信用证中价格含佣,有的含折扣,有的还要求显示运费、保险费,所以在制作发票总金额一栏时要注意以下几点。

(1)如果信用证总金额和单价都是含佣价,而商业发票没有要求扣佣,则发票按含佣价制作。

例：

DESCRIPTION	QUANTITY	UNIT PRICE	AMOUNT
MEN'S SHIRTS	1,000PCS	CIFC5% NEW YORK USD10.00/PC	USD10,000.00
TOTAL:	1,000PCS		USD10,000.00

（2）如果信用证总金额和单价都是含佣价，而商业发票要求显示净价或明确要求扣除佣金，则发票显示扣佣过程。

例1：CIFC5% NEW YORK　USD10.00/PC

SIGNED COMMERCIAL INVOICE IN DUPLICATE INDICATING CIF NET VALUE.

则扣佣，大写含佣价。如下表：

DESCRIPTION	QUANTITY	UNIT PRICE	AMOUNT
MEN'S SHIRTS	1,000PCS	CIFC5% NEW YORK USD10.00/PC	USD10,000.00
TOTAL:	1,000PCS	LESS C5% CIF NET VALUE	USD10,000.00 USD500.00 USD9,500.00

TOTAL AMOUNT(IN WORDS)：SAY U.S.DOLLARS TEN THOUSAND ONLY.

（注：若L/C要求INDICATING/SHOWING/BEARING COMMISSION，则只需显示，表示为，例：INCLUDING C5%　USD500.00）

例2：CIFC5% NEW YORK　USD10.00/PC

5% COMMISSION TO BE DEDUCTED / LESS FROM THE INVOICE VALUE.

则扣佣，大写净价。如下表：

DESCRIPTION	QUANTITY	UNIT PRICE	AMOUNT
MEN'S SHIRTS	1,000PCS	CIFC5% NEW YORK USD10.00/PC	USD10,000.00
TOTAL:	1,000PCS	LESS C5% CIF NET VALUE	USD10,000.00 USD500.00 USD9,500.00

TOTAL AMOUNT(IN WORDS)：SAY U.S.DOLLARS NINE THOUSAND FIVE HUNDRED ONLY.

（3）如果信用证单价是含佣价，而总金额是净价，则发票显示扣佣过程，金额大写也是净价。

（显示过程同"例2"）

（4）如果信用证价格为含折扣价，则要显示扣除折扣的过程，金额大写为净价。如下表：

DESCRIPTION	QUANTITY	UNIT PRICE	AMOUNT
MEN'S SHIRTS	1,000PCS	CIFD5% NEW YORK USD10.00/PC	USD10,000.00
TOTAL:	1,000PCS	LESS D5% CIF NET VALUE	USD10,000.00 USD500.00 USD9,500.00

TOTAL AMOUNT(IN WORDS):SAY U.S.DOLLARS NINE THOUSAND FIVE HUNDRED ONLY.

（5）如果发票条款要求SHOWING FREIGHT CHARGE,PREMIUM AND FOB VALUE SEPARATELY.

例：

DESCRIPTION	QUANTITY	UNIT PRICE	AMOUNT
MEN'S SHIRTS	1,000PCS	CIF NEW YORK USD10.00/PC	USD10,000.00
TOTAL:	1,000PCS	FREIGHT CHARGE PREMIUM CIF NET VALUE	USD10,000.00 USD500.00 USD100.00 USD9,400.00

注意：（1）运费、保险费和净价不一定填在TOTAL一栏中,具体参看标号在哪里,就填哪里。

（2）只是要求显示运费、保险费和净价,金额大写仍是原价格金额。

（3）保险费的计算:保险费=CIF×（1+投保加成率）×保险费率。

（4）保佣不保折,即出现含佣价,按含佣价计算保险费;出现折扣,则取出折扣后的净价计算保险费。

11. 发票上加注各种特殊文句

（1）显示运费、保险费、FOB金额;

（2）注明特殊号码,如进口证号、配额许可证号等;或注明"COUNTRY OF CHINA";

（3）编制证明句,如:WE HEREBY CERTIFY/DECLARE/EVIDENCE THAT…;

例1:SIGNED COMMERCIAL INVOICE IN FIVE FOLDS CERTIFYING THAT GOODS ARE AS PER CONTRACT NO.12345 OF MAR.11,2004,QUOTING L/C NUMBER AND BTN/HS NO. SHOWING ORIGINAL INVOICE AND A COPY TO ACCOMPANY ORIGINAL SET OF DOCUMENTS.

译:签字发票一式五份,证明货物是根据2004年3月11日号码为12345的合同,并注明信用证号码和布鲁塞尔税则分类号码,显示正本发票和一份副本随附原套单证。

例2:COMMERCIAL INVOICE IN TRIPLICATE SHOWING SEPARATELY FOB VALUE,FRIGHT CHARGES,PREMIUM,CIF VALUE AND COUNTRY OF ORIGIN.

译:商业发票一式三份,分别显示FOB价值、运费、保险费、CIF总值和原产地国。

（4）发票认证条款

例:SIGNED COMMERCIAL INVOICE IN 2-FOLD ORIGINAL OF WHICH SHOULD BE CERTIFIED BY CHAMBER OF COMMERCE OR CCPIT AND LEGALIZED BY UAE EMBASSY AT BENEFICIARY'S COUNTRY.

译:签字发票一式两份,其中一份正本由受益人所在国的商会或贸促会认证,再经由阿拉伯联合酋长国大使馆认证。

(5)发票由收货人回签条款

例:COMMERCIAL INVOICE IN TRIPLICATE DULY SIGNED BY BENEFICIARY AND COUNTER SIGNED BY MR. JASON AS APPLICANT'S LEGAL REPRESENTIVE WHOSE AUTOGRAPH SIGNATURE WE ARE SENDING YOU BY DHL AS INTEGRAL PART OF THIS L/C.

译:受益人签字发票一式三份,该发票需由作为申请人合法代表的贾森先生回签。我们正用DHL将他的亲笔签名快邮给贵方,并将其作为信用证不可分割的一部分。

12. 出单人名称及签名(SIGNATURE)

发票条款中出现MANUALLY或IN INK,意为手签,则法人名字写好后,旁边注明手签。例:张明(手签);若发票条款中出现STAMPED,意为盖章,则法人名字写好后,旁边注明章。例:张明(章)。

13. 商业发票的份数

(1)正本 ORIGINAL(S)　　　副本 COPY(COPIES)

(2)一式X份

六、商业发票易错点集锦

1. 公司名称和地址要分栏写。

2. 如果发票条款或装箱单条款中有指定抬头,或信用证特殊条款中说明所有单据的抬头是***,则发票抬头应为该指定抬头。

3. 如实际有转运,则在目的港后面注明转运港。

4. 唛头中如有UP,应该为具体的最大包装件数。

5. 货描的填写应根据实际填写。如允许分批装运或溢短装,发票只需填写实际装运的那一部分。货描显示所有45A列出的条款,包括AS PER S/C NO.、包装方式等。

6. 金额小写保留2位小数。若有小数位,则金额大写注意辅币的应用;金额大写,整数与小数点之间必须加"AND"。

7. 金额根据信用证要求扣除佣金、折扣或去除运费、保费,显示净价等。

8. 发票条款中出现MANUALLY或IN INK,意为手签,则法人名字写好后,旁边注明手签;若发票条款中出现STAMPED,意为盖章,则法人名字写好后,旁边注明章。

9. 注意特殊条款的描述和位置,特殊条款应写全。如:L/C NO....,WE HEREBY CERTIFY THAT...

七、专项练习

练习一

ISSUING BANK:DAS BANK LTD.,TOKYO

L/C NO:9426

DATE:JUNE 15,2018

APPLICANT:DRF INTERNATIONAL FOOD CO.,26 TORIMI—CHO NISHI-PU NAGOYA 546,JAPAN

BENEFICIARY:NINGBO INT PRODUCTS CO.,NO.115 DONGFENG ROAD,NINGBO,CHINA

CONTRACT NO.:NP180501

CONTRACT DATE:MAY 01,2018

COVERING:20M/T FRESH BAMBOO SHOOTS FROM NINGBO TO NAGOYA AT CIF NAGOYA USD1,080.00 PER M/T AND 30 M/T FRESH ASPARAGUS AT CIF NAGOYA 1,600.00 PER M/T

SHIPPING MARKS:NO MARKS

INVOICE NO.:NP180620

INVOICE DATE:JUNE 20,2018

SELLER	商业发票 COMMERCIAL INVOICE				
BUYER	INVOICE NO.			INVOICE DATE	
	L/C NO.			S/C DATE	
	S/C NO.			PRICE TERM	
	FROM			TO	
MARKS	DESCRIPTION OF GOODS	QUANTITY		UNIT PRICE	AMOUNT
		TOTAL:			
TOTAL AMOUNT IN WORDS:					

练习二

FROM:BANK OF CHINA,LONDON,UK.

TO:BANK OF CHINA,SHANGHAI,CHINA

SEQUENCE OF TOTAL   27:1/1

FORM OF DOC. CREDIT   40:IRREVOCABLE

DOC. CREDIT NUMBER   20:LC-21683

DATE OF ISSUE   31C:180501

EXPIRY	31D:DATE:180725 PLACE:CHINA

EXPIRY 31D:DATE:180725   PLACE:CHINA

APPLICANT 50:DFG TRADING CO.,LTD,
117-2 QUEEN STREET,LONDON,UK

BENEFICIARY 59:ZHEJIANG YUANDONG CO.,LTD,
NO.1121,YAN'AN ROAD,HANGZHOU,CHINA

AMOUNT 32B:CURRENCY USD AMOUNT 105,722.50

AVAILABLE WITH 41D:ANY BANK IN CHINA BY NEGOTIATION

DRAFT AT... 42C:SIGHT FOR 100 PCT OF INVOICE VALUE

DRAWEE 42D:BANK OF CHINA,LONDON,UK.

PARTIAL SHIPMENT 43P:NOT ALLOWED

TRANSSHIPMENT 43T:ALLOWED AT HONG KONG

LOADING IN CHARGE 44A:CHINESE PORT

FOR TRANSPORT TO 44B:LONDON,UK

LATEST DATE OF SHIPMENT 44C:180630

DESCRIPT. OF GOODS 45A:100% COTTON LADIES' DRESS AS PER S/C NO.BP13-2594

SPECIFICATION	QUANTITY	UNIT PRICE	AMOUNT
LD-501	3,350PCS	USD14.55/PC	48,742.50
SH-401	2,800PCS	USD20.35/PC	56,980.00

TRADE TERM:CIFC2% LONDON

SHIPPING MARKS:DFG/BP13-2594/LONDON/NO.1-UP

DOCUMENTS REQUIRED 46A:+SIGNED COMMERCIAL INVOICE IN TRIPLICATE IN THE NAME OF ABC TRADING CO.,LTD. INDICATING CIF NET VALUE

DETAILS OF CHARGES 71B:ALL BANKING CHARGES OUTSIDE LONDON ARE FOR THE ACCOUNT OF THE BENEFICIARY

PRESENTATION PERIOD 48:DOCUMENTS TO BE PRESENTED WITHIN 15 DAYS AFTER THE DATE OF SHIPMENT,BUT WITHIN THE VALIDITY OF THE CREDIT.

其他资料

合同签约日:2018年4月23日

发票号码:BPCH13-23   发票日期:2018年6月5日

装运港:上海   卖方法人代表:李宏

运费:2,000.00美元   保险费:1,800.00美元

PACKING:PACKED IN CARTONS OF 50PCS EACH

SELLER	商业发票 COMMERCIAL INVOICE			
BUYER	INVOICE NO.		INVOICE DATE	
	L/C NO.		S/C DATE	
	S/C NO.		PRICE TERM	
	FROM		TO	
MARKS	DESCRIPTION OF GOODS	QUANTITY	UNIT PRICE	AMOUNT
		TOTAL:		
TOTAL AMOUNT IN WORDS:				

练习三

ADVISING BANK:BANK OF COMMUNICATIONS SHANGHAI(HEAD OFFICE)

OPENING BANK:BANGKOK BANK PUBLIC COMPANY LIMITED,BANGKOK

SEQUENCE TOTAL   *27:1/1

FORM DOC. CREDIT   *40A:IRREVOCABLE

DOC. CREDIT NUM.   *20:0011LC123756

DATE OF ISSUE   31C:181103

EXPIRY   *31D:DATE:190114   PLACE:BENEFICIARIES' COUNTRY

APPLICANT   *50:MOUN CO.,LTD.,
                             NO. 443,249 ROAD,BANGKOK,THAILAND

BENEFICIARY   59:SHANGHAI FOREIGN TRADE CORP.,SHANGHAI,CHINA

AMOUNT   *32B:CURRENCY USD AMOUNT 18,000

AVAILABLE WITH   *41D:ANY BANK IN CHINA BY NEGOTIATION

DRAFTS AT   42C:SIGHT IN DUPLICATE INDICATING THIS L/C NUMBER

DRAWEE   43D:ISSUING BANK

PARTIAL SHIPMENT   43P:NOT ALLOWED

TRANSSHIPMENT   43T:ALLOWED

LOADING ON BOARD   44A:CHINA MAIN PORT,CHINA

TRANSPORT TO   44B:BANGKOK,THAILAND

LATEST SHIPMENT   44C:181220

GOODS DESCRIPT.   45A:2,000KGS ISONIAZID BP98 AT USD9.00 PER KG CFRC5% BANGKOK

DOCS. REQUIRED   46A:+COMMERCIAL INVOICE IN ONE ORIGINAL PLUS 5 COPIES INDICATING FOB VALUE,FREIGHT CHARGES SEPARATELY AND THIS L/C NUMBER AND B/L NUMBER,ALL OF WHICH MUST BE MANUALLY SIGNED

+FULL SET OF 3/3 CLEAN ON BOARD OCEAN BILL OF LADING AND TWO NON-NEGOTIABLE COPIES MADE OUT TO ORDER OF BANGKOK BANK PUBLIC COMPANY LIMITED, BANGKOK MARKED FREIGHT PREPAID AND NOTIFYING APPLICANT AND INDICATING THIS L/C NUMBER

+PACKING LIST IN ONE ORIGINAL PLUS 5 COPIES IN THE NAME OF ABC COMPANY,ALL OF WHICH MUST BE MANUALLY SIGNED

+CERTIFICATE OF ANALYSIS IN ONE ORIGINAL PLUS ONE COPY

AD. CONDITIONS   47A:A DISCREPANCY FEE OF USD50.00 WILL BE IMPOSED ON EACH SET OF DOCUMENTS PRESENTED FOR NEGOTIATION UNDER THIS L/C WITH DISCREPANCY AND THE FEE WILL BE DEDUCTED FROM THE BILL AMOUNT

CHARGES   71B:ALL BANK CHARGES OUTSIDE THAILAND INCLUDING REIMBURSING BANK COMMISSION AND DISCREPANCY FEE(IF ANY) ARE FOR BENEFICIARIES' ACCOUNT

相关资料

发票号码:SHE 02/1845   发票日期:2018年11月26日

提单号码:SCOISG7564   提单日期:2018年11月29日

合同号码:S/C00112233   合同日期:2018年10月25日

公司法人:张丽

货物装箱情况:50KGS/DRUM   总毛重:2,200KGS

总净重:2,000KGS   总体积:50M³

集装箱:1x40' FCL CFS/CFS   运费:USD0.08/KG

UXXU4240250 0169255

SELLER	商业发票 COMMERCIAL INVOICE				
BUYER	INVOICE NO.			INVOICE DATE	
	L/C NO.			S/C DATE	
	S/C NO.			PRICE TERM	
	FROM			TO	
MARKS	DESCRIPTION OF GOODS	QUANTITY		UNIT PRICE	AMOUNT
		TOTAL:			
TOTAL AMOUNT IN WORDS:					

练习四

FROM：

UNION BANK OF CALIFORNIA,N.A.

SOUTHERN CALIFORNIA TRADE SERVICE OPERATIONS

IMPORT LETTERS OF CREDIT

1980 SA TURN STREET

MONTEREY PARK,CA. 91755

DATE：180706

LETTER OF CREDIT NO.：309M116905

ADVISING BANK：BANK OF CHINA,SHANGHAI BRANCH

BENEFICIARY：

SHANGHAI GARMENTS IMP. AND EXP. CO.,LTD.

309 SUZHOU ROAD NORTH,SHANGHAI,CHINA

APPLICANT：

POWER PLAY INC.

2ND FLOOR,NO. 137E,33ROAD STREET,

LOS ANGELES,CA. 90011

U.S.A.

WE HEREBY ISSUE OUR IRREVOCABLE LETTER OF CREDIT NUMBER 309M116905 IN FAVOR OF THE ABOVE NAMED BENEFICIARY IN THE AMOUNT OF USD66,726.00(SAY U.S.DOLLARS SIXTY-SIX THOUSAND SEVEN HUNDRED AND TWENTY-SIX ONLY.)

EXPIRATION DATE:SEPTEMBER 05,2018

EXPIRY PLACE:IN CHINA

SHIPMENT FROM:SHANGHAI,CHINA

SHIPMENT TO:LONG BEACH CA,USA

LATEST SHIPMENT DATE:180821

PARTIAL SHIPMENTS ARE ALLOWED,TRANSSHIPMENT IS PROHIBITED,CREDIT IS AVAILABLE WITH ANY BANK BY NEGOTIATION AGAINST BENEFICIARY'S.

DRAFTS AT SIGHT DRAWN ON US FOR 100 PCT OF THE INVOICE VALUE BEARING THE CLAUSE: DRAWN UNDER UNION BANK OF CALIFORNIA,N.A., CREDIT NO. 309M116905 WITH ACCOMPANIED BY THE FOLLOWING DOCUMENTS:

1. COMMERCIAL INVOICE IN TRIPLICATE CERTIFYING THAT THE QUALITY COLOR SIZE AND STYLE ON EACH ITEM ARE AS PER S/C NO. PS11E06F025 DATED 180625.

2. PACKING LIST IN TRIPLICATE SHOWING THAT ONE SET INTO ONE PP BAG,12 SET INTO ONE EXPORT CARTON.

3. CERTIFICATE OF ORIGIN IN DUPLICATE ISSUED BY CCPIT.

4. FULL SET CLEAN ON BOARD OCEAN BILL OF LADING MADE OUT TO OUR ORDER MARKED FREIGHT PREPAID NOTIFY APPLICANT WITH FULL NAME AND ADDRESS.

5. CERTIFICATE OF QUALITY INSPECTION SIGNED BY MR. MARK LALEAH DATED PRIOR TO THE ACTUAL SHIPMENT DATE.

6. SHIPPING ADVICE ISSUED BY BENEFICIARY TO APPLICANT ON FAX NUMBER001-949-3623623 STATING ALL SHIPPING DETAILS ONE DAY BEFORE THE SHIPMENT.

MERCHANDISE DESCRIPTION:

MEN'S SHIRTS AND PANTS

ITEM NO.7001　2,220SETS　USD19.35 PER SET

ITEM NO.7002　780SETS　USD20.35 PER SET

ITEM NO.7003　420SETS　USD18.80 PER SET

CFR LONG BEACH INCOTERMS 2010

SPECIAL CONDITIONS:

1. ALL DOCUMENTS MUST INDICATE THIS CREDIT NUMBER.

2. DOCUMENTS PRESENTED WITH DISCREPANCIES WILL BE DEDUCTED A DISCREPANCY FEE OF USD75.00 PER EACH SET OF DOCUMENT.

3. ONE ADDITIONAL COPY OF DOCUMENTS IS REQUIRED TO BE PRESENTED TOGETHER

WITH THE DOCUMENTS FOR ISSUING BANKS RETENTION USD20.00 WILL BE DEDUCTED IF NO SUCH COPY PRESENTED.

4. INSURANCE TO BE EFFECTED BY THE BUYER.

5. DRAFTS AND DOCUMENTS MUST BE PRESENTED FOR NEGOTIATION WITHIN 15 DAYS AFTER THE DATE OF BILL OF LADING BUT WITHIN THE VALIDITY OF THIS CREDIT.

6. ALL BANKING CHARGES OTHER THAN THOSE OF THE ISSUING BANK ARE FOR THE ACCOUNT OF THE BENEFICIARY.

7. THIS CREDIT IS SUBJECT TO THE UNIFORM CUSTOMS AND PRACTICE FOR DOCUMENTARY CREDITS(2007 REVISION) INTERNATIONAL CHAMBER OF COMMERCE PUBLICATION NO 600.

8. WE ENGAGE WITH YOU THAT ALL DRAFTS DRAWN UNDER AND IN COMPLIANCE WITH THE TERMS OF THIS CREDIT WILL BE HONORED AND OR REMITTED ON MATURITY ON DELIVERY OF DOCUMENTS AS SPECIFIED IF PRESENTED AT THIS OFFICE INSTRUCTIONS TO PAYING/ACCEPTING/NEGOTIA TING BANK：NEGOTIA TING BANK IS REQUESTED TO FORWARD THE DOCUMENTS IN ONE MAIL BY COURIER A TTN：TRADE SERVICE OPERA TIONS（V01-518），1980 SA TURN STREET，MONTEREY PARK，CA 91755 USA.

有关资料：

男式休闲短袖上衣与中裤(套装),法定商检产品

其中货号7001只出运了2,160套,另两款全部出运

一套一个塑料袋(PP BAG),12套一箱

毛重:13公斤/箱　　净重:11公斤/箱

纸箱尺码:58×50×30cms	发票号码:11SG09-301	发票日期:2018年8月7日
提单号码:SHLB1108201	提单日期:2018年8月20日	
集装箱号码:TRLU856092	集装箱封号:487092	1×20'FCL,CY/CY
海运费:2,100.00美元	船名:OOCL TRADE UNION,V.803E	

受益人中文:上海服装进出口有限公司

发票签署:李晓雨

唛头:

POWER PLAY

PS11E06F025

LONG BEACH

NO.1-280

MADE IN CHINA

SELLER	商业发票 COMMERCIAL INVOICE			
BUYER	INVOICE NO.		INVOICE DATE	
	L/C NO.		S/C DATE	
	S/C NO.		PRICE TERM	
	FROM		TO	
MARKS	DESCRIPTION OF GOODS	QUANTITY	UNIT PRICE	AMOUNT
		TOTAL:		
TOTAL AMOUNT IN WORDS:				

练习五

ISSUING BANK:METITA BANK LTD.,FINLAND

DOC. CREDIT NO.:IRREVOCABLE

CREDIT NUMBER:LRT9802457

DATE OF ISSUE:180428

EXPIRY:DATE:180616   PLACE:FINLAND

APPLICANT:F.T.C. CO. AKEKSANTERINK AUTO P.O.BOX 9,FINLAND

BENEFICIARY:GREAT WALL TRADING CO.,LTD.,

            RM201,HUASHENG BUILDING,NINGBO,P.R. CHINA

AMOUNT:USD19,090,00

AVAILABLE WITH:ANY BANK IN ADVISING COUNTRY BY NEGOTIATION

DRAFT AT:DRAFTS AT 30 DAYS AFTER B/L DATE FOR 100% INVOICE VALUE

PARTIAL SHIPMENTS:NOT ALLOWED

TRANSSHIPMENT:ALLOWED

LOADING IN CHARGE:NINGBO

FOR TRANSPORT TO:HELSINKI

SHIPMENT PERIOD:AT THE LATEST MAY 30,2018

DESCRIP. OF GOODS:P.P INJECTION CASES ZL0322+BC05 230SETS @USD42.00/SET USD9,660.00

P.P INJECTION CASES ZL0319+BC01 230SETS @USD41.00/SET USD9,430.00

AS PER SALES CONTRACT GW2005M06 DATED APR. 22,2018,CIFC5% HELSINKI

DOCUMENTS REQUIRED:+ SIGNED COMMERCIAL INVOICE 1 ORIGINAL AND 5 COPIES, 5% COMMISSION TO BE DEDUCTED FROM THE INVOICE VALUE

+PACKING LIST IN 2 COPIES

+ FULL SET OF CLEAN ON BOARD MARINE BILL OF LADING, MADE OUT TO ORDER,MARKED FREIGHT PREPAID AND NOTIFY APPLICANT AND US(AS INDICATE ABOVE)

+CERTIFICATE OF ORIGIN IN 2 COPIES

+ INSURANCE POLICY / CERTIFICATE COVERING ALL RISKS AND WAR RISKS OF P.I.C.C. UP TO FINAL DESTINATION AT HELSINKI, FOR AT LEAST 110 PCT OF CIF VALUE

+SHIPPING ADVICES MUST BE SENT TO APPLICANT WITH 2 DAYS AFTER SHIPMENT ADVISING NUMBER OF PACKAGES, GROSS & NET WEIGHT, VESSEL NAME,BILL OF LADING NO. AND DATE, CONTRACT NO.,VALUE

+CERTIFICATE TO SHOW THAT THE REQUIRED SHIPMENT SAMPLES HAVE BEEN SENT BY DHL TO THE APPLICANT

PRESENTATION PERIOD:15 DAYS AFTER ISSUANCE DATE OF SHIPPING DOCUMENT

ADDITIONAL INSTRUCTION:

1. BOTH QUANTITY AND AMOUNT 10 PERCENT MORE OR LESS ARE ALLOWED.

2. ALL DOCUMENTS MUST INDICATE THIS CREDIT NUMBER.

CHARGES:ALL BANKING CHARGES OUTSIDE THE OPENING BANK ARE FOR BENEFICIARY'S ACCOUNT.

CONFIRMATION:WITHOUT

INSTRUCTIONS:THE NEGOTIATION BANK MUST FORWARD THE DRAFTS AND ALL DOCUMENTS BY REGISTEREDAIRMAIL DIRECT TO US IN TWO CONSECUTIVE LOTS,UPON RECEIPT OF THE DRAFTS AND CUMENTS IN ORDER,WE WILL REMIT THE PROCEEDS AS INSTRUCTED BY THE NEGOTIATING BANK.

补充资料

我国长城贸易公司与芬兰某公司就注塑箱(P.P INJECTION CASES)达成协议,签订合同。填单所需其他信息:

1. 发票号码:GW2005M06-2

2. 发票日期:2018年5月22日

3. 装运期：2018年5月29日

4. 唛头：ROYAL

　　　05AR225031

　　　JEDDAH

　　　C/N：1-UP

5. 包装：每套/纸箱

SELLER				
	商业发票 COMMERCIAL INVOICE			
BUYER	INVOICE NO.		INVOICE DATE	
	L/C NO.		S/C DATE	
	S/C NO.		PRICE TERM	
	FROM		TO	
MARKS	DESCRIPTION OF GOODS	QUANTITY	UNIT PRICE	AMOUNT
		TOTAL:		
TOTAL AMOUNT IN WORDS:				

第四节　装箱单的填制

*一、装箱单的概念及意义

装箱单（PACKING LIST），又称包装单，是最常用的包装单据，是用以说明货物包装细节的清单。装箱单具体列明每批货物的包装形式和实际装箱情况，包括从最小包装到最大包装所有使用的包装材料、包装方式等。对于重量和尺码内容，在装箱单中一般只体现它们的累计总额。

装箱单是发票的补充单据，它列明了信用证（或合同）中买卖双方约定的有关包装事宜的细节，便于国外买方在货物到达目的港时供海关检查和核对货物。通常买方可以将其有关内容加列在商业发票上，但是在信用证有明确要求时，就必须严格按信用证约定制作装箱单。

装箱单名称应按照信用证规定使用，通常用"PACKING LIST""PACKING SPECIFICATION"或"DETAILED PACKING LIST"。

二、装箱单模板

装箱单没有统一的格式，每家公司都有自己的装箱单格式，但其基本内容基本相似。

1. 高考指定装箱单模板

SELLER			装箱单 PACKING LIST			
BUYER			NO.		DATE:	
			S/C NO.		L/C NO.	
			FROM		TO	
			MARKS & NOS.			
C/NOS.	DESCRIPTION OF GOODS	NUMBERS & KIND OF PACKAGE	QUANTITY	G.W. （KGS）	N.W. （KGS）	MEAS. （CBM）
	TOTAL:					
TOTAL PACKAGES(IN WORDS):						

2. 其他模板

PACKING LIST

ORIGINAL

TO: DATE:

INVOICE NO.:

CONTRACT NO.:

FROM	TO	LETTER OF CREDIT NO.			
ISSUED BY					
MARKS & NUMBERS	DESCRIPTION & QUANTITY	PACKAGE	WEIGHT		MEASUREMENT
			NET	GROSS	

SPECIAL CONDITIONS

NAME & SIGNATURE

三、装箱单条款概述

1. 出单方：出单人的名称与地址，一般指信用证中的受益人。

2. 受单方：受单方的名称与地址，一般指信用证中的开证申请人。

3. 发票号：填发票号码。

4. 日期："装箱单"缮制日期，一般与商业发票日期一致。

5. 运输标志：又称唛头，是出口货物包装上的装运标记和号码。

6. 包装种类和件数、货物描述：填写货物及包装的详细资料，包括货物名称、规格、数量和包装说明等内容。

7. 填写货物的毛重、净重，在列明单件毛重、净重时，还需计算出总毛重、总净重；体积按货物的实际体积填列，均应符合信用证的规定。

8. 自由处理区：自由处理区位于单据格式下方，用于表达格式中其他栏目不能或不便表达的内容。

四、装箱单详解

1. 装箱单名称（PACKING LIST）

应按照信用证规定使用，通常用"Packing List""Packing Specification""Detailed Packing List"。如果来证要求用中性包装单（Neutral Packing List），则包装单名称打"Packing List"，但装箱单内不打卖方名称。

2. 出票人的名称和地址（SELLER）

此栏填制出口公司的名称和详细地址，应与商业发票一致，注意名称、地址分栏填写。

在信用证支付方式下，一般填受益人的名称和地址（L/C 中 59），通常也将此项内容事先印制在装箱单的正上方。

3. 收货人（TO）

此栏填进口商的名称和地址，与商业发票上同一栏目相同。在信用证支付方式下，一般填信用证开证申请人信息(L/C中50)。

4. 装箱单号码(NO.)

与商业发票号码一致,若题目中出现装箱单号码,则填装箱单号。

5. 日期(DATE)

与商业发票日期一致,若题目中出现装箱单日期,则填装箱单日期。装箱单日期等于或迟于商业发票日期。

6. 合同号(S/C NO.)

此栏填制此批货物相应的合同号码。

7. 信用证号码(L/C NO.)

在信用证支付方式下,此栏填制相应的信用证号码。否则,此栏空白。

8. 起运地(FROM)

此栏按实际运输情况填制货物的起运地(装运港)的名称,与商业发票或提单同一栏目相同(L/C中44A)。

9. 目的地(TO)

此栏按实际运输情况填制货物的目的地(目的港)的名称,与商业发票或提单同一栏目相同(L/C中44B)。

10. 唛头及号码(MARKS & NOS.)

此栏按合同或者信用证规定的唛头填制,若没有,则写N/M。所填内容与商业发票、提单等其他单据保持一致。

11. 箱号(C/NOS.)

又称包装件号码。在单位包装货量或品种不固定的情况下,需注明每个包装件内的包装情况,因此包装件应编号。例如:

C/NOS.	DESCRIPTION OF GOODS
	RAINCOATS
C/NO.1—100 (表示1—100箱为M1204号货物,共100箱)	M1204
C/NO.101—200 (表示101—200箱为M1205号货物,共100箱)	M1205
C/NO.201—300 (表示201—300箱为M1206号货物,共100箱)	M1206

12. 货描(DESCRIPTION OF GOODS)

与信用证货描(L/C中45A)相一致。若信用证中只出现货名总称,但补充资料中出现详细型号、规格等信息,也应注明。

13. 包装种类与件数(NUMBERS & KIND OF PACKAGE)

此栏应填制最大包装的种类与件数,并与前11、12项栏目相对应。

14. 数量(QUANTITY)

此栏填制每箱实际所装货物的数量及总的货物数量。例如:@10PCS/350PCS(每箱装10件,总共350件);@1PC/25PCS(每箱装1件,总共25件)。

注意:只有一件时,不需要加"S"。

15. 毛重(G.W.)

此栏填制包装后每件货物的毛重及货物的总毛重,以千克为单位,保留两位小数。

例如:@15.00KGS/4500.00KGS。

16. 净重(N.W.)

此栏填制包装后每件货物的净重及货物的总净重,以千克为单位,保留两位小数。

例如:@10.00KGS/3000.00KGS。

17. 体积(MEASUREMENT)

此栏填制包装后每件货物的体积及货物的总体积,以立方米为单位,保留三位小数。

例如:@0.032CBM/9.660CBM。

18. 总计(TOTAL)

在填制装箱单时,为了使商品的总包装件数、净重、毛重和体积更加清晰明了,都要在装箱单中予以总计。注:若大包装的计量单位不一致,在总计时,计量单位写"PKGS"(PACKAGES)。详见易错点3。

19. 合计件数(TOTAL PACKAGES IN WORDS)

此栏填制最大包装的总件数。SAY+件数+包装材料(全称)+ONLY。

20. 出票人签章

此栏需填制出口公司的名称(英)和负责人的签字或手签印章。

21. 申明文句及其他内容(DECLARATION AND OTHER CONTENTS)

此区域填制装箱单条款和附加条款中需额外写在装箱单中的内容,若补充资料中也出现关于包装的内容,也应书写进去。

五、装箱单易错点集锦

1. 装箱单收货人,即抬头,往往是BUYER,但是若商业发票中或附加条款中出现MADE OUT IN THE NAME OF... / MADE IN THE NAME OF... / CONSIGNED TO...等,即使装箱单条款中未出现相应语句,装箱单抬头也需做成"..."中所代表的公司。总之装箱单跟着商业发票走,是发票的补充。

2. 若信用证中出现不同型号,且数量、毛重、净重、体积都不一样,则须分开写清楚。如:

DESCRIPTION OF GOODS	QUANTITY	G.W. (KGS)	N.W. (KGS)	MEAS. (CBM)
RAINCOATS ART.NO.07 ART.NO.08	@5PCS 100PCS @4PCS 120PCS	@23.00KGS 460.00KGS @25.00KGS 750.00KGS	@20.00KGS 400.00KGS @22.00KGS 660.00KGS	@0.125CBM 2.500CBM @0.146CBM 4.380CBM
TOTAL:	220PCS	1210.00KGS	1060.00KGS	6.880CBM

3. 若大包装的计量单位不一致,在总计时,计量单位写"PKGS"(PACKAGES)。如:

DESCRIPTION OF GOODS	NUMBERS & KIND OF PACKAGE
RAINCOATS ART.NO.07 ART.NO.08	350CTNS 400BOXES
TOTAL:	750PKGS

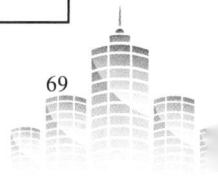

4. 若在信用证出现的商品总数量为"50M/TS",但补充资料中,商品的包装方式为"20KGS/CTNS",则在填制"数量(QUANTITY)"这一栏目时,需将单位化成"千克",即总数量为"50,000KGS"。

5. 若信用证来证要求包装为"中性包装(NEUTRAL PACKING)",则"出票人"一栏与签章处空白。

6. 包装单据可以不需要签署,但包装单据含有"……证明(CERTIFICATE OF...)"证明文句时,则应该签署。

7. 若信用证中规定要列明内包装情况(INNER PACKING),则必须在单据中充分显示出来。

六、专项练习

练习一

```
RECEIVED FROM:BANK OF CHINA,BARCELONA BRANCH
TO:BANK OF CHINA,HANGZHOU BRANCH
SEQUENCE OF TOTAL          *27:1/1
FORM OF DOC. CREDIT        *40A:IRREVOCABLE
DOC. CREDIT NUMBER         *20:5248FG5210
DATE OF ISSUE              *31C:190218
DATE/PLACE EXP.            *31D:DATE:190415    PLACE:IN THE BENEFICIARY'S COUNTRY
APPLICANT                  *50:HOP TONG HAI(PIE) LTD.,
                               BLK 15,SOUTH BRIPDE ROAD,
                               #04-9370 BARCELONA SPAIN
                               100032
                               FAX:459862
BENEFICIARY                *59:ZHEJIANG BAIMEI GARMENTS
                               IMP. & EXP. CO.,LTD.,
                               JINAN MANSION 762 HONGDA ROAD,
                               XIAOSHAN DISTRICT,HANGZHOU,
                               ZHEJIANG,CHINA
                               A/C NO:856324136-00213
AMOUNT                     *32B:CURRENCY EUR AMOUNT 37,850.00
AVAILABLE WITH             *41D:ANY BANK BY NEGOTIATION
DRAFTS AT                  42C:80 DAYS AFTER SIGHT
DRAWEE                     42D:BANK OF CHINA,NEW YORK BRANCH
PARTIAL SHIPMENT           43P:ALLOWED
TRANSSHIPMENT              43T:ALLOWED
PORT OF LOADING            44A:NINGBO,CHINA
PORT OF DISCHARGE          44B:BARCELONA PORT,SPAIN
                               WITH TRANSSHIPMENT AT SINGAPORE
```

LATEST SHIPMENT   44C:190405

GOODS DISCRIPT   45A:1600 DOZEN 80% COTTON OVERALLS,SHIRTS AND SINGLETS AS PER S/C NO.02EC301302 DATED 23-01-2019 AS DETAILS BELOW:

(1)300 DOZEN 80% COTTON OVERALLS AT EUR45.00 PER DOZEN；

(2)1,200 DOZEN 80% COTTON SHIRTS AT EUR16.50 PER DOZEN；

(3)100 DOZEN 80% COTTON SINGLETS AT EUR9.50 PER DOZEN；

TRADE TERMS:CFRC3 BARCELONA AS PER INCOTERMS 2010

PACKING:TO BE PACKED IN CARTONS,80% COTTON OVERALLS:30DOZ/CTN;

        80% COTTON SHIRTS:120DOZ/CTN;80% COTTON SINGLETS:20DOZ/CTN

DOCUMENTS REQUIRED   *46A:

+ MANUALLY SIGNED COMMERCIAL INVOICE IN THREE FOLDS SHOWING FREIGHT CHARGES,INSURANCE PREMIUM AND FOB VALUE,AND THE COUNTRY OF ORIGIN IS P.R. CHINA

+ SIGNED PACKING LIST INDICATING THE G.W,N.W, MEASUREMENT OF PER CARTON,AND BEARING THE CLAUSE:WE HEREBY CERTIFY THAT EACH PACKAGE IS MARKED THE SHIPPING MARK:C.T.H./BARCELONA/ NO:1-UP

+CERTIFICATE OF ORIGIN

+INSURANCE POLICY/CERTIFICATE IN DUPLICATE ENDORSED IN BLANK FOR 110% OF CIF VALUE,COVERING ALL RISKS AND WAR RISK OF C.I.C. OF PICC(1/1/1981), WAREHOUSE TO WAREHOUSE AND SHOWING THE CLAIMING CURRENCY IS THE SAME AS CURRENCY OF CREDIT

+ FULL SET OF CLEAN ON BOARD OCEAN BILLS OF LADING MADE OUT TO ORDER OF SHIPPER MARKED FREIGHT PREPAID AND NOTIFY APPLICANT

+SHIPMENT ADVICE SHOULD SENT TO APPLICANT WITHIN 10 DAYS AFTER THE DATE OF BILL OF LADING

ADDITIONAL CONDITIONS   *47A:

+ MORE OR LESS 10PCT OF QUANTITY OF GOODS AND CREDIT AMOUNT IS ALLOWED

+ THE NUMBER AND THE DATE OF THIS CREDIT AND THE NAME OF ISSUING BANK MUST BE QUOTED ON

ALL DOCUMENTS

+SHIPMENT MUST BE EFFECTED BY 1×20' FCL CONTAINER LOAD PACKING LIST TO SHOW OF THIS EFFECT IS REQUIRED

+ONE SET OF NON-NEGOTIABLE SHIPPING DOCUMENTS TO BE FAXED TO APPLICANT WHININ 3 DAYS AFTER SHIPMENT BENEFICIARY'S CERTIFICATE TO THIS EFFECT IS REQUIRED

+SHIPPING MARKS：C.T.H./BARCELONA/NO.：1-UP

DETAILS OF CHARGES   71B：ALL CHARGES AND COMMISSIONS OUTSIDE ARE FOR BENEFICIARY ACCOUNT

PRESENTATION PERIOD   48：WITHIN 10 DAYS AFTER THE DATE OF SHIPMENT, BUT WITHIN THE VALIDITY OF EXPIRY DATE OF THIS CREDIT

CONFIRMATION   *49：WITHOUT

相关背景资料

1. PACKING INFORMATION

COMMODITY & SPECIFICATION	PACKAGE	G.W.	N.W.	MEAS.
80% COTTON OVERALLS	10CTNS	5,520.00KGS	5,040.00KGS	19.200CBM
80% COTTON SHIRTS	10CTNS	1,980.00KGS	1,860.00KGS	4.000CBM
80% COTTON SINGLETS	5CTNS	2,480.00KGS	240.00KGS	24.200CBM

2. INVOICE NO.ANC20170018   INVOICE DATE：MARCH 25,2019

3. FREIGHT CHARGE：USD1,020.00/20'FT CONTAINER

INSURANCE COST：USD400.00

4. 公司法人代表：金胜利

SELLER		
	装箱单 PACKING LIST	
BUYER	NO.	DATE
	S/C NO.	L/C NO.
	FROM	TO
	MARKS & NOS.	

C/NOS.	DESCRIPTION OF GOODS	NUMBERS & KIND OF PACKAGES	QUANTITY	G.W. (KGS)	N.W. (KGS)	MEAS. (CBM)
	TOTAL:					

TOTAL PACKAGES(IN WORDS):

练习二

SEQUENCE OF TOTAL	*27:1/1
FORM OF DOC. CREDIT	*40A:IRREVOCABLE
DOC. CREDIT NUMBER	*20:1920/742
DATE OF ISSUE	31C:190828
EXPIRY	*31D:DATE:191003 PLACE:SHANGHAI
APPLICANT	*50:SEMPREVIVO SRL IMPORT EXPORT CO. I/B 90123 PALERMO
APPLICANT BANK	51:ISTITUTO BANCARIO SAN PAOLO DI,TORINO S.P.A, PALERMO
BENEFICIARY	*59:SHANGHAI ZHEN YUAN IMP. AND EXP. CO.,LTD., RM 302-305,700 JIANGUODONG RD., SHANGHAI,CHINA
AMOUNT	*32B:CURRENCY USD AMOUNT 24,290.00
POS./NEG. TOL.(%)	*39A:05/05
AVAILABLE WITH	*41D:ANY BANK BY NEGOTIATION
DRAFTS AT	*42C:SIGHT
DRAWEE	*42D:ISTITUTO BANCARIO SAN PAOLO DI,TORINO S.P.A.,PALERMO,ITALY
PARTIAL SHIPMENT	43P:NOT ALLOWED
TRANSSHIPMENT	43T:ALLOWED
PORT OF LOADING	44E:SHANGHAI,CHINA

PORT OF DISCHARGE	44F:PALERMO,ITALY
LATEST DATE OF SHIP.	44C:190918
DESCRIPT. OF GOODS	45A:SPORTS MUG AS PER SALES CONTRACT

NO.17SHSS199 DATED 10-JULY-19 CIF PALERMO

DOCUMENTS REQUIRED 46A:+SIGNED COMMERCIAL INVOICE IN THREE FOLDS
EVIDENCING THAT GOODS SHIPPED AND INVOICED
FULLY CONFORM TO THOSE DESCRIBED ON
PROFORMA INVOICED NO.5330703199 DATED 31
JULY 2019, MADE IN THE NAME OF STRONG
SAN PAOLO DI,TORINO S.P.A.

+FULL SET CLEAN ON BOARD MARINE BILL OF
LADING MADE OUT TO ORDER AND BLANK
ENDORSED, MARKED FREIGHT PREPAID AND
NOTIFY APPLICANT AND E. AGNEL ECO. SRL,
VIA ROMA NO.48990139,PALERMO

+PACKING LIST IN THREE FOLDS SHOWING G.W.,
N.W. AND MEAS. OF EACH PACKAGE

+ CERTIFICATE OF ORIGIN FORM A PLUS ONE
COPY ISSUED BY COMPETENT AUTHORITY OF THE
PEOPLE'S REPUBLIC OF CHINA,SPECIFYING THE
CONTRACT NO.

+ INSURANCE POLICY OR CERTIFICATE ENDORSED
IN BLANK ISSUED FOR 110 PERCENT INVOICE
VALUE COVERING ALL RISKS AND WAR RISK
AS PER O.M.C.C. OF PICC DATED 01/01/1982
INCLUDING W/W CLAUSE CLAIMS PAYABLE AT
DESTINATION

+CERTIFICATE SENT BY BENEFICIARY TO APPLICANT,
EVIDENCING THAT COPIES OF INVOICE,BILL OF
LADING AND PACKING LIST HAVE BEEN FAXED TO
APPLICANT ON FAX NO.01-5824-3470 WITHIN 3
DAYS OF BILL OF LADING DATE

ADDITIONAL COND. 47A:DOCUMENTARY CREDIT NO. AND NAME OF ISSUING
BANK MUST BE QUOTED ON ALL DOCUMENTS

PRESENTATION PERIOD 48:WITHIN 15 DAYS AFTER THE DATE OF SHIPMENT
BUT IN THE VALIDITY OF THE CREDIT

CONFIRMATION 49:WITHOUT

INSTRUCTION 78:ON RECEIPT OF DOCUMENTS CONFIRMING TO THE TERMS OF THIS DOCUMENTARY CREDIT, WE UNDERTAKE TO REIMBURSE YOU IN THE CURRENCY OF THE CREDIT IN ACCORDANCE WITH YOUR INSTRUCTIONS, WHICH SHOULD INCLUDE YOUR UID NUMBER AND THE ABA CODE OF THE RECEIVING BANK

相关背景资料

补充货物明细：

货号	数量	计量单位	单价	包装方式	包装种类	毛重	净重	尺码（长×宽×高）
DL-001A	3,600	PC	USD3.65	24	CARTON	12KGS	10KGS	40×30×25CM
DL-002A	3,600	PC	USD2.96	24	CARTON	15KGS	13KGS	50×36×28CM
YQB-A315	2,000	PC	USD1.25	40	CARTON	17KGS	16KGS	63×55×20CM
YQB-A500	4,000	PC	USD2.01	40	CARTON	19KGS	15KGS	60×50×25CM

发票号码：ZYIE1702　　　　发票日期：2019年8月20日

提单号码：COSCOTEC192　　装船日期：2019年9月15日

包装：所有货物用硬纸板箱包装

装运船只：TUO HE　　　　航次：V.25

唛头：

SEMPREVIVO

5330703199

PAI ERMO

C/NO.1-UP

商业发票和汇票的授权签字人：王晓

SELLER	装箱单 PACKING LIST	
BUYER	NO.	DATE
	S/C NO.	L/C NO.
	FROM	TO
	MARKS & NOS.	

续表

C/NOS.	DESCRIPTION OF GOODS	NUMBERS & KIND OF PACKAGES	QUANTITY	G.W.(KGS)	N.W.(KGS)	MEAS.(CBM)
	TOTAL:					

TOTAL PACKAGES(IN WORDS):

练习三

APPLICATION HEADER	51:BANK OF TOKYO,LTD.,TOKYO,JAPAN
USER HEADER	* BANK OF CHINA,NINGBO,CHINA
SEQUENCE OF TOTAL	*27:1/1
FORM OF DOC. CREDIT	*40A:IRREVOCABLE
DOC. CREDIT NUMBER	*20:H486-20194730
DATE OF ISSUE	31C:190608
EXPIRY	*31D:DATE:190815 PLACE:CHINA
APPLICANT	*50:DAIHATSU TRADE CORPORATION
	17-6,NISHIOGU,ARAWAKAN,TOKYO,JAPAN
BENEFICIARY	*59:NINGBO HUAFENG FOOD CO.,LTD.
	NO. 215 JIEFANF ROAD,NINGBO,CHINA
AMOUNT	*32B:CURRENCY USD AMOUNT 40,000.00
POS./NEG. TOL.(%)	39A:05/10
AVAILABLE WITH	*41D:ADVISING BANK BY NEGOTIATION
DRAFTS AT	42C:SIGHT
DRAWEE	42D:BANK OF MITSUBISHI,LTD. TOKYO,JAPAN
PARTIAL SHIPMENT	43P:ALLOWED
TRANSSHIPMENT	43T:PROHIBITED
PORT OF LOADING	44E:NINGBO,CHINA
PORT OF DISCHARGE	44F:TOKYO,JAPAN
LATEST DATE OF SHIP.	44C:190720

DESCRIPT. OF GOODS

45A:20M/T FROZEN SOYBEANS CIF TOKYO,JAPAN
USD2,000.00 PER M/T AS PER S/C NO. HD012
DATED MAY 15,2019

DOCUMENTS REQURED

46A:

+COMMERCIAL INVOICE IN TWO FOLDS

+FULL SET CLEAN ON BOARD MARINE BILL OF LADING MADE OUT TO OUR ORDER AND BLANK ENDORSED,MARKED FREIGHT PREPAID AND NOTIFY TO APPLICANT

+PACKING LIST IN THREE FOLDS INDICATING G.W.,N.W.,AND MEAS. OF CARTON

+CERTIFICATE OF ORIGIN

+FULL SET OF INSURANCE POLICY OR CERTIFICATE ENDORSED IN BLANK ISSUED FOR 110 PERCENT OF INVOICE VALUE COVERING F.P.A. AND WAR RISK AS PER C.I.C. DATED 01/01/1981

ADDITIONAL COND.

47A:

1. T/T REIMBURSEMENT PROHIBITED.

2. THE GOODS TO BE PACKED IN SEAWORTHY CARTONS.

3. SHIPPING MARK:DAIHATSU/MADE IN CHINA/ NO.1-UP.

背景资料:

1. 发票号码:HF192026

2. 发票日期:JULY 10,2019　　箱单日期:JULY 13,2019

3. PACKING:PACKED IN SEAWORTHY CARTONS, SIZE:35CM*30CM*28CM WITH 10KGS IN EACH CARTON. N.W.:10KGS/CTN,G.W.:11KGS/CTN.

4. 公司法人:王冰

SELLER		装箱单 PACKING LIST				
BUYER		NO.		DATE		
		S/C NO.		L/C NO.		
		FROM		TO		
		MARKS & NOS.				

C/NOS.	DESCRIPTION OF GOODS	NUMBERS & KIND OF PACKAGES	QUANTITY	G.W. （KGS）	N.W. （KGS）	MEAS. （CBM）
	TOTAL:					

TOTAL PACKAGES(IN WORDS):

_____

_____

练习四

ISSUING BANK:CYPRUS POPULAR BANK LTD.,LARNAKA

ADVISING BANK:BANK OF CHINA,SHANGHAI BRANCH

SEQUENCE OF TOTAL   *27:1/1

FORM OF DOC. CREDIT   *40A:IRREVOCABLE

DATE OF ISSUE   31C:190105

EXPIRY   *31D:DATE:190229   PLACE:CHINA

APPLICANT   *50:LAIKI PERAGORA ORPHANIDES LTD.,

                              020 STRATIGOU TIMAGIA AVE.,

                              6046,LARNAKA,CYPRUS

BENEFICIARY	*59:SHANGHAI GARDEN PRODUCTS
	IMP. AND EXP. CO.,LTD.,
	27 ZHONGSHAN DONGYI ROAD,SHANGHAI,CHINA
AMOUNT	*32B:CURRENCY USD AMOUNT 6,115.00
AVAILABLE WITH	*41D:ANY BANK BY NEGOTIATION
DRAFTS AT	42C:SIGHT
DRAWEE	*42D:LIKICY2NXXX,CYPRUS POPULAR BANK LTD.,
	LARNAKA
PARTIAL SHIPMENT	43P:ALLOWED
TRANSSHIPMENT	43T:ALLOWED
LOADING IN CHARGE	44A:SHANGHAI PORT
FOR TRANSPORT TO	44B:LIMASSOL PORT
LATEST DATE OF SHIP.	44C:190214
DESCRIPT. OF GOODS	45A:LADIES' SHIRT AND LADIES' SKIRT
	S/C NO. E03FD121
	CFR LIMASSOL PORT,INCOTERM 2010
DOCUMENTS REQUIRED	46A:

+ COMMERCIAL INVOICE IN QUADRUPLICATE ALL STAMPED AND SIGNED BY BENEFICIARY

+FULL SET OF CLEAN ON BOARD BILL OF LADING MADE OUT TO ORDER OF SHIPPER AND BLANK ENDORSED,MARKED FREIGHT PREPAID AND NOTIFY APPLICANT

+PACKING LIST IN TRIPLICATE SHOWING PACKING DETAILS SUCH AS CARTON NO. AND CONTENTS OF EACH CARTON AND CERTIFYING THAT THE GOODS ARE OF CHINESE ORIGIN

+CERTIFICATE STAMPED AND SIGNED BY BENEFICIARY STATING THAT THE ORIGINAL INVOICE AND PACKING LIST HAVE BEEN DISPATCHED TO THE APPLICANT BY COURIER SERVICE 2 DAYS BEFORE SHIPMENT

ADDITIONAL COND.	47A:

+EACH PACKING UNIT BEARS AN INDELIBLE MARK INDICATING THE COUNTRY OF ORIGIN OF THE GOODS. PACKING LIST TO CERTIFY THIS

+ALL DRAFTS MUST SHOW THE B/L NO.

+5PCT BOTH IN QUANTITY AND AMOUNT ALLOWED

	+L／C NO. AND DATE MUST BE QUOTED ON ALL DOCS
DETAILS OF CHARGES	71B:ALL BANK CHARGES OUTSIDE CYPRUS ARE FOR THE ACCOUNT OF THE BENEFICIARY
PRESENTATION PERIOD	48:WITHIN 15 DAYS AFTER THE DATE OF SHIPMENT BUT WITHIN THE VALIDITY OF THE CREDIT
CONFIRMATION	*49:WITHOUT
INSTRUCTION	78:ON RECEIPT OF DOCUMENTS CONFIRMING TO THE TERMS OF THIS DOCUMENTARY CREDIT, WE UNDERTAKE TO REIMBURSE YOU IN THE CURRENCY OF THE CREDIT IN ACCORDANCE WITH YOUR INSTRUCTIONS, WHICH SHOULD INCLUDE YOUR UID NUMBER AND THE ABA CODE OF THE RECEIVING BANK

相关资料

发票号码:19SGHTRY3023　　　　发票日期:2019年2月9日

提单号码:SHGH5732　　　　　　提单日期:2019年2月12日

LADIES' SHIRT 的 H.S. CODE:469863542

QUANTITY:580PCS,USD8.90/PC,4PCS/箱

纸箱尺码:56x12x27CM

毛重:16.3KGS/箱

净重:12.8KGS/箱

LADIES' SKIRT 的 H.S. CODE:469863556

QUANTITY:720PCS,USD5.00/PC,6PCS/箱

纸箱尺码:32x38x29CM

毛重:17.4KGS/箱

净重:15.6KGS/箱

唛头:

L.P.O.L.

DC. NO. FG26/19/358

MADE IN CHINA

NO.1-UP

SELLER			装箱单 PACKING LIST			
BUYER			NO.		DATE	
			S/C NO.		L/C NO.	
			FROM		TO	
			MARKS & NOS.			
C/NOS.	DESCRIPTION OF GOODS	NUMBERS & KIND OF PACKAGES	QUANTITY	G.W.（KGS）	N.W.（KGS）	MEAS.（CBM）
	TOTAL:					
TOTAL PACKAGES(IN WORDS):						

练习五

SEQUENCE OF TOTAL	27:1/1
FORM OF DOCUMENTARY CREDIT	40A:IRREVOCABLE
DOCUMENTARY CREDIT NUMBER	20:LC1JD624
DATE OF ISSUE	31C:181228
DATE AND PLACE OF EXPIRY	31D:190320,CHINA
APPLICANT BANK	51A:BANK OF GOOD COLOMBO
APPLICANT	50:ELEC TRADE CO. LTD., THE FIRST STREET,COLOMBO,SRI LANKA
BENEFICIARY	59:ZHENGCHANG TRADING CO. LTD., NO.168 XUESHI ROAD,HUZHOU,ZHEJIANG,CHINA

AMOUNT	32B:CURRENCY EUR13,625.00
AVAILABLE WITH	41D:BANK OF CHINA,HUZHOU BRANCH
DRAFTS AT	42C:SIGHT
DRAWEE	42D:BANK OF GOOD COLOMBO
PARTIAL SHIPMENT	43P:NOT ALLOWED
TRANSSHIPMENT	43T:ALLOWED
LOADING FROM	44A:SHANGHAI,CHINA
FOR TRANSPORTATION TO	44B:COLOMBO,SRI LANKA
LATEST DATE OF SHIPMENT	44C:190228
DESCRIPT. OF GOODS	45A:

COMMODITY:TRAVELING BAGS

ITEM NO.:

PG6520	3,000PCS	EUR1.50/PC
DG6359	2,500PCS	EUR1.80/PC
TQ3523	2,500PCS	EUR1.85/PC

TOTAL VALUE:CIF COLOMBO,EUR13,625.00

SHIPPING MARKS:

E.L.E.

HZ0114

COLOMBO

C/NO. 1-160

DOCUMENTARY REQUIRED	46A:

1. SIGNED COMMERCIAL INVOICE IN TRIPLICATE MADE OUT IN THE NAME OF COFCO HUZHOU CEREALS AND OILS CO. LTD.

2. PACKING LIST IN TRIPLICATE IN INK SHOWING THE TOTAL WEIGHT AND MEASUREMENT CERTIFYING THAT GOODS ARE IN ACCORDANCE WITH CONTRACT NO. HZ0114.

3. CERTIFICATE OF ORIGIN IN ONE ORIGINAL AND TWO COPIES ISSUED BY CHINA COUNCIL FOR PROMOTION OF INTERNATIONAL TRADE.

4. 3/3 SET OF CLEAN ON BOARD MARINE BILLS OF LADING MADE OUT TO ORDER AND BLANK ENDORSED, MARKED FREIGHT PREPAID NOTIFY THE APPLICANT.

5. INSURANCE CERTIFICATE COVERING ALL RISKS

FOR 110% INVOICE VALUE SUBJECTED TO THE OCEAN MARINE CARGO CLAUSE OF THE P.I.C.C. DATED 1981/1/1.

6. BENEFICIARY'S CERTIFICATE CERTIFYING THAT EACH COPY OF SHIPPING DOCUMENTS HAVE BEEN FAXED TO THE APPLICANT WITHIN 48 HOURS AFTER SHIPMENT.

7. SHIPPING ADVICE MUST SENT TO THE APPLICANT WITHIN 48 HOURS AFTER SHIPMENT IN FULL DETAILS.

ADDITIONAL CONDITIONS 47A:

+ ALL BANKING CHARGES OUTSIDE THE OPENING BANK ARE FOR BENEFICIARY'S ACCOUNT

+ TRANSSHIPMENT AT HONG KONG

+ H.S. CODE MUST BE MARKED ON ALL DOCUEMNTS EXCEPT PACKING LIST

PERIOD FOR PRESENTATIONS 48:

DOCUMENTS MUST BE PRESENTED FOR NEGOTIATION WITHIN 15 DAYS AFTER BILL OF LADING DATE, BUT WITHIN THE VALIDITY OF THIS L/C

INSTRUCTION 78:

ON RECEIPT OF DOCUMENTS CONFIRMING TO THE TERMS OF THIS DOCUMENTARY CREDIT, WE UNDERTAKE TO REIMBURSE YOU IN THE CURRENCY OF THE CREDIT IN ACCORDANCE WITH YOUR INSTRUCTIONS, WHICH SHOULD INCLUDE YOUR UID NUMBER AND THE ABA CODE OF THE RECEIVING BANK

相关资料

1. 发票号码:VGDET42KLJ 发票日期:2019年1月11日

2. 包装情况:1PC/BOX,50BOXES/CTN

每箱净重9.5千克,两个纸盒重0.05千克,一个纸箱重0.2千克

每箱尺码(MEAS.):0.018CBM/CTN

3. 所有货物被装进1×20' CONTAINER

4. 装船日期:2019年2月28日,提单日期同装船日期,提单号:COS0190116

5. H.S CODE:85352100

单证员:王丽 法人代表:徐汇

SELLER					装箱单 PACKING LIST		
BUYER			NO.		DATE		
			S/C NO.		L/C NO.		
			FROM		TO		
			MARKS & NOS.				
C/NOS.	DESCRIPTION OF GOODS	NUMBERS & KIND OF PACKAGES	QUANTITY	G.W.（KGS）	N.W.（KGS）	MEAS.（CBM）	
	TOTAL:						
TOTAL PACKAGES(IN WORDS):							

第五节 订舱委托书的填制

一、托运

托运是指出口商委托承运人将出口货物运送至合同约定的目的地而办理的单货交接手续。它是出口商履行合同交货义务的一个重要环节。在我国,出口商既可以直接向承运人订舱出运,也可以委托货运代理人办理出口货物托运业务,后者居多。出口货物托运涉及出口商、货运代理和承运人,他们之间具有不同的委托代理关系或契约关系。

二、出口商托运程序

以集装箱海运为例,出口商托运程序:订舱→缮制托运单→装运→取得转船文件。

外贸人员应根据信用证的最迟装运期及货源情况安排委托运输,一般情况应提前5天左右或更长的时间安排托运,缮制订舱委托书委托货代或者直接向船公司订舱。

三、订舱委托书(Booking Note)的含义

订舱委托书简称托书,是进/出口商为了买卖商品,通过船公司和货代公司进行船运订舱的申请书。订舱委托书没有固定格式,不同进出口公司缮制的托书不尽相同,但主要内容都基本包括托运人、收货人、装货港、卸货港、唛头、货物描述、货物毛重、货物体积、运费的支付方式、所订船期等。

注意事项:

(1)确认委托书所载品名是否为危险品或液体,确认是否对该产品存在海关监管条件。

(2)确认件数,确认货物尺寸、体积是否超过装载装箱能力,确认重量是否有单件货物超过3吨,如果超过3吨需要和仓库确认是否能有装箱能力。

(3)托书是预配舱单以及提单确认的初步依据,如果一次性正确可为提单确认省去许多麻烦。如需要投保、熏蒸、打托缠膜、拍照、换单、买单,要在订舱委托书显要位置注明。

(4)所订船期受到外商订购合同、备货时间、商检时间等制约,根据时间合理安排订舱日期。

(5)遇到拼箱出口未能按时出运,并未按时撤载,会产生亏舱费。

四、订舱委托书模板

(一)高考模板

Shipper:	订舱委托书
Consignee:	To: 开船日: 箱型、箱量:

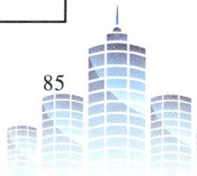

Notify:	合同号:
	运费:
	Vessel/Voyage:

Port of Loading	Port of Discharge	Transshipment	Partial Shipment

Marks & Numbers	Description of Goods	No. of Packages	Gross Weight	Meas.

TOTAL NUMBERS OF CONTAINERS OR PACKAGES:

客户要求

□送货　　　□产装　　　□代理报关　　　□代理报检　　　□投保

产装信息	产装地址及预计日期:	订舱公司:
	单位名称:	联系人:
	地址:	电话:
	联系人:	传真:
	电话:	

特殊要求	

(二)其他模板

模板一:

出口货物订舱委托书

公司编号:		日期:
1. 发货人	4.信用证号码	
	5.开证银行	
	6.合同号码	7.成交金额
	8. 装运口岸	9.目的港
2. 收货人	10.转船运输	11.分批装运
	12.信用证效期	13.装船期限
	14.运费	15.成交条件
	16.公司联系人	17.电话/传真

3. 通知人	18.公司开户行		19.银行账号				
	20.特别要求						
21)标记唛码	22)货号规格	23)包装件数	24)毛重	25)净重	26)数量	27)单价	28)总价
	29)总件数　　30)总毛重　　31)总净重　　32)总体积　　33)总金额						
34)备注							

模板二：

海(空)运出口委托书
BOOKING CONFIRMATION

发货人 Shipper					
收货人 Consignee					
通知人 Notify Party					
起运港 Port of Loading					
目的港 Port of Discharge					
集装箱 预配数			运费支付方式		
唛头 Marks & Numbers	件数 NO. of PCS	货物名称和HS编码 Description of Goods	毛重 Gross Weight	净重 Net Weight	货物体积 Measurement

其他要求：请订　　月　　号的船期

(　　)CY TO CY　　(　　)CY TO DOOR　　(　/　)DOOR TO DOOR　　(　　)DOOR TO CY

备注:细节请按照实际操作

续表

制单员联系方式：
电话：
传真：
邮箱：
联系人：
地址：
签名或盖章：_____
制单日期：_____

五、订舱委托书条款概述

1. 托运人(Shipper)：此栏一般情况下填写出口商或受益人的名称和地址。

2. 收货人(Consignee)：按信用证或合同的规定填写，一般情况下为指示性抬头。

3. 被通知人(Notify Party)：按信用证或合同规定填写，一般为信用证开证申请人(买方)的名称和地址。

4. 开船日/船期：填写要求装运出口的日期。

5. 箱型、箱量：填写出运集装箱的数量、箱型、装箱方式等内容。

6. 合同号：填写该批货物的外销合同号码。

7. 运费支付方式：根据贸易术语填写或者看信用证提单条款。

8. 海运船只(Ocean Vessel)和航次(Voyage No.)：按实际情况填写承担本次运输货物的船舶的名称和航次。

9. 装货港(Port of Loading)：本栏填写货物的实际装船的港口名称，即起运港。

10. 卸货港(Port of Discharge)：本栏填写海运承运人终止承运责任的港口名称。

11. 转运(Transshipment)和分批装运(Partial Shipment)：按信用证或合同规定填制。

12. 标志和号码(Marks and Nos)：又称唛头，必须按信用证或合同的规定填写。如无唛头规定时，可注N/M。

13. 货物描述(Description of Goods)：填写出口货物的中英文品名和H.S.编码。

14. 件数(No. of Packages)：填写货物的最大包装件数。

15. 毛重(Gross Weight)：填写该批货物的总毛重。

16. 净重(Net Weight)：填写该批货物的总净重。

17. 体积(Measurement)：填写该批货物的总体积。

18. 大写件数(Total Numbers of Containers or Packages)：用大写表示集装箱或其他形式最大外包装件数。

19. 客户要求：按实际情况填写。

20. 产装信息：集装箱整箱出运需要填写，拼箱出运留空。

21. 订舱公司：根据实际情况填写委托订舱的公司信息。

22. 特殊要求：填写要求签发的提单份数，以及合同中或信用证中对提单的具体要求。

六、订舱委托书填制详解(以高考模板信用证下制单为例)

1. 托运人(Shipper):出口商或信用证没有特殊规定时,此栏应填写信用证受益人的名称和地址。如果信用证提单条款中要求以第三者为托运人,则必须按信用证的要求予以缮制。如 ABC COMPANY AS SHIPPER,则托运人一栏填写 ABC COMPANY。

2. 收货人(Consignee):收货人的名称必须按信用证的规定填写。看提单条款中 MADE OUT / ISSUED TO / CONSIGNED TO 后面的内容,如果是 ISSUED / CONSIGNED TO APPLICANT,开证申请人为 EASTERN TRADING CORP.,此栏填 EASTERN TRADING CORP.;如果是 ISSUED / CONSIGNED TO ORDER OF APPLICANT,此栏填 TO ORDER OF EASTERN TRADING CORP.。

3. 被通知人(Notify Party):按信用证提单条款 NOTIFY 后面的内容填写。如果是 APPLICANT,则要把开证申请人替代进去;如果有具体明确的通知人,照抄条款。

4. TO:写货代/联系人,用中文,在补充资料里找。

5. 开船日:在补充资料中找提单日、开船日、装运日、发运日等信息,可以填中文或英文,建议根据所给资料填。

6. 箱型、箱量:按照货物的总毛重或总体积来确定。如果是一个20英尺整箱,填写20'FCL×1,以此类推;如果是拼箱,填写 LCL 和箱数,如 LCL 80CTNS。20立方以上都填20英尺小柜,50立方以上都填40英尺平柜。

7. 合同号:填写该批货物的外销合同号码,在信用证45A或46A或47A或补充资料里找。

8. 运费支付方式:看信用证提单条款中 MARKED 后面,一般情况下 FOB 填 FREIGHT COLLECT,CFR 或 CIF 填 FREIGHT PREPAID。

9. 海运船只(Ocean Vessel)和航次(Voyage No.):本栏按实际情况填写承担本次运输货物的船舶的名称和航次,在补充资料里找,照抄。

10. 装货港(Port of Loading):本栏填写货物的实际装船的港口名称,即起运港。信用证中如果是具体明确的港口,照抄;如果是笼统规定,如 ANY CHINESE PORT,要看补充资料里的出货港口,填港口和国家,如 SHANGHAI,CHINA。

11. 卸货港(Port of Discharge):本栏填写海运承运人终止承运责任的港口名称,写法同上。

12. 转运(Transshipment)和分批装运(Partial Shipment):按信用证规定填制。如果货物有转运,如在香港中转,在 Transshipment 一栏中填 ALLOWED VIA HONG KONG。

13. 标志和号码(Marks and Nos):又称唛头,必须按信用证规定填写。如果唛头里件号是 UP,要替代成具体的包装件数,如 NO.1-UP,已知总件数为500件,则改成 NO.1-500;如无唛头规定时,可注 N/M。

14. 货物描述(Description of Goods):填写出口货物的中英文品名和 H.S. 编码,无须填写规格,不同 H.S. 编码的商品分开写。

15. 件数(No. of Packages):填写货物的最大包装件数,可以依据装箱单填制。如果货物 H.S. 编码不一样,分开填写,最后合计总件数。两种或两种以上货物单位不一样,合计单位要写 PACKAGES。

16. 毛重(Gross Weight):填写该批货物的总毛重,可以依据装箱单填制。如果货物 H.S. 编码不一样,分开填写,最后合计总毛重。

17. 体积(Measurement):填写该批货物的总体积,可以依据装箱单填制。如果货物 H.S. 编码不一样,分

开填写,最后合计总体积。

第14、15、16、17条举例如下:

DESCRIPTION OF GOODS	NO. OF PACKAGES	GROSS WEIGHT	MEAS.
BATH TOWEL 浴巾 4879550000	500CTNS	5,600.00KGS	18.450CBM
BLANKET 毛毯 4785500000	480BOXES	5,200.00KGS	16.478CBM
TOTAL:	980PKGS	10,800.00KGS	34.928CBM

18. 大写件数(Total Numbers of Containers or Packages):用大写表示集装箱或其他形式最大外包装件数。一般填大包装件数格式为"SAY...ONLY."。

19. 客户要求:按实际情况填写。如果是整箱,产装前打"√",要填产装信息;如果是拼箱,送货前打"√",产装信息不用填。无论是产装还是送货,代理报关前都要打"√",再看补充资料里有没有要求货代代理报检、投保等内容,有的话打"√"。

20. 产装信息:集装箱整箱出运需要填写,拼箱出运留空。首先看补充资料是否给了出口公司名称、地址的中文,如果有中文,则写中文,预计日期和产装地址都写成中文,产装地址填出口商所在地城市,预计产装日期一般写提单日前五天,联系人和电话要写出口商的单证员和电话;如果没有给中文,也不用翻译,照抄英文公司名称、地址。如果补充资料里有工厂名称或产装地址,产装地址则要写工厂或产装所在地的城市,单位名称和地址要写工厂名称和产装地址,联系人写产装联系人;如果没有,写出口公司的单证员。

21. 订舱公司:填写出口商名称,单证员和公司电话、传真,有中文写中文,没有中文写英文。

22. 特殊要求:填写信用证提单条款中对提单签发的份数及要求。如FULL SET(3/3) OF CLEAN ON BOARD OCEAN BILL OF LADING,则写签全套3份正本清洁已装船海运提单。如果信用证中对单据及提单有特殊要求,也要在此注明,如THE NUMBER AND THE DATE OF THIS CREDIT AND THE NAME OF ISSUING BANK MUST BE QUOTED ON ALL DOCUMENTS.,则在特殊要求里要分别注明THE NUMBER OF CREDIT:789922,THE DATE OF CREDIT:DEC.12,2018 和 THE NAME OF ISSUING BANK:ABC BANK。

七、订舱委托书易错点集锦

1. 注意有没有指定SHIPPER,如果有,不能填受益人或卖方。

2. CONSIGNEE一定要根据信用证填写,出现APPLICANT要替代。

3. 箱型、箱量要根据货物的重量或体积确定,注意不要有计算错误。

4. 有多个唛头要分开写清楚。

5. 不同的H.S.编码商品要分开写。

6. 总件数要填最大的包装件数,写明包装单位。单位不一致,合计单位写PACKAGES,缩写为PKGS。

7. 毛重和体积要写单位,不要计算错误,重量保留两位小数,体积保留三位小数。

8. 大写件数不要遗漏,最后要以ONLY结尾。

9. 产装信息中有工厂信息要填工厂信息,不能填出口商信息。

10. 特殊要求中一定要把所有跟提单有关的特殊要求进行备注,不要遗漏。

八、专项练习

练习一

ISSUING BANK:THE CENTER OF CANADA BANK

APPLICANT:AST NATIONAL TRADING COMPANY,CANADA

AMOUNT:USD40,000.00

BENEFICIARY:HANGZHOU ABC IMPORT & EXPORT LTD.,

　　　　　　NO. 40 BINGWEN ROAD,HANGZHOU,CHINA,310053

L/C NO.:FD878/38DES

LATEST DATE OF SHIPMENT:OCT. 15,2010

EXPIRY DATE:OCT. 20,2010

PORT OF LOADING:SHANGHAI,CHINA

PORT OF DISCHARGE:MONTREAL

PARTIAL SHIPMENT:ALLOWED

TRANSSHIPMENT:ALLOWED

DESCRIPTION OF GOODS:LEATHER COMPUTER CASES(PO:234569)

TYPE 1　5,000PCS

TYPE 2　15,000PCS

QUANTITY OF GOODS:20,000PCS

UNIT PRICE:USD20.00 PER PC CIF MONTREAL

+3/3 SET OF CLEAN ON BOARD OCEAN BILL OF LADING MADE OUT TO ORDER,BLANK ENDORSED MARKED FREIGHT PREPAID AND NOTIFY APPLICANT

+INSURANCE POLICY OF CERTIFICIAL IN DUPLICATE BLANK ENDORSED COVERING MARINE INSTITUTE CARGO CLAUSE(ALL RISKS)AND WAR CLAUSE AND SRCC FOR 110% INVOICE VALUE UP TO FINAL DESTINATION IN NEPAL AND INSURANCE POLICY OR CERTIFICATE MUST BE VALID FOR 60 DAYS AFTER THE DISCHARGE OF GOODS FROM THE VESSEL AT THE PORT OF DESTINATION CLAIMS,IF ANY,PAYABLE AT MONTREAL

+ALL DOCS MUST BE SHOWED THIS L/C NO.

相关资料

PACKING:25PCS/CTN

GROSS WEIGHT:@22KGS/CTN

NET WEIGHT:@20KGS/CTN

MEASUREMENT：@（48×35×20）CM/CTN

皮质电脑套的海关编码为8754211100

装箱地点及联系人：门对门装箱，地址为浙江杭州市滨康路450号　　　联系人：吴森琦

联系电话：18767169488　　装箱时间：2010年10月11日

出口公司：杭州ABC进出口公司

集装箱箱号和封号：OOLU3012356/978812，OOLU2012356/967712　无唛头

出口公司单证员王可联系杭州大地物流公司的小王订2010年10月15日的"DONGFANG　V.589"号轮从上海出运。

Shipper:		订舱委托书		
Consignee:		To: 开船日： 箱型、箱量：		
Notify:		合同号：		
		运费：		
		Vessel/Voyage：		
Port of Loading	Port of Discharge	Transshipment		Partial Shipment
Marks & Numbers	Description of Goods	No. of Packages	Gross Weight	Meas.
TOTAL NUMBERS OF CONTAINERS OR PACKAGES:				
		客户要求		
	□送货　　□产装　　□代理报关　　□代理报检　　□投保			
产装信息	产装地址及预计日期： 单位名称： 地址： 联系人： 电话：		订舱公司： 联系人： 电话： 传真：	
特殊要求				

练习二

DOCUMENTARY CREDIT

SEQUENCE OF TOTAL	*27:1/1
FORM OF DOC. CREDIT	*40A:IRREVOCABLE
DOC. CREDIT NUMBER	*20:AHT100263
DATE OF ISSUE	31C:140525
DATE/PLACE OF EXPIRY	*31D:140805,IN COUNTRY OF BENEFICIARY
ISSUING BANK	52A:NATIONAL AUSTRALIA BANK LIMITED,SYDNEY
APPLICANT	*50:THE CLOTHING COMPANY AUSTRALIA PTY LTD.,
	10 BURWOOD HIGHWAY,BURWOOD VIC 3125
BENEFICIARY	*59:ZHEJIANG TEXTILES IMPORT & EXPORT
	TRADE CORPORATION,
	201 BAOCHU ROAD,HANGZHOU,CHINA
AMOUNT	*32B:CURRENCY USD AMOUNT 3,280.00
POS./NEG. TOL.(%)	39A:5/5
AVAILABLE WITH	*41D:ANY BANK BY PAYMENT
DRAFTS AT	42C:30 DAYS AFTER SIGHT
DRAWEE	*42D:NATIONAL AUSTRALIA BANK LIMITED,SYDNEY
PARTIAL SHIPMENT	43P:ALLOWED
TRANSSHIPMENT	43T:NOT ALLOWED
LOADING IN CHARGE	44A:SHANGHAI,CHINA
FOR TRANSPORT TO	44B:MELBOURNE,AUSTRALIA
LATEST DATE OF SHIPMENT	44C:140715
DESCRIPTION OF GOODS	45A:

KNITTED GARMENTS AS PER S/C NO. 8612 DATED MAY. 8,2014

400PCS USD8.20/PC　　USD3,280.00

CFR MELBOURNE,AUSTRALIA

DOCUMENTS REQUIRED　　46A:

+ FULL SET OF ORIGINAL CLEAN ON BOARD MARINE BILL OF LADING MADE OUT TO THE ORDER OF SHIPPER, BLANK ENDORSED,MARKED FREIGHT PREPAID, NOTIFY TIVOLI PRODUCTS PLC COMPANY AND US

+ SIGNED COMMERCIAL INVOICE IN TWO ORIGINALS AND FIVE COPIES

+PACKING LIST IN QUADRUPLICATE

+CERTIFICATE OF ORIGIN IN DUPLICATE

+CUSTOMS INVOICE IN DUPLICATE

+BENEFICIARY'S CERTIFICATE STATING THAT SHIPPING ADVICE MUST BE SENT TO APPLICANT AFTER SHIPMENT ADVISING L/C NO.,SHIPMENT DATE,VESSEL NAME,TOTAL QUANTITY AND WEIGHT OF GOODS

+INSURANCE POLICY IN DUPLICATE FOR 120% OF THE INVOICE VALUE COVERING WPA AND T.P.N.D. AS PER CIC DATED 01/01/1981, CLAIM TO BE PAYABLE AT DESTINATION IN THE CURRENCY OF THE DRAFTS

ADDITIONAL COND.　　　47A:

+DOCUMENTS NEGOTIATED WITH ANY DISCREPANCY WILL ATTRACT A HANDLING FEE OF USD40.00. THIS FEE WILL BE DEDUCTED FROM PROCEEDS REMITTED BY OURSELVES

+SHIPPING MARKS:NABLS/NO.8612SH/MELBOURNE/NO.1-UP

DETAILS OF CHARGES　　　71B: ALL BANK CHARGES OUTSIDE AUSTRALIA, PLUS ADVISING AND REIMBURSING COMMISSION, ARE FOR THE ACCOUNT OF BENEFICIARY

PRESENTATION PERIOD　　　48: WITHIN 15 DAYS AFTER THE DATE OF B/L BUT WITHIN THE VALIDITY OF THIS CREDIT

CONFIRMATION　　　*49: ADVISING BANK IS NOT REQUESTED TO CONFIRM THE CREDIT

INSTRUCTION　　　78: ON RECEIPT OF DOCUMENTS CONFIRMING TO THE TERMS OF THIS DOCUMENTARY CREDIT, WE UNDERTAKE TO REIMBURSE YOU IN THE CURRENCY OF THE CREDIT IN ACCORDANCE WITH YOUR INSTRUCTIONS, WHICH SHOULD INCLUDE YOUR UID NUMBER AND THE ABA CODE OF THE RECEIVING BANK

ADVISING THROUGH BANK　　　57A:BANK OF CHINA,HANGZHOU BRANCH

相关资料

1. 发票号:KGC508

2. 发票日期:2014年5月27日

3. 包装:10件装一纸箱

4. G.W:26.00KGS/CTN

　　N.W:25.00KGS/CTN

　　体积:25*30*40cm

5. 船名航次:VICTORY V.123

6. 卖方公司法人代表：吴敏

7. 委托上海外运/小李托运、代理报关、代理报检，于2014年7月1日装船出运。

8. 针织衫的海关编码为4785200010

9. 卖方公司单证员：李丹　　　电话：0571-88546000

　　　　　　　　　　　　传真：0571-88546500

Shipper:		订舱委托书		
Consignee:		To: 开船日： 箱型、箱量：		
Notify:		合同号：		
		运费：		
		Vessel/Voyage：		
Port of Loading	Port of Discharge	Transshipment		Partial Shipment
Marks & Numbers	Description of Goods	No. of Packages	Gross Weight	Meas.
TOTAL NUMBERS OF CONTAINERS OR PACKAGES:				
客户要求				
□送货　　　□产装　　　□代理报关　　　□代理报检　　　□投保				
产装信息	产装地址及预计日期： 单位名称： 地址： 联系人： 电话：	订舱公司： 联系人： 电话： 传真：		
特殊要求				

ADVISING BANK:BANK OF COMMUNICATIONS SHANGHAI(HEAD OFFICE)

OPENING BANK:BANGKOK BANK PUBLIC COMPANY LIMITED,BANGKOK

SEQUENCE OF TOTAL	*27:1/1
FORM OF DOC. CREDIT	*40A:IRREVOCABLE
DOC. CREDIT NUM.	*20:0011LC123756
DATE OF ISSUE	31C:001103
DATE/PLACE EXPIRY	*31D:DATE:010114 PLACE:BENEFICIARIES' COUNTRY
APPLICANT	*50:MOUN CO.,LTD.,
	NO. 443,249 ROAD,
	BANGKOK,THAILAND
BENEFICIARY	*59:SHANGHAI FOREIGN TRADE CORP.,
	SHANGHAI,CHINA
AMOUNT	*32B:CODE USD AMOUNT 18,000
AVAILABLE WITH	*41D:ANY BANK IN CHINA BY NEGOTIATION
DRAFTS AT	42C:SIGHT IN DUPLICATE INDICATING THIS L/C NUMBER
DRAWEE	43D:ISSUING BANK
PARTIAL SHIPMENT	43P:NOT ALLOWED
TRANSSHIPMENT	43T:ALLOWED
LOADING ON BOARD	44A:CHINA MAIN PORT,CHINA
TRANSPORT TO	44B:BANGKOK,THAILAND
LATEST SHIPMENT	44C:001220
GOODS DESCRIPT.	45A:2,000KGS. ISONIAZID BP98
	AT USD9.00 PER KG. CFRC5% BANGKOK
DOCUMENTS REQUIRED	46A:+COMMERCIAL INVOICE IN ONE ORIGINAL

PLUS 5 COPIES INDICATING FOB VALUE,

FREIGHT CHARGES SEPARATELY AND THIS

L/C NUMBER,ALL OF WHICH MUST BE

MANUALLY SIGNED

+FULL SET OF 3/3 CLEAN ON BOARD OCEAN BILLS OF

LADING AND TWO NON-NEGOTIABLE COPIES MADE

OUT TO ORDER OF BANGKOK BANK PUBLIC COMPANY

LIMITED, BANGKOK MARKED FREIGHT PREPAID AND

NOTIFY APPLICANT AND INDICATING THIS L/C NUMBER

+PACKING LIST IN ONE ORIGINAL PLUS 5 COPIES, ALL

OF WHICH MUST BE MANUALLY SIGNED

+ CERTIFICATE OF ANALYSIS IN ONE ORIGINAL PLUS ONE COPY

ADDITIONAL CONDITIONS   47A：A DISCREPANCY FEE OF USD50.00 WILL BE IMPOSED ON EACH SET OF DOCUMENTS PRESENTED FOR NEGOTIATION UNDER THIS L/C WITH DISCREPANCY.THE FEE WILL BE DEDUCTED FROM THE BILL AMOUNT

CHARGES   71B：ALL BANK CHARGES OUTSIDE THAILAND INCLUDING REIMBURSING BANK COMMISSION AND DISCREPANCY FEE (IF ANY)ARE FOR BENEFICIARIES' ACCOUNT

相关资料

发票号码：SHE 02/1845   发票日期：2000年11月26日

提单号码：SCOISG7564   提单日期：2000年11月29日

合同号码：S/C00112233   合同日期：2000年10月25日

货运代理联系人：金丰货代/小金

海关编码：29333999 无唛头

船名：JENNY V.03   装运港：上海港

产装预计日期：2000年11月27日

订舱公司：上海对外贸易有限公司

地址：中国上海东一路387号

联系人：张丽   电话：021-88665768   传真：021-88665769

货物装箱情况：50KGS/DRUM   总毛重：2,200KGS

总净重：2000KGS   总体积：50M^3

集装箱：1x40' FCL   运费：USD0.08/KG

UXXU4240250 0169255

Shipper:	订舱委托书
Consignee:	To: 开船日： 箱型、箱量：
Notify:	合同号： 运费： Vessel/Voyage：

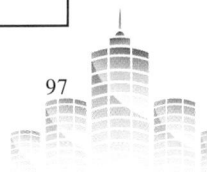

续表

Port of Loading	Port of Discharge	Transshipment	Partial Shipment	
Marks & Numbers	Description of Goods	No. of Packages	Gross Weight	Meas.

TOTAL NUMBERS OF CONTAINERS OR PACKAGES:

<table>
<tr><td colspan="2" align="center">客户要求</td></tr>
<tr><td colspan="2" align="center">□送货　　□产装　　□代理报关　　□代理报检　　□投保</td></tr>
<tr><td rowspan="5">产装信息</td><td>产装地址及预计日期：</td><td>订舱公司：</td></tr>
<tr><td>单位名称：</td><td>联系人：</td></tr>
<tr><td>地址：</td><td>电话：</td></tr>
<tr><td>联系人：</td><td>传真：</td></tr>
<tr><td>电话：</td><td></td></tr>
<tr><td>特殊要求</td><td colspan="2"></td></tr>
</table>

练习四

FROM:HABIB BANK LTD.,DUBAI

TO:BANK OF CHINA,NANJING BRANCH

FORM OF DOC. CREDIT	*40A:IRREVOCABLE
DOC. CREDIT NUMBER	*20:LC-2008-1098
DATE OF ISSUE	31C:171010
EXPIRY	*31D:DATE:171230　　PLACE:CHINA
APPLICANT	*50:AL-HADON TRADING COMPANY
	P.O.BOX NO. 1198,DUBAI,U.A.E.
BENEFICIARY	*59:NANJING GARMENTS IMP. AND EXP. CO.,LTD.,
	NO. 301 ZHEN'ANTONG ROAD,NANJING,210002,CHINA
AMOUNT	*32B:CURRENCY USD AMOUNT 40,750.00
POS./NEG. TOL.(%)	39A:5/5
AVAILABLE WITH	*41D:ANY BANK BY NEGOTIATION
DRAFTS AT	42C:60 DAYS AFTER SIGHT FOR FULL INVOICE VALUE
DRAWEE	42A:HABIB BANK LTD.,DUBAI,
	TRADING SERVICES,BOX 1106,DUBAI U.A.E.

PARTIAL SHIPMENT   43P:ALLOWED

TRANSSHIPMENT   43T:ALLOWED

PORT OF LOADING   44E:NANJING,CHINA

PORT OF DISCHARGE   44F:DUBAI,U.A.E.

LATEST DATE OF SHIP.   44C:171215

DESCRIPT. OF GOODS   45A:MEN'S 2PCS SET,CFR DUBAI

ART NO. 3124A,U. PRICE USD52.50/DOZ,300DOZ

ART NO. 3125A,U. PRICE USD50.00/DOZ,500DOZ

ALL OTHER DETAILS AS PER PROFORMA INVOICE NO. HT-2578 OF M/S. HALLSON TRADING P. O. BOX 2512 DUBAI U.A.E.

DOCUMENTS REQUIRED   46A:

+SIGNED COMMERCIAL INVOICE IN TRIPLICATE

+PACKING AND ASSORTMENT LIST IN TRIPLICATE STATING THAT THE GOODS OF SIZE S,M,L,XL ARE PACKED INTO 4 DOZ PER ONE EXPORT CARTON,EACH SIZE EACH DOZEN

+MANUALLY SIGNED CERTIFICATE OF ORIGIN IN TRIPLICATE SHOWING B/L NOTIFY PARTY AS CONSIGNEE AND INDICATING THE NAME OF THE MANUFACTURER

+FULL SET OF CLEAN ON BOARD BILLS OF LADING MADE OUT TO ORDER OF SHIPPER AND BLANK ENDORSED AND MARKED FREIGHT PREPAID,NOTIFY M/S HALLSON TRADING,P.O.BOX NO. 2512 DUBAI U.A.E. AND ALSO SHOWING THE NAME,ADDRESS,TEL. NO. OR FAX NO. OF THE CARRYING VESSEL'S AGENT AT PORT OF DISCHARGE

+A SEPARATE CERTIFICATE FROM THE SHIPPING CO. OR ITS AGENT CERTIFYING THAT THE CARRYING VESSEL IS ALLOWED BY ARAB AUTHORITIES TO CALL AT ARABIAN PORTS AND IS NOT SCHEDULED TO CALL AT ANY ISRAELI PORTS DURING ITS TRIP TO ARABIAN COUNTRIES

+ SHIPPING ADVICE MUST BE SENT TO THE DUBAI INSURANCE COMPANY ON FAX NO. 82354322 SHOWING THE SHIPPING DETAILS

+ ONE SET OF NON-NEGOTIABLE SHIPPING DOCUMENTS AND SHIPMENT SAMPLES SHOULD BE SENT DIRECTLY TO THE OPENERS AND A CERTIFICATE AND RELATIVE

POST RECEIPT FOR THIS EFFECT IS REQUIRED

ADDITIONAL CONDITIONS 47A：

1. INSURANCE TO BE EFFECTED BY BUYER

2. REIMBURSEMENT UNDER THIS CREDIT IS SUBJECT TO UNIFORM RULES FOR BANK TO BANK REIMBURSEMENT UNDER DOCUMENTARY ICC PUBLICATION NO. 525

3. WE SHALL ARRANGE REMITTANCE OF THE PROCEEDS TO YOU ON RECEIPT OF DOCUMENTS COMPLYING WITH THE TERMS OF THIS L/C CONFIRMING THAT THE DRAFT AMOUNT HAS BEEN ENDORSED ON THIS LETTER OF CREDIT

4. AMOUNT AND QUANTITY 5 PCT MORE OR LESS ARE ALLOWED

5. ALL DOCUMENTS MUST SHOW OUR L/C NUMBER

6. THIS L/C IS UNRESTRICTED FOR NEGOTIATION

DETAILS OF CHARGES 71B：ALL BANKING CHARGES OUTSIDE DUBAI ARE FOR A/C OF BENEFICIARY

PRESENTATION PERIOD 48：DOCUMENTS TO BE PRESENTED WITHIN 15 DAYS AFTER THE DATE OF SHIPMENT,BUT WITHIN THE VALIDITY OF THE CREDIT

相关资料

发票号码：2017-1500　　　　　　　发票日期：2017年11月30日

提单号码：HSKK50088　　　　　　　提单日期：2017年12月10日

船名：CMA CROWN V. 987　　　　　集装箱：1×20' LCL CFS/CFS

集装箱号：TRIU287756　　　　　　　封号：80709

原产地证号：08NJ98699　　　　　　　商品编号：6302.2900

包装：4DOZ/CTN　　　　　　　　　　体积：58×40×25CMS

净重：20.00KGS/CTN　　　　　　　　毛重：22.00KGS/CTN

合同号：NG08-2578　　　　　　　　　预约保单号：08-236147

议付银行：中国银行南京分行(BANK OF CHINA,NANJING BRANCH)

生产厂家：南京佳美服装厂(NANJING JUSTMADE GARMENTS FACTORY)

货代公司：南京远洋货运公司　　　　货代联系人：王一南

唛头：

HALLSON

HT-2578

DUBAI

NO. 1-200

Shipper:	订舱委托书			
Consignee：	To： 开船日： 箱型、箱量：			
Notify：	合同号：			
	运费：			
	Vessel/Voyage：			
Port of Loading	Port of Discharge	Transshipment		Partial Shipment
Marks & Numbers	Description of Goods	No. of Packages	Gross Weight	Meas.
TOTAL NUMBERS OF CONTAINERS OR PACKAGES：				
客户要求 □送货　　　□产装　　　□代理报关　　　□代理报检　　　□投保				
产装信息	产装地址及预计日期： 单位名称： 地址： 联系人： 电话：	订舱公司： 联系人： 电话： 传真：		
特殊要求				

练习五

FORM OF DOC. CREDIT	*40A:IRREVOCABLE
DOC. CREDIT NUMBER	*20:7440-0093471
DATE OF ISSUE	*31C:DATE:20150615 PLACE:SHANGHAI
EXPIRY	*31D:20150929
APPLICANT	*50:SIS & BRO TRADING CO.,LTD.,
	8230 AADYYHOEJ
BENEFICIARY	*59:SHANGHAI TOYSON IMPORT AND EXPORT CO.,
	27 ZHONGSHAN ROAD,E.1 CN-200002 SHANGHAI,CHINA
AMOUNT	*32B:CURRENCY USD AMOUNT USD95,902.50
AVAILABLE WITH	*41D:ANY BANK IN CHINA BY NEGOTIATION
DRAFTS AT	*42C:30 DAYS SIGHT
DRAWEE	*42A:OURSELVES
PARTIAL SHIPMENT	*43P:PROHIBITED
TRANSSHIPMENT	*43T:ALLOWED
LOADING IN CHARGE	*44A:SHANGHAI
LATEST DATE OF SHIP	*44C:20150730
FOR TRANSPORT TO	*44B:CIF AARHUS
DESCRIPT. OF GOODS	*45A:TOWELS
	ART NO. 2021 ABOUT 14,500DOZ AT USD2.77
	ART NO. 2151 ABOUT 12,250DOZ AT USD4.55
	AS PER S/C NO. 4CA3068
DOCUMENTS REQUIRED	*46A:

+SIGNED COMMERCIAL INVOICE IN 5 ORIGINALS SHOWING THE VALUE OF THE MENTIONED GOODS AND STATING "WE THEREBY CERTIFY THAT THE GOODS HEREIN INVOICED CONFIRM WITH 4CA3068 ART. 2021,2151"

+COMPLETE SET OF NOT LESS THAN 3 ORIGINALS AND 1 NON-NEGOTIABLE COPY OF "ON BOARD" BILL OF LOADING ISSUED TO ORDER AND BLANK ENDORSED, MARKED "FREIGHT PREPAID" AND EVIDENCING SHIPMENT FROM SHANGHAI VIA HONG KONG TO AARHUS NOTIFYING APPLICANT

+ INSURANCE POLICY OR CERTIFICATE IN DUPLICATE BLANK ENDORSED FOR 110% OF INVOICE VALUE INCLUDING INSTITUTE CARGO CLAUSES A,AND INSTITUTE

WAR CLAUSES, CLAIMS TO BE PAYABLE IN DENMARK
IN THE CURRENCY OF THE DRAFTS

+PACKING LIST

+GSP CERTIFICATE OF ORIGIN FORM A

PRESENTATION PERIOD　　　*48: NOT LATER THAN 15 DAYS AFTER THE DATE OF
ISSUANCE OF THE SHIPPING DOCUMENTS BUT WITHIN
THE VALIDITY OF THE CREDIT

ADDITIONAL COND.　　　*47A:

+ THE NUMBER AND THE DATE OF THIS CREDIT
AND THE NAME OF OUR BANK MUST BE QUOTED
ON ALL DRAFTS REQUIRED

相关资料

1. INVOICE NO. AND DATE: HT980418, JUN. 30, 2015

2. B/L NO. AND DATE: MOL8003816, JUL. 25, 2015

3. VESSEL'S NAME AND VOYAGE: NAM KING, V.987

4. REFERENCE NO.: Y0310

5. H.S. CODE: 61171000

6. S/C DATE: 20050610

7. SHIPPING MARKS:

REV　　　　　　　　　　JSL
240553　　　　　　　　　857235
AARHUS DENMARK　　　　AARHUS DENMARK
ART. NO. 2021　　　　　ART. NO. 2151
NO. 1-290　　　　　　　NO. 291-535

8. PACKING: ONE DOZEN IN A PLASTIC BAG, 50 DOZEN TO AN EXPORT CARTON
@ GW: 27KGS @NW: 23KGS@MEAS: (60×26×46)CM

9. 该批货物委托上海扬帆海运公司的小王订舱出运。

Shipper:	订舱委托书
Consignee:	To: 开船日： 箱型、箱量：

Notify:	合同号：		
	运费：		
	Vessel/Voyage：		

Port of Loading	Port of Discharge	Transshipment	Partial Shipment

Marks & Numbers	Description of Goods	No. of Packages	Gross Weight	Meas.

TOTAL NUMBERS OF CONTAINERS OR PACKAGES:

客户要求

□送货　　　□产装　　　□代理报关　　　□代理报检　　　□投保

产装信息	产装地址及预计日期：	订舱公司：
	单位名称：	联系人：
	地址：	电话：
	联系人：	传真：
	电话：	
特殊要求		

第六节　汇票的填制

一、汇票的概念、种类及使用意义

1. 汇票的概念

汇票(BILL OF EXCHANGE,简称 BILL 或 DRAFT 或 EXCHANGE)是出票人签发的,委托付款人在见票时或者在指定日期无条件支付确定的金额给收款人或者持票人的票据。

2. 种类

(1)银行汇票　　银行签发,银行付款的汇票。

(2)商业汇票　　由出口企业签发,向国外进口人或银行收取货款时使用的汇票。

3. 汇票在国际贸易中的使用

(1)银行汇票:多用于票汇(D/D)业务,一般为光票,结汇方式为顺汇。

(2)商业汇票:多用于托收和信用证业务,一般为跟单汇票,结汇方式为逆汇。

由于在国际贸易中托收和 L/C 的支付方式占了很大比例,因此在国际贸易中大多数使用的是商业汇票。

汇票通常签发一式两份,两份具同等效力,但付款人仅对其中的一份进行付款或承兑,先到先付,后到无效。汇票上通常写明"付一不付二"(SECOND OF EXCHANGE BEING UNPAID)或"付二不付一"(FIRST OF EXCHANGE BEING UNPAID)。

【拓展】

汇票是随着国际贸易的发展而产生的。国际贸易的买卖双方相距遥远,所用货币各异,不能像国内贸易那样方便地结算。从出口方发运货物到进口方收到货物,中间有一个较长的过程。在这段时间,一定有一方向另一方提供信用,不是进口商提前支付货款,就是出口商赊销货物。若没有强有力的中介人担保,进口商怕付了款收不到货,出口商怕发了货收不到款,这样国际贸易就难以顺利进行。后来银行参与国际贸易,作为进出口双方的中介人,进口商通过开证行向出口商开出信用证,向出口商担保:货物运出后,只要出口商按时向议付行提交全套信用证单据就可以收到货款;议付行开出以开证行为付款人的汇票发到开证行,开证行保证见到议付行汇票及全套信用证单据后付款,同时又向进口商担保,能及时收到他们所进口的货物单据,到港口提货。

二、汇票样本模板

1. 高考汇票样本

BILL OF EXCHANGE

凭
Drawn under _____

信用证　第　　　　号
L/C No. _____

日期
Dated _____ 支取 Payable with interest@

_____% per annum 按年息_____付款

号码
No. _____

汇票金额
Exchange for _____

中国XX　　年　　月　　日
China

见票

At _____

日后(本汇票之副本未付)付交

sight of this FIRST of Exchange(Second of Exchange

金额

being unpaid) Pay to the order of _____

the sum of

款已收讫

Value received

此致

To:

_____

_____

_____

signature

2. 其他汇票样本

汇票

BILL OF EXCHANGE

凭

DRAWN UNDER _____

信用证　第　　　　号

L/C NO. _____

日期　　　　　　　　　　年　　月　　日

DATED _____

按息付款

Payable with interest@_____% per annum

号码　　　　　　　汇票金额　　　　　　　上海　　年　　月　　日

NO. _____ Exchange for_____ SHANGHAI_____

见票　　　　　　日后(本汇票之副本未付)付

At _____ sight this FIRST of Exchange(Second of Exchange being unpaid)

Pay to the order of _____或其指定人

金额

The sum of _____

此致

To：

_____

_____

signature

三、汇票的项目及内容填写

(一)汇票的必要项目

一张有效的汇票必须具备以下8个项目：

1. 写明汇票"BILL OF EXCHANGE OR DRAFT"字样。

2. 小写与大写的货币名称和金额。

3. 出票日期与地点。

4. 适当的文句表明无条件支付的命令。

5. 付款期限。

6. 收款人的名称和地址。

7. 付款人的名称和地址。

8. 出票人的名称和负责人的签字或印章。

（二）汇票各栏目内容及填制方法

1. 出票条款（DRAWN UNDER）：此栏按要求填写开证银行的名称和地址。

2. L/C NO.填信用证号码。

3. 日期（DATED）填开证日期。

4. 号码（NO.）填发票号码。

5. 汇票小写金额。

如信用证规定"DRAFT FOR 100% OF THE INVOICE VALUE（按照发票金额的100%开立汇票），则汇票金额等于发票金额。

如信用证规定"INVOICE SHOWING CIFC3，AT THE TIME OF NEGOTIATION 3% COMMISSION MUST BE DEDUCTED FROM DRAWING UNDER THE CREDIT（发票显示CIF3%含佣价，在议付时3%佣金必须从该信用证下汇票中扣除），则这时汇票金额小于发票金额。

6. 出票日期和地点：出票日期即交单期，根据信用证中交单期条款period of presentation（代码48）内容推算，如WITHIN 15 DAYS AFTER THE DATE OF SHIPMENT BUT WITHIN THE VALIDITY OF CREDIT（交单期为装运日后15日内，但要在信用证有效期内），则在货物实际装运日基础上加上15天，算出单据的有效期，然后与信用证有效期相比，看哪个有效期更早，更早的那个就是最晚交单日，也就是该汇票的最晚出票日期。如果信用证中没有交单期条款，则按照国际惯例，按照装运日后21日去算单据的有效期。

出票地点一般为卖方所在地。如：SHANGHAI，CHINA。

7. 几种常见的汇票付款期限：

（1）见票即付

DRAFT AT SIGHT

填写：AT ***** SIGHT

（2）见票后若干天付款

DRAFT AT 30 DAYS AFTER SIGHT

填写：AT ___30 DAYS AFTER___ SIGHT

（3）提单日后若干天付款

DRAFT AT 45 DAYS AFTER B/L DATE

填写：AT ___45 DAYS AFTER B/L DATE___，同时注明B/L DATE：MAY 14TH，2017

8. 汇票大写金额：SAY开始，ONLY结尾，货币名称全称写在金额前。

如：USD23,978.50

大写金额：SAY US DOLLARS TWENTY-THREE THOUSAND NINE HUNDRED AND SEVENTY-

EIGHT AND POINT FIFTY ONLY.

其中小数点后数字0.55的表达方法有以下几种：

（1）AND CENTS FIFTY-FIVE，注意整数与小数之间加"AND"一词；

（2）POINT FIFTY-FIVE，注意使用POINT，就不必再加CENTS；

（3）55% OR 55/100。

9. 收款人（PAY TO THE ORDER OF _____）：该栏填写先看信用证条款AVAILABLE WITH，如果是具体的银行名称，此为限制议付信用证，则照着填写；如果是ANY BANK IN CHINA，此为自由议付信用证，则填BANK OF CHINA，...BRANCH（即中国银行卖方所在地分行）。

10. 付款人（TO）：看信用证条款DRAWEE，如未规定，一般填写开证行。

（三）填制汇票的注意事项

（1）除非信用证另有规定，否则汇票金额应与发票金额一致。

（2）如信用证规定汇票金额为发票金额的百分之几，例如97%，那么发票金额应为100%，汇票金额为97%，其差额3%一般为应付的佣金。这种做法通常用于中间商代开信用证的场合。信用证支付方式项下的汇票，除了严格按信用证缮制以外，还要符合票据的规范。

（3）如信用证规定部分信用证付款，部分托收，则分做两套汇票：信用证下支付的汇票按信用证允许的金额填制，其余部分为托收项下汇票的金额，两者之和等于发票金额。

（4）如信用证要求两张汇票分别支付一笔交易金额，则在两张汇票上打上信用证所要求的金额。

（5）汇票中的大小金额和币制必须相同，并符合信用证的规定。汇票的缮制应做到单证一致，要整洁美观，不得有涂改现象。

四、汇票易错点集锦

1. 出票时间和地点：地点要写出口商所在城市拼音。如果有确定的交单期，写资料中的交单期；如果没有，则必须根据信用证交单期条款推算出最晚交单日期；如果信用证无交单期条款，就默认为装运日后21天，并且在信用证有效期内。

2. PAY TO THE ORDER OF（抬头）：后面要看信用证条款中的AVAILABLE WITH，如果那里是ANY BANK BY NEGOTIATION，一般写成通知行；如果没有通知行，写BANK OF CHINA，** BRANCH，其中**指的是出口商所在地的城市拼音。如果这里还出现其他银行的，则把这里出现的银行填上。

3. TO后面填写的内容看DRAWEE条款后面的内容。

4. 出票人填写出口公司英文名称和法人代表签名。

5. 开证银行地址：如果上面有大地址，而在附加条款或者特殊条款中出现详细地址，这个详细地址可以不抄。

6. 汇票期限：按信用证规定填写，看DRAFT AT条款，如果是30 DAYS AFTER THE DATE OF B/L，则把原句填写上之后（这种情况下可以把SIGHT划掉，也可以不划），还要注明提单日期。注意：如果在大写金额下面有标号，而汇票中没有其他东西要补充的，则要把提单日期写在标号处；如果大写金额下面没有标号，标在AT后面。

五、专项练习

练习一

APPLICATION HEADER:BANK OF CHINA,LONDON

USER HEADER:BANK OF CHINA,SHANGHAI

SEQUENCE OF TOTAL	27:1/1
FORM OF DOC. CREDIT	40A:IRREVOCABLE
APPLICABLE RULES	40E:UCP LATEST VERSION
DOC. CREDIT NUMBER	20:LC-17G021
DATE OF ISSUE	31C:170318
EXPIRY	31D:DATE:170710 PLACE:CHINA
APPLICANT	50:GREAT BRITAIN TRADING INC.
	#2125-3 QUEEN AVENUE,LONDON,BRITAIN
BENEFICIARY	59:SHANGHAI BAOJING COMPANY
	NO. 1270,ZHEJIANG ROAD,SHANGHAI,CHINA
AMOUNT	32B:CURRENCY USD AMOUNT 190,800.00
AVAILABLE WITH	41D:ANY BANK IN CHINA BY NEGOTIATION
DRAFTS AT	42C:SIGHT FOR FULL INVOICE COST VALUE
DRAWEE	42A:BANK OF CHINA,LONDON
PARTIAL SHIPMENT	43P:NOT ALLOWED
TRANSSHIPMENT	43T:ALLOWED
LOADING IN CHARGE	44A:CHINESE PORTS
FOR TRANSPORT TO	44B:LONDON
LATEST DATE OF SHIP.	44C:170625
DESCRIPT. OF GOODS	45A:

7200 GROSS NBB0021 PROPELLING PENCILS AS PER S/C NO.:GB1703

CIFC3% LONDON,BRITAIN USD26.50 PER GROSS

SHIPPING MARK:GB/LONDON/NO.1-UP

DOCUMENTS REQUIRED   46A:

+ORIGINAL SIGNED COMMERCIAL INVOICE IN 3 COPIES

+ORIGINAL PACKING LIST IN 3 COPIES

+CERTIFICATE OF ORIGIN IN 2 COPIES

+CERTIFICATE OF QUALITY IN 3 COPIES ISSUED BY CIQ

+FULL SET 3/3 OF SIGNED CLEAN ON BOARD OCEAN

  BILLS OF LADING MADE OUT TO THE ORDER OF CIYI

BANK N.A., NEW YORK, NOTIFYING APPLICANT INDICATING OUR LETTER OF CREDIT NUMBER AND MARKED FREIGHT PREPAID

+INSURANCE POLICY IN TRIPLICATE FOR 110 PERCENT OF THE INVOICE VALUE SHOWING CLAIMS SETTING AGENT AT DESTINATION PORT AND THE CLAIMS ARE PAYABLE IN THE CURRENCY OF THE DRAFT, COVERING ALL RISKS, WAR RISKS AND S.R.C.C.

ADDITIONAL INSTRUCTIONS: 47A: ALL DOCUMENTS MUST INDICATE CONTRACT NO. AND L/C NO.

DETAILS OF CHARGES 71B: ALL BANKING CHARGES OUTSIDE BRITAIN ARE FOR THE ACCOUNT OF THE BENEFICIARY

PRESENTATION PERIOD 48: DOCUMENTS TO BE PRESENTED WITHIN 15 DAYS AFTER THE DATE OF SHIPMENT, BUT WITHIN THE VALIDITY OF THE CREDIT

补充资料

发票号码:BP-BJ023

法人代表:蔡佩琪

交单日期:JUNE 28,2017

BILL OF EXCHANGE

凭
Drawn under _____

信用证　第　　　号
L/C No. _____

日期
Dated _____ 支取 Payable with interest@

% per annum 按年息_____付款

号码
No. _____

汇票金额
Exchange for ▓▓▓▓▓▓▓

中国XX　　年　　月　　日
China

见票
At _____

日后(本汇票之副本未付)付交
sight of this FIRST of Exchange(Second of Exchange

金额

being unpaid) Pay to the order of _____

the sum of

款已收讫
Value received
此致
To:

_____

_____

_____

signature

练习二

APPLICATION HEADER：BANK OF CHINA，LONDON

USER HEADER：BANK OF CHINA，SHANGHAI

SEQUENCE OF TOTAL　　　27：1/1

FORM OF DOC. CREDIT　　40A：IRREVOCABLE

APPLICABLE RULES　　　　40E：UCP LATEST VERSION

DOC. CREDIT NUMBER　　 20：LC-17G021

DATE OF ISSUE　　　　　 31C：170318

EXPIRY　　　　　　　　　31D：DATE：170710　PLACE：CHINA

APPLICANT　　　　　　　 50：GREAT BRITAIN TRADING INC.

　　　　　　　　　　　　　　#2125-3 QUEEN AVENUE，LONDON，BRITAIN

BENEFICIARY　　　　　　 59：SHANGHAI BAOJING COMPANY

　　　　　　　　　　　　　　NO. 1270，ZHEJIANG ROAD，SHANGHAI，CHINA

AMOUNT　　　　　　　　　32B：CURRENCY EUR AMOUNT 190,800.00

AVAILABLE WITH　　　　　41D：ANY BANK IN CHINA BY NEGOTIATION

DRAFTS AT　　　　　　　 42C：SIGHT

DRAWEE　　　　　　　　　42A：LONDON COMMERCIAL BANK，LONDON

PARTIAL SHIPMENT　　　　43P：NOT ALLOWED

TRANSSHIPMENT　　　　　 43T：ALLOWED

LOADING IN CHARGE　　　 44A：CHINESE PORTS

FOR TRANSPORT TO　　　　44B：LONDON

LATEST DATE OF SHIP.　　44C：170625

DESCRIPT. OF GOODS　　　45A：

　　　　　　　　　　　　　7200 GROSS NBB0021 PROPELLING PENCILS AS PER S/C NO.：GB1703

　　　　　　　　　　　　　CIFC3% LONDON，BRITAIN USD26.50 PER GROSS

　　　　　　　　　　　　　SHIPPING MARK：GB/LONDON/NO.1-UP

DOCUMENTS REQUIRED　　　46A：

　　　　　　　　　　　　　+ ORIGINAL SIGNED COMMERCIAL INVOICE IN 3 COPIES INDICATING CIF VALUE INCLUDING 3% COMMISSION，AT THE TIME OF NEGOTIATION 3% COMMISSION MUST BE DEDUCTED FROM DRAWINGS UNDER THIS CREDIT

　　　　　　　　　　　　　+ORIGINAL PACKING LIST IN 3 COPIES

　　　　　　　　　　　　　+CERTIFICATE OF ORIGIN IN 2 COPIES

　　　　　　　　　　　　　+CERTIFICATE OF QUALITY IN 3 COPIES ISSUED BY CIQ

　　　　　　　　　　　　　+ FULL SET 3/3 OF SIGNED CLEAN ON BOARD OCEAN

BILLS OF LADING MADE OUT TO THE ORDER OF CIYI BANK N.A., NEW YORK, NOTIFYING APPLICANT INDICATIING OUR LETTER OF CREDIT NUMBER AND MARKED FREIGHT PREPAID

+INSURANCE POLICY IN TRIPLICATE FOR 110 PERCENT OF THE INVOICE VALUE SHOWING CLAIMS SETTING AGENT AT DESTINATION PORT AND THE CLAIMS ARE PAYABLE IN THE CURRENCY OF THE DRAFT, COVERING ALL RISKS, WAR RISKS AND S.R.C.C.

DETAILS OF CHARGES   71B: ALL BANKING CHARGES OUTSIDE BRITAIN ARE FOR THE ACCOUNT OF THE BENEFICIARY

PRESENTATION PERIOD   48: DOCUMENTS TO BE PRESENTED WITHIN 15 DAYS AFTER THE DATE OF SHIPMENT, BUT WITHIN THE VALIDITY OF THE CREDIT

补充资料

发票号码:BP-BJ023

法人代表:蔡佩琪

交单日期:JUNE 28,2017

BILL OF EXCHANGE

凭
Drawn under _____

信用证 第 号
L/C No. _____

日期
Dated _____ 支取 Payable with interest@

% per annum 按年息_____付款

号码
No. _____

汇票金额
Exchange for [_____]

中国XX 年 月 日
China

见票
At _____

日后(本汇票之副本未付)付交
sight of this FIRST of Exchange(Second of Exchange

金额

being unpaid) Pay to the order of _____

the sum of

款已收讫
Value received
此致
To:

_____

_____

_____

signature

练习三

APPLICATION HEADER:BANK OF CHINA,LONDON

USER HEADER:BANK OF CHINA,SHANGHAI

SEQUENCE OF TOTAL   27:1/1

FORM OF DOC. CREDIT   40A:IRREVOCABLE

APPLICABLE RULES   40E:UCP LATEST VERSION

DOC. CREDIT NUMBER   20:LC-17G021

DATE OF ISSUE   31C:170318

EXPIRY   31D:DATE:170710 PLACE:CHINA

APPLICANT   50:GREAT BRITAIN TRADING INC.

    #2125-3 QUEEN AVENUE,LONDON,BRITAIN

BENEFICIARY   59:SHANGHAI BAOJING COMPANY

    NO. 1270,ZHEJIANG ROAD,SHANGHAI,CHINA

AMOUNT   32B:CURRENCY USD AMOUNT 20,977.45

AVAILABLE WITH   41D:ANY BANK IN CHINA BY NEGOTIATION

DRAFTS AT   42C:60 DAYS FROM THE DATE OF INVOICE

DRAWEE   42A:OURSELVES

PARTIAL SHIPMENT   43P:NOT ALLOWED

TRANSSHIPMENT   43T:ALLOWED

LOADING IN CHARGE   44A:CHINESE PORTS

FOR TRANSPORT TO   44B:LONDON

LATEST DATE OF SHIP.   44C:170625

DESCRIPT. OF GOODS   45A:

    7111GROSS NBB0021 PROPELLING PENCILS AS PER S/C NO.:GB1703

    CIF LONDON,BRITAIN USD2.95 PER GROSS

    SHIPPING MARK:GB/LONDON/NO.1-UP

DOCUMENTS REQUIRED   46A:

    +ORIGINAL SIGNED COMMERCIAL INVOICE IN 3 COPIES

    +ORIGINAL PACKING LIST IN 3 COPIES

    +CERTIFICATE OF ORIGIN IN 2 COPIES

    +CERTIFICATE OF QUALITY IN 3 COPIES ISSUED BY CIQ

    +FULL SET 3/3 OF SIGNED CLEAN ON BOARD OCEAN BILLS OF LADING MADE OUT TO THE ORDER OF CIYI BANK N.A.,NEW YORK,NOTIFYING APPLICANT INDICATING OUR LETTER OF CREDIT NUMBER AND MARKED FREIGHT

PREPAID

+INSURANCE POLICY IN TRIPLICATE FOR 110 PERCENT OF THE INVOICE VALUE SHOWING CLAIMS SETTING AGENT AT DESTINATION PORT AND THE CLAIMS ARE PAYABLE IN THE CURRENCY OF THE DRAFT, COVERING ALL RISKS, WAR RISKS AND S.R.C.C.

DETAILS OF CHARGES   71B: ALL BANKING CHARGES OUTSIDE BRITAIN ARE FOR THE ACCOUNT OF THE BENEFICIARY

PRESENTATION PERIOD   48: DOCUMENTS TO BE PRESENTED WITHIN 15 DAYS AFTER THE DATE OF SHIPMENT, BUT WITHIN THE VALIDITY OF THE CREDIT

补充资料

发票号码：BP-BJ023

发票日期：MAY 15, 2017

法人代表：蔡佩琪

交单日期：JUNE 28, 2017

BILL OF EXCHANGE

凭
Drawn under _____

信用证　第　　号
L/C No. _____

日期
Dated _____ 支取 Payable with interest@ _____ % per annum 按年息_____付款

号码
No. _____

汇票金额
Exchange for ▓▓▓▓▓▓▓

中国XX　年　月　日
China

见票
At _____ sight of this FIRST of Exchange(Second of Exchange

日后(本汇票之副本未付)付交

金额

being unpaid) Pay to the order of _____

the sum of

款已收讫
Value received

此致
To:

_____

_____

_____

| signature |

练习四

APPLICATION HEADER：BANK OF CHINA, LONDON

USER HEADER：BANK OF CHINA, SHANGHAI

SEQUENCE OF TOTAL   27:1/1

FORM OF DOC. CREDIT	40A:IRREVOCABLE
APPLICABLE RULES	40E:UCP LATEST VERSION
DOC. CREDIT NUMBER	20:LC-17G021
DATE OF ISSUE	31C:170318
EXPIRY	31D:DATE:170710 PLACE:CHINA
APPLICANT	50:GREAT BRITAIN TRADING INC.
	#2125-3 QUEEN AVENUE,LONDON,BRITAIN
BENEFICIARY	59:SHANGHAI BAOJING COMPANY
	NO. 1270,ZHEJIANG ROAD,SHANGHAI,CHINA
AMOUNT	32B:CURRENCY USD AMOUNT 190,800.00
AVAILABLE WITH	41D:ANY BANK IN CHINA BY NEGOTIATION
DRAFTS AT	42C:45 DAYS AFTER THE B/L DATE
DRAWEE	42A:LONDON COMMERCIAL BANK,LONDON
PARTIAL SHIPMENT	43P:ALLOWED
TRANSSHIPMENT	43T:ALLOWED
LOADING IN CHARGE	44A:CHINESE PORTS
FOR TRANSPORT TO	44B:LONDON
LATEST DATE OF SHIP.	44C:3600 GROSS TO BE SHIPPED BY THE END OF MAY,AND THE BALANCE TO BE SHIPPED DURING JUNE
DESCRIPT. OF GOODS	45A:

45A:

7200 GROSS NBB0021 PROPELLING PENCILS AS PER S/C NO.:GB1703

CIF LONDON,BRITAIN USD26.50 PER GROSS

SHIPPING MARK:GB/LONDON/NO.1-UP

DOCUMENTS REQUIRED　　46A:

+ORIGINAL SIGNED COMMERCIAL INVOICE IN 3 COPIES

+ORIGINAL PACKING LIST IN 3 COPIES

+CERTIFICATE OF ORIGIN IN 2 COPIES

+CERTIFICATE OF QUALITY IN 3 COPIES ISSUED BY CIQ

+FULL SET 3/3 OF SIGNED CLEAN ON BOARD OCEAN BILLS OF LADING MADE OUT TO THE ORDER OF CIYI BANK N.A.,NEW YORK,NOTIFYING APPLICANT INDICATING OUR LETTER OF CREDIT NUMBER AND MARKED FREIGHT PREPAID

+INSURANCE POLICY IN TRIPLICATE FOR 110 PERCENT OF THE INVOICE VALUE SHOWING CLAIMS SETTING AGENT AT DESTINATION PORT AND THE CLAIMS ARE

PAYABLE IN THE CURRENCY OF THE DRAFT, COVERING ALL RISKS, WAR RISKS AND S.R.C.C.

DETAILS OF CHARGES   71B: ALL BANKING CHARGES OUTSIDE BRITAIN ARE FOR THE ACCOUNT OF THE BENEFICIARY

PRESENTATION PERIOD   48: DOCUMENTS TO BE PRESENTED WITHIN 15 DAYS AFTER THE DATE OF SHIPMENT, BUT WITHIN THE VALIDITY OF THE CREDIT

补充资料

发票号码:BP-BJ023

法人代表:蔡佩琪

第一批于2017年5月25日装船发货,第二批开航日期为JUNE 15,2017。

BILL OF EXCHANGE

凭
Drawn under _____

信用证 第 号
L/C No. _____

日期
Dated _____ 支取 Payable with interest@   % per annum 按年息_____付款

号码
No. _____

汇票金额
Exchange for ▢▢▢▢▢

中国XX 年 月 日
China

见票
At _____

日后(本汇票之副本未付)付交
sight of this FIRST of Exchange(Second of Exchange

金额

being unpaid) Pay to the order of _____ the sum of

款已收讫
Value received

此致
To:

_____

_____

_____

▢▢▢▢▢▢▢
signature

BILL OF EXCHANGE

凭
Drawn under _____

信用证 第 号
L/C No. _____

日期
Dated _____ 支取 Payable with interest@   % per annum 按年息_____付款

号码
No. _____

汇票金额
Exchange for ▢▢▢▢▢

中国XX 年 月 日
China

见票
At _____

日后(本汇票之副本未付)付交
sight of this FIRST of Exchange(Second of Exchange

金额

being unpaid) Pay to the order of _____ the sum of

款已收讫
Value received
此致
To:

_____
_____
_____

signature

练习五

APPLICATION HEADER:BANK OF CHINA,LONDON

USER HEADER:BANK OF CHINA,SHANGHAI

SEQUENCE OF TOTAL	27:1/1
FORM OF DOC. CREDIT	40A:IRREVOCABLE
APPLICABLE RULES	40E:UCP LATEST VERSION
DOC. CREDIT NUMBER	20:LC-17G021
DATE OF ISSUE	31C:170318
EXPIRY	31D:DATE:170710 PLACE:CHINA
APPLICANT	50:GREAT BRITAIN TRADING INC.
	#2125-3 QUEEN AVENUE,LONDON,BRITAIN
BENEFICIARY	59:SHANGHAI BAOJING COMPANY
	NO. 1270,ZHEJIANG ROAD,SHANGHAI,CHINA
AMOUNT	32B:CURRENCY USD AMOUNT 190,800.00
AVAILABLE WITH	41D:ANY BANK IN CHINA BY NEGOTIATION
DRAFTS AT	42C:DRAFT FOR 70% INVOICE VALUE PAYABLE AT SIGHT AND FOR REMAINING 30% PAYABLE AT 30 DAYS AFTER SIGHT FREE OF INTEREST
DRAWEE	42A:BANK OF CHINA,LONDON
PARTIAL SHIPMENT	43P:NOT ALLOWED
TRANSSHIPMENT	43T:ALLOWED
LOADING IN CHARGE	44A:CHINESE PORTS
FOR TRANSPORT TO	44B:LONDON
LATEST DATE OF SHIP.	44C:170625
DESCRIPT. OF GOODS	45A:
	7200 GROSS NBB0021 PROPELLING PENCILS AS PER S/C NO.:GB1703
	DIF LONDON,BRITAIN USD26.50 PER GROSS
	SHIPPING MARK:GB/LONDON/NO.1-UP
DOCUMENTS REQUIRED	46A:……

DETAILS OF CHARGES   71B: ALL BANKING CHARGES OUTSIDE BRITAIN ARE FOR THE ACCOUNT OF THE BENEFICIARY

PRESENTATION PERIOD   48: DOCUMENTS TO BE PRESENTED WITHIN 15 DAYS AFTER THE DATE OF SHIPMENT, BUT WITHIN THE VALIDITY OF THE CREDIT

补充资料

发票号码: BP-BJ023

法人代表: 蔡佩琪

交单日期: JUNE 28, 2017

BILL OF EXCHANGE

凭
Drawn under _____

信用证 第 号
L/C No. _____

日期
Dated _____ 支取 Payable with interest@

% per annum 按年息_____付款

号码
No. _____

汇票金额
Exchange for █████████

中国XX 年 月 日
China

见票
At _____

日后(本汇票之副本未付)付交
sight of this FIRST of Exchange(Second of Exchange

金额

being unpaid) Pay to the order of _____

the sum of

███████████████████████████████████

款已收讫
Value received
此致
To:

_____

_____

_____

signature

BILL OF EXCHANGE

凭
Drawn under _____

信用证 第 号
L/C No. _____

日期
Dated _____ 支取 Payable with interest@

% per annum 按年息_____付款

号码
No. _____

汇票金额
Exchange for █████████

中国XX 年 月 日
China

见票
At _____

日后(本汇票之副本未付)付交
sight of this FIRST of Exchange(Second of Exchange

金额

being unpaid) Pay to the order of _____

the sum of

███████████████████████████████████

款已收讫
Value received
此致
To：

signature

第一节　外贸技能综合练习(一)

一、合同填制

请根据所提供的背景材料将下列合同填写完整。

卖方:香港洋娃娃进出口公司　　　联系人:李琳

买方:伦敦洋娃娃进出口公司　　　联系人:LUCY

品名:洋娃娃　　款号:05、06、08　　数量:1000件、2000件、2000件

价格:05:10美元/件　1000件;06:15美元/件　2000件　06:12美元/件　2000件

采用《2010通则》中的FOB术语

支付条款:20%电汇预付订金,剩余货款在装运前电汇

包装:外包装按买方的出口标准纸箱包装,内包装按卖方的礼盒包装,包装设计和内装物由买方提供

装运:7月份由香港发运

唛头:卖方自制并要求"marked in circle"

保险:按发票金额加保10%投保一切险和战争险

SALES CONTRACT

TO:　　　　　　　　　　　　　　　　　　S/C NO.:SH20151014

DATE:OCT.14,2015

We hereby confirm having sold to you the following goods on terms and conditions as stated below:

Commodity & Specifications	Quantity	Unit Price	Amount
TOTAL:			
TOTAL CONTRACT VALUE:			

SHIPPING MARK：

PACKING：

PORT OF SHIPMENT：

PORT OF DESTINATION：

TIME OF SHIPMENT：

TRANSSHIPMENT：ALLOWED

PARTIAL SHIPMENT：NOT ALLOWED

TERMS OF PAYMENT：

INSURANCE：

Signed by：

THE SELLER：香港洋娃娃进出口公司　　　THE BUYER：LONDON DOLL IMPORT & EXPORT CO.,LTD.

　　　　　　　李琳　　　　　　　　　　　　　　　　　LUCY

二、信用证分析表填制

ISSUE OF DOCUMENTARY CREDIT

SEQUENCE OF TOTAL	27：1/1
FORM OF DOC. CREDIT	40A：IRREVOCABLE
DOC. CREDIT NUMBER	20：KLMU1234
DATE OF ISSUE	31C：190728
APPLICABLE RULES	40E：UCP LATEST VERSION
DATE AND PLACE OF EXPIRY	31D：DATE：190915　　PLACE：CHINA
APPLICANT BANK	51D：NATIONAL COMMERCIAL BANK,JEDDAH
APPLICANT	50：ALOSMNY INTERNATIONAL TRADE CO.,
	177 ALHRAM STREET SECOND FLOOR-G102A EGYPT,
	12111
BENEFICIARY	59：ABC COMPANY,SHANGHAI,
	NO.11 CHANGCHUN ROAD,SHANGHAI,CHINA
AMOUNT	32B：CURRENCY USD AMOUNT 28,820.00
AVAILABLE WITH	41A：ANY BANK IN CHINA BY NEGOTIATION
DRAFTS AT	42C：SIGHT FOR FULL INVOICE VALUE
DRAWEE	42A：ISSUING BANK
PARTIAL SHIPMENT	43P：NOT ALLOWED
TRANSSHIPMENT	43T：NOT ALLOWED
PORT OF LOADING	44E：SHANGHAI,CHINA
PORT OF DISCHARGE	44F：SAID,EGYPT

LATEST DATE OF SHIPMENT   44C:190830

DESCRIPTION OF GOODS   45A:

ABT 48,000 CANS OF MEILING BRAND CANNED ORANGE JAM,PACKED IN SEAWORTHY CARTONS.250 GRAM PER CAN,12CANS IN A CARTON

UNIT PRICE:USD6.55/CTN CFR JEDDAH

COUNTRY OF ORIGIN:P.R.CHINA

DOCUMENTS REQUIRED   46A:

1.COMMERCIAL INVOICE IN 3 COPIES DATED THE SAME DATE AS THAT OF L/C ISSUANCE DATE INDICATING COUNTRY OF ORIGIN THE GOODS AND CERTIFIED TO BE TRUE AND CORRECT INDICATING CONTRACT NO. SUM356/19 AND L/C NO.

2.NEUTRAL PACKING LIST INDICATING QUANTITY, N.W.AND G.W OF EACH PACKAGE,TTL QUANTITY, N.W AND G.W,AND PACKING CONDITIONS AS REQUIRED BY L/C

3.BENEFICIANY'S CERTIFIED COPY OF SHIPPING ADVICE TO THE APPLICANT ADVISING MERCHANDISE, SHIPMENT DATE,GROSS INVOICE VALUE, NAME AND VOYAGE OF VESSEL, CARRIERS NAME, PORT OF LOADING AND PORT OF DISCHARGE LMMEDIATELY ON THE DATE OF SHIPMENT

4.FULL SET OF BILL ONE OF WHICH SHOULD BE SENT TO APPLICANT MADE OUT TO ORDER NOTIFY APPLICANT SHOWING THE B/L NO.

ADDITIONAL CODITIONS   47A:

1.ALL DOCUMENTS MUST INDICATE SHIPPINGMARKS.

2.ALL DOCUMENTS MUST BE MADE OUT IN THE NAME OF DEF CO., LTD., UNLESS OTHERWISE STIPULATED BY THE L/C.

CHARGES   71B:ALL CHANGES AND COMMISSIONS OUTSIDE EGYPT ARE FOR ACCOUNT OF BENEFICIARY

PERIOD FOR PERSENTATION   48:WITHIN 15 DAYS AFTER THE DATE OF SHIPMENT, BUT WITHIN THE VALIDITY OF THIS CREDIT

CONFIRMATION INSTRUCTION   49:WITHOUT

信用证号		合约号			受益人			
开证银行			开证申请人					
开证日期		兑付方式	起运口岸			目的地		
金额			可否转运			成交方式		
汇票付款人			可否分批					
汇票期限	见票_____天期		装运期限			唛头		
			有效期					
			有效地点					
			提单日_____天内议付		_____天内寄单			

单证名称	提单	副本提单	商业发票	海关发票	装箱单	重量数量单	尺码单	保险单	产地证	普惠制产地证	贸促会产地证	出口许可证	装船通知书	投保通知	寄投保通知邮据	寄单证明	寄样证明	品质证明书
提交银行																		
提交客户																		

注:在"提交银行"或"提交客户"对应的栏目中填写应提交的单据份数,信用证要求提交的单据没有注明份数,默认为1份。

提单	抬头		保险	险种	
	通知				
运费支付方式(预付或到付)(17)				投保加成率	赔款地点

注:如果提供的信用证的内容没有涉及信用证分析表的某些栏目,该栏目为空。

三、国际贸易单证填制

请根据上述信用证和下列相关补充资料完成商业发票、装箱单、订舱委托书和汇票的缮制。

补充资料:

SHIPPING MARK:A.I.T.C.

SUM356/19

SAID

C/NO.1-UP

发票号码:123QWE　　发票日期:2019.7.28　　装箱单日期:2019.8.19

受益人授权签字人:李丰　　买方委托德安物流/王明办理租船订舱手续。

供货商出仓单显示:

52800 CANS OF MEILING BRAND CANNED ORANGE JAM

N.W.3KG/CARTONS

G.W.4KG/CARTONS

MEAS. 20*30*40CM/CARTON

船名:MOONRIVER V.987

装船日期:2019.8.30

REFERENCE NO.:A009870121F10007　　　SEAL NUMBER:JPL2894

B/L NO.:F456872

S/C DATE:2019-6-19　　H.S.CODE:2132233288

SELLER	商业发票 COMMERCIAL INVOICE			
BUYER	INVOICE NO.		INVOICE DATE	
	L/C NO.		S/C DATE	
	S/C NO.		PRICE TERM	
	FROM		TO	
MARKS	DESCRIPTION OF GOODS	QUANTITY	UNIT PRICE	AMOUNT
		TOTAL:		
TOTAL AMOUNT IN WORDS:				

SELLER						
		装箱单 PACKING LIST				
BUYER		INVOICE NO..		DATE		
		S/C NO.		L/C NO.		
		FROM		TO		
		MARKS & NOS.				
C/NOS.	DESCRIPTION OF GOODS	NUMBERS & KIND OF RACKAGE	QUANTITY	G.W.（KGS）	N.W.（KGS）	MEAS.（CBM）
	TOTAL:					
TOTAL PACKAGES(IN WORDS):						

Shipper:	订舱委托书		
Consignee:	To: 开船日: 箱型、箱量:		
Notify:	合同号:		
	运费:		
	Vessel/Voyage:		
Port of Loading	Port of Discharge	Transshipment	Partial Shipment
Marks & Numbers	Description of Goods	No. of Packages	Gross Weight	Meas.
A.I.T.C. SUM356/19 SAID C/NO.1~4400				

TOTAL NUMBERS OF CONTAINERS OR PACKAGES:

客户要求

□送货   □产装   □代理报关   □代理报检   □投保

产装信息	产装地址及预计日期: 单位名称: 地址: 联系人: 电话:	订舱公司: 联系人: 电话: 传真:
特殊要求		

BILL OF EXCHANGE

凭
Drawn under _____

信用证　　　第　　　号
L/C No. _____KLMU1234_____

日期
Dated _____　支取 Payable with interest@　　　% per annum 按年息_____付款

号码　　　　汇票金额　　　　　　　　　　　中国XX　　年　　月　　日
No. _____　Exchange for ▓▓▓▓▓▓▓▓▓　China

见票　　　　日后(本汇票之副本未付)付交
At _____　sight of this FIRST of Exchange(Second of Exchange　　金额

being unpaid) Pay to the order of _____　the sum of

▓▓▓▓▓▓▓▓▓▓▓▓▓▓▓▓▓▓▓▓▓▓▓▓▓▓▓▓▓▓▓▓▓▓▓

款已收讫
Value received
此致
To:

_____

_____

_____

signature

第二节　外贸技能综合练习(二)

一、合同填制

请根据所提供的背景材料将下列合同填写完整。

2019年1月,上海纺织品进出口有限公司(SHANGHAI TEXTILES IMP. AND EXP. CORPORATION, 27 ZHONGSHAN ROAD E,1,SHANGHAI,CHINA)销售经理陈彤与日本一客户(ITOCHU CORPORATION, OSAKA,JAPAN,OSACY SECTION)负责人JAC-KIE CHANG就8736条纯棉围裙进行磋商,内容如下:

1. 原定FOB价格的纯棉围裙(100% PURE COTTON APRON):型号为49394(014428)共3216件,单价1美元;型号为49393(014428)共3960件,单价1美元;型号为55306(014429)共1560件,单价1.25美元;

2. 运输标志为ITOCHU/OSAKA/NO.1-728;

3. 货物全部装于适合长距离海运的出口纸箱中,每件套一个塑料袋,12袋装一箱,共728箱;

4. 货物于收到信用证后的45天之内,并不迟于2019年5月,通过海运从上海运往日本大阪,允许分批装运,只允许在青岛中转;

5. 双方最终于1月20日签订一份销售合同AN120,协定依据2010通则,卖方负责运输(每件0.05美元)和保险(每件0.02美元);

6. 双方用保兑的不可撤销的信用证即期支付,信用证由买方开立,于2019年4月15日之前开到卖方,在装船后的15天内在中国议付有效。由于信用证迟到,卖方对延迟装运不负责任并有权撤销合同和/或提出损害赔偿;

7. 由卖方按照中国保险条款依据CIF成交金额的120%投保一切险、战争险和罢工险,额外的保费由买方承担。

SALES CONTRACT

TO:　　　　　　　　　　　　　　　　　　　　　　　　　S/C NO.:

DATE:

We hereby confirm having sold to you the following goods on terms and conditions as stated below:

Commodity & Specifications	Quantity	Unit Price	Amount
TOTAL:			
TOTAL CONTRACT VALUE:			

SHIPPING MARK:

PACKING:

PORT OF SHIPMENT:

PORT OF DESTINATION:

TIME OF SHIPMENT:

TRANSSHIPMENT:

PARTIAL SHIPMENT:

TERMS OF PAYMENT:

INSURANCE:

Signed by:

THE SELLER: THE BUYER:

二、信用证分析表填制

MSG TYPE:700(ISSUE OF A DOCUMENTARY CREDIT)

APPLICANT HEADER:45071932

CIYIBANK N.A.,NEW YORK

SEQUENCE TOTAL	*27:1/1
FORM OF DOCUMENTARY CREDIT	*40A:IRREVOCABLE
LETTER OF CREDIT NUMBER	*20:ADK/32921/05
DATE OF ISSUE	31C:190220
DATE AND PLACE OF EXPIRY	*31D:DATE:190421 PLACE:CHINA
APPLICANT	*50:GRUEN FRED CO.,LTD.,
	6270N PORT WASHINGTON ROAD, MILWAUKEE WI 53217 UNITED STATES
BENEFICIARY	*59:
	DALIAN LIGHT INDUSTRIAL PRODUCTS IMPORT AND EXPORT CORPORATION, NO. 23 FUGUI STREET ZHONGSHAN DISTRICT,DALIAN,CHINA
AMOUNT	*32B:CURRENCY USD AMOUNT 276,331,00
AVAILABLE WITH	*41D:BANK OF CHINA,DALIAN BY NEGOTIATION
DRAFTS AT	42C:SIGHT FOR 80PCT OF INVOICE VALUE
DRAWEE	42D:CIYIBANK N.A.,NEW YORK
PARTIAL SHIPMENT	43P:PROHIBITED
TRANSSHIPMENT	43T:PROHIBITED
SHIPPING ON BOARD/DISPATCH/LOADING	44A:IN CHARGE AT/FROM CHINESE MAIN PORT
TRANSPORTATION TO	44B:NEW YORK,USA
LATEST DATE OF SHIPMENT	44C:190331
DESCRIPTION OF GOODS OR SERVICES	45A:
	COMMODITY:ENERGY SAVING LAMPS

CONTRACT NO.:DLLI5739

PRICE TERM:CIF NEW YORK,USA

DOCUMENTS REQUIRED   46A:

+ SIGNED COMMERCIAL INVOICE IN 01 / 02 (ORIGINAL/COPIES) IN THE NAME OF ABC CO., INDICATING CONTRACT NO. AND L/C NO.

+ ORIGINAL PACKING LIST IN TRIPLICATE BEAR THE DETAIL CONTENTS OF EACH PACKAGE

+ CERTIFICATE OF ORIGIN IN 2 COPIES

+ GSP CERTIFICATE OF ORIGIN FORM A,CERTIFY GOODS OF ORIGIN IN CHINA, ISSUED BY COMPETENT AUTHORITIES

+ CERTIFICATE OF QUALITY IN 3 COPIES ISSUED BY CIQ

+ 2/3 SETS SIGNED CLEAN ON BOARD OCEAN BILLS OF LADING MADE OUT TO THE ORDER OF CIYIBANK N.A., NEW YORK, NOTIFYING APPLICANT INDICATING OUR LETTER OF CREDIT NUMBER AND MARKED FREIGHT PREPAID

+ INSURANCE POLICY IN TRIPLICATE FOR 120 PERCENT OF THE INVOICE VALUE SHOWING CLAIMS SETTING AGENT AT DESTINATION PORT AND THE CLAIMS ARE PAYABLE IN THE CURRENCY OF THE DRAFT,COVERING ALL RISKS,WAR RISK AND S.R.C.C.

+ SHIPPING ADVICE MUST BE SENT TO APPLICANT WITHIN 2 DAYS AFTER SHIPMENT ADVISING NUMBER OF PACKAGES,GROSS & NET WEIGHT, VESSEL NAME,BILL OF LADING NO. AND DATE, CAONTRACT NO.,VALUE

ADDITIONAL INSTRUCTIONS   47A:

1. THIS L/C IS NOT TRANSFERABLE

2. BOTH QUANTITY AND AMOUNT 10 PERCENT MORE OR LESS ARE ALLOWED

3. ALL DOCUMENTS MUST INDICATE THIS CREDIT

NUMBER AND B/L NUMBER

4. SHIPPING MARKS:ROLISA/LEIXOES/1-UP

5. 1/3 ORIGINAL B/L MUST BE SENT DIRECTLY TO APPLICANT IN 3 DAYS AFTER B/L DATE AND SENT BY FAX

PERIOD FOR PRESENTATION	48:

DOCUMENTS MUST BE PRESENTED WITHIN 21 DAYS AFTER SHIPMENT BUT WITHIN THE VALIDITY OF THE LETTER OF CREDIT

CONFIRMATION INSTRUCTIONS	*49:WITHOUT
INSTRUCTIONS TO THE PAYING/ ACCEPTING/NEGOTIATING BANK	78:

1. ALL DOCUMENTS MUST BE FORWARDED TO US IN ONE AIRMAIL

2. A DISCREPANT DOCUMENT FEE OF USD35.00 BE DEDUCTED FROM PROCEEDS IF THE DISCREPANCIES ARE ACCEPTED

3. UPON RECEIPT OF ALL DOCUMENTS AND DRAFT IN CONFORMITY WITH THE TERMS AND CONDITIONS OF THIS CREDIT, WE SHALL REMIT THE PROCEEDS TO THE BANK DESIGNATED BY YOU

ADVISING THROUGH BANK	57D:DALIAN FINANCE,CORPRATION 59,DAQING ROAD DALIAN CHINA
CHARGES	71B: ALL BANKING CHARGES OUTSIDE THE OPENING BANK ARE FOR BENEFICIARY'S ACCOUNT
SENDER TO RECEIVER INFORMATION	72:

THIS CREDIT IS ISSUED SUBJECT TO UNIFORM CUSTOMS AND PRACTICE FOR DOCUMENTARY CREDITS（2007 REVISION）ICC PUBLICATION NO.600

信用证号		合约号				受益人			
开证银行				开证申请人					
开证日期		兑付方式		起运口岸				目的地	
金额				可否转运				成交方式	
汇票付款人				可否分批					
汇票期限	见票＿＿＿天期			装运期限				唛头	
				有效期					
				有效地点					
				提单日＿＿＿天内议付		＿＿＿天内寄单			

单证名称	提单	副本提单	商业发票	海关发票	装箱单	重量数量单	尺码单	保险单	产地证	普惠制产地证	贸促会产地证	出口许可证	装船通知书	投保通知	寄投保通知邮据	寄单证明	寄样证明	品质证明书
提交银行																		
提交客户																		

注:在"提交银行"或"提交客户"对应的栏目中填写应提交的单据份数,信用证要求提交的单据没有注明份数,默认为1份。

提单	抬头			保险	险种				
	通知								
运费支付方式(预付或到付)					投保加成			赔款地点	

注:如果提供的信用证的内容没有涉及信用证分析表的某些栏目,该栏目为空。

三、国际贸易单证填制

请根据上述信用证和下列相关补充资料完成商业发票、装箱单、订舱委托书和汇票的缮制。

补充资料：

2019年2月8日，美国某公司(GRUEN FRED CO.,LTD.,6270N PORT WASHINGTON ROAD,MILWAUKEE WI 53217 UNITED STATES)与大连轻工业品进出口公司(DALIAN LIGHT INDUSTRIAL PRODUCTS IMPORT AND EXPORT CORPORATION,NO.23 FUGUI STREET ZHONGSHAN DISTRICT, DALIAN, CHINA)就节能灯(ENERGY SAVING LAMPS,H.S.CODE:8539319900)经过几个回合的磋商，达成如下交易条件：

规格	成交数量	单价
8 WATT	25,000PCS	USD2.45
10 WATT	27,000PCS	USD2.98
12 WATT	30,000PCS	USD3.65

货物委托汇通货代办理报关、托运事宜，货代联系人李云；货物于2019年3月19日从大连港装运出口，集装箱号及封号：FBZU3077952/79452 20'CY/CY，提单号：JTX562/0003

1. 发票号码：DAL12345

2. 发票日期：2019年3月12日

3. 运输货物的船名航次：TIAN LI SHAN V.562E

4. 包装条件：每支/纸盒，500支/纸箱，共164纸箱。每支节能灯重0.038KGS，每个纸盒重0.001KGS，每个纸箱重0.50KGS，纸箱长宽高为68*46*45CM。

5. 公司法人：张莉

6. 单证员：王琦

SELLER	商业发票 COMMERCIAL INVOICE		
BUYER	INVOICE NO.		INVOICE DATE
	L/C NO.		S/C DATE
	S/C NO.		PRICE TERM
	FROM		TO
MARKS	DESCRIPTION OF GOODS	QUANTITY	UNIT PRICE	AMOUNT

		TOTAL:		

TOTAL AMOUNT IN WORDS:

SELLER		
	装箱单 PACKING LIST	
BUYER	INVOICE NO.	DATE
	S/C NO.	L/C NO.
	FROM	TO
	MARKS & NOS.	

C/NOS.	DESCRIPTION OF GOODS	NUMBERS & KIND OF PACKAGE	QUANTITY	G.W. (KGS)	N.W. (KGS)	MEAS. (CBM)
	TOTAL:					

TOTAL PACKAGES(IN WORDS):

Shipper:		订舱委托书		
Consignee：		To： 开船日： 箱型、箱量：		
Notify：		合同号：		
		运费：		
		Vessel/Voyage：		
Port of Loading	Port of Discharge	Transshipment		Partial Shipment
Marks & Numbers	Description of Goods	No. of Packages	Gross Weight	Meas.

TOTAL NUMBERS OF CONTAINERS OR PACKAGES:

<table>
<tr><td colspan="2">客户要求</td></tr>
<tr><td colspan="2">□送货　　　□产装　　　□代理报关　　　□代理报检　　　□投保</td></tr>
<tr><td rowspan="2">产装信息</td><td>产装地址及预计日期：
单位名称：
地址：
联系人：
电话：</td><td>订舱公司：
联系人：
电话：
传真：</td></tr>
</table>

特殊要求	

BILL OF EXCHANGE

凭
Drawn under _____

信用证　第　　　号
L/C No. _____

日期
Dated _____ 支取 Payable with interest@

% per annum 按年息_____ 付款

号码　　　　　汇票金额
No. _____　　Exchange for ▓▓▓▓▓▓

中国XX　　年　　月　　日
China

见票
At _____

日后(本汇票之副本未付)付交
sight of this FIRST of Exchange(Second of Exchange

金额

being unpaid) Pay to the order of _____

the sum of

▓▓▓▓▓▓▓▓▓▓▓▓▓▓▓▓▓▓▓▓▓▓▓▓▓▓▓▓▓▓

款已收讫
Value received
此致
To:

_____
_____
_____

signature

第三节 外贸技能综合练习(三)

一、合同填制

请根据所提供的背景材料将下列合同填写完整。

卖方:上海纺织进出口公司(SHANGHAI TEXTILES IMP. & EXP. CORP.) 　　联系人:王晶

买方:CROMBONGO TEXTILES CO.,LTD. 　　联系人:MARY

品名:印花布(PRINTED SHIRTING) 　　款号:82、72、84

数量:4000码

价格:82:0.4美元/码 1000码　　　72:0.45美元/码 1000码　　　84:0.5美元/码 2000码

CIF 拉各斯

支付条款:保兑的不可撤销的信用证在出示装运单据时凭即期汇票付款

包装:卷装,每卷100码

装运:7月份由上海发运

唛头:由卖方决定

保险:按发票金额的110%投保一切险和战争险

SALES CONTRACT

TO: 　　　　　　　　　　　　　　　　　S/C NO.:SH20151014

　　　　　　　　　　　　　　　　　　　DATE:OCT. 14,2015

We hereby confirm having sold to you the following goods on terms and conditions as stated below:

Commodity & Specifications	Quantity	Unit Price	Amount
TOTAL:			
TOTAL CONTRACT VALUE:			

SHIPPING MARK:

PACKING:

PORT OF SHIPMENT:SHANGHAI,CHINA

PORT OF DESTINATION:

TIME OF SHIPMENT:

TRANSSHIPMENT:ALLOWED

PARTIAL SHIPMENT:NOT ALLOWED

TERMS OF PAYMENT:

INSURANCE：

Signed by：

THE SELLER：   THE BUYER：

二、信用证分析表填制

ISSUE OF A DOCUMENTARY CREDIT

ISSUING BANK:SPANIARD-BANK BERLIN,POTSDAM GERMANY

ADVISING BANK:BANK OF CHINA,JIAXING BRANCH

SEQUENCE OF TOTAL	27:1/1
FORM OF DOC. CREDIT	40A:IRREVOCABLE
DOC. CREDIT NUMBER	20:XJF+5682135
DATE OF ISSUE	31C:140206
EXPIRY	31D:DATE:140430　　PLACE:CHINA
APPLICANT	50:TGT IMPORT & EXPORT COMPANY POTSDAM GERMANY, WIESENHOF 12 POTSDAM BRANDENBURG GERMANY
BENEFICIARY:	59:JIAXING GUANGYUAN IMPORT & EXPORT CO.,LTD., NO.563 YOUDIAN ROAD,JIAXING ZHEJIANG,CHINA
CURRENCY CODE AMOUNT	32B:EUR495,620.00
AVAILABLE WITH	4ID:ANY BANK BY NEGOTIATION
DRAFT AT	42C:30 DAYS AFTER THE DATE OF B/L
DRAWEE	42D:SPANIARD-BANK BERLIN,POTSDAM GERMANY
PARTIAL SHIPMENT	43P:ALLOWED
TRANSSHIPMENT	43T:NOT ALLOWED
LOADING IN CHARGE	44A:ANY PORT IN CHINA
FOR TRANSPORT TO	44B:HAMBURG,GERMANY
LATEST DATE OF SHIPMENT	44C:140315
DESCRIPTION OF GOODS	45A:

GOOD DAY BRAND TRAVELLING BAGS AS PER S/C NO.OP45 DD.140129

ART. QESW-12 800PCS AT EUR 10.50/PC

ART. QESW-13 600PCS. AT EUR 12.70/PC

ART. QESW-14 500PCS. AT EUR 13.00/PC

CFR HAMBURG

DOCUMENTS REQUIRED   46A:

+COMMERCIAL INVOICE IN TRIPLICATE ALL STAMPED AND SIGNED BY BENEFICIARY

+FULL SET OF CLEAN ON BOARD BILL OF LADING

MADE OUT TO ORDER AND BLANK ENDORSED, MARKED FREIGHT PREPAID AND NOTIFY APPLICANT

+PACKING LIST IN TRIPLICATE SHOWING PACKING DETAILS SUCH AS CARTON NO. AND CONTENTS OF EACH CARTON

+A CERTIFICATE OF BENEFICIARY STAMPED AND SIGNED BY BENEFICIARY STATING THAT THE ORIGINAL INVOICE AND PACKING LIST HAVE BEEN DISPATCHED TO THE APPLICANT BY COURIER SERVICE ONE DAY BEFORE THE SHIPMENT

+SHIPPING ADVICE TO THE APPLICANT SHOWING ALL SHIPPING DETAILS

ADDITIONAL CONDITION   47A:

+A USD50.00 DISCREPANCY FEE, FOR BENEFICIARY'S ACCOUNT, WILL BE DEDUCTED FROM THE REIMBURSEMENT CLAIM FOR EACH PRESENTATION OF DISCREPANT DOCUMENTS UNDER THIS CREDIT

+5% MORE OR LESS BOTH IN QUANTITY AND AMOUNT ARE ALLOWED

+ALL DOCUMENTS SHOULD SHOW THE COUNTRY OF ORIGIN

+THE PACKING LIST AND THE INVOICE MUST MADE IN THE NAME OF GFT IMPORT & EXPORT POTSDAM GERMANY

DETAILS OF CHARGES   71B:

ALL BANKING CHARGES OUTSIDE GERMANY ARE FOR THE ACCOUNT OF BENEFICIARY

PRESENTATION PERIOD   48: DOCUMENTS MUST BE PRESENTED WITHIN 15 DAYS AFTER THE DATE OF SHIPMENT BUT WITHIN VALIDITY OF THE CREDIT

CONFIRMATION   49: WITHOUT

INSTRUCTION   78: ON RECEIPT OF DOCUMENTS CONFIRMING TO THE TERMS OF THIS DOCUMENTARY CREDIT. WE UNDERTAKE TO REIMBURSE YOU IN THE CURRENCY OF THE CREDIT IN ACCORDANCE WITH YOUR INSTRUCTIONS, WHICH SHOULD INCLUDE YOUR UID NUMBER AND THE ABA CODE OF THE RECEIVING BANK. THIS CREDIT IS

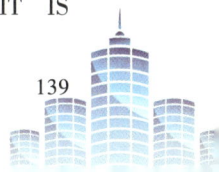

ISSUED SUBJECT TO UNIFORM CUSTOMS AND PRACTICE FOR DOCUMENTARY CREDIT（2006 REVISION） ICC PUBLICATION 600

信用证号		合约号	0P45	受益人		
开证银行			开证申请人			
开证日期		兑付方式	起运口岸		目的地	
金额			可否转运		成交方式	
汇票付款人			可否分批			
汇票期限	见票____天期		装运期限		唛头	
			有效期			
			有效地点			
			提单日____天内议付	____天内寄单		

单证名称	提单	副本提单	商业发票	海关发票	装箱单	重量数量单	尺码单	保险单	产地证	普惠制产地证	贸促会产地证	出口许可证	装船通知书	投保通知	寄投保通知邮据	寄单证明	寄样证明	品质证明书
提交银行																		
提交客户																		

注：在"提交银行"或"提交客户"对应的栏目中填写应提交的单据份数，信用证要求提交的单据没有注明份数，默认为1份。

提单	抬头		保险	险种	
	通知				
运费支付方式（预付或到付）				投保加成率	赔款地点

注：如果提供的信用证的内容没有涉及信用证分析表的某些栏目，该栏目为空。

三、国际贸易单证填制

请根据上述信用证和下列相关补充资料完成商业发票和汇票的缮制。

其他参考资料：

嘉兴广元进出口公司在2014年2月8号收到信用证后,立即组织货源。由于货源充足,价格有利,故决定每批货物都多装5%的数量,但由于遇到台风天气,故于2014年3月1号将QESW-12和QESW-13这两批货物装于HUANGHE NO.1轮船在上海港出运,于2014年3月11号将QESW-14货物装于HUANGHE NO.2轮船在宁波港出运。请代公司业务员郑明敏在2月16号开立第一批货物项下编号为DIM/7-595的商业发票以及相应汇票、发票和汇票的授权签字人为郑明敏。

SELLER				
	商业发票 COMMERCIAL INVOICE			
BUYER	INVOICE NO.		INVOICE DATE	
	L/C NO.		S/C DATE	
	S/C NO.		PRICE TERM	
	FROM		TO	
MARKS	DESCRIPTION OF GOODS	QUANTITY	UNIT PRICE	AMOUNT
	TOTAL:			
TOTAL AMOUNT IN WORDS:(18)				

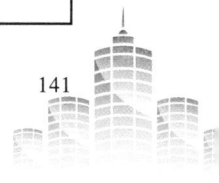

BILL OF EXCHANGE

凭　　　　　　　　　　　　　　　　　　　　　　　　信用证　　　　第　　　号
Drawn under ______________________________ L/C No. ______________

日期
Dated ____________ 支取 Payable with interest @ 　　% per annum 按年息__________付款

号码　　　　　　汇票金额　　　　　　　　　　　中国XX　　　年　　　月　　　日
No. __________ Exchange for ____________ China

见票　　　　　　　　　　日后(本汇票之副本未付)付交
At __________ sight of this FIRST of Exchange(Second of exchange
being unpaid) Pay to the order of ______________________________

金额 the sum of

款已收讫
Value received
此致
To:

____

____

____

signature

第四节　外贸技能综合练习(四)

一、合同填制

请根据所提供的背景材料将下列合同填写完整。

卖方南京丽华纺织品进出口公司(NANJING LIHUA TEXTILES IMP. & EXP. CORP.)和买方加拿大(PARMIX SPORTSWEAR INC.,591 EAST LAMEN STREET,TORONTO,CANADA)经过反复交易磋商,最终决定购买1000套女式服装(以FOB价成交),分别为50PCT NYLON/50PCT RAYON,WOVEN LADIES 2-PCE SUIT—JACKET L/S/FULLY LINED PANT W/BELT LOOPS STYLE 167C/168C TOTAl500 SETS AT USD10.00/SET,LADIES 2PCE ENSEMBLE—TAILORED WAISTCOAT/SKIRT,STYLE FULLY LINED 585A/169C TOTAL500 SETS AT USD8.00/SET,具体参见第585号购买订单。包装方式采用挂装。最迟于2015年8月底从中国上海运至加拿大多伦多,不允许分批装运,允许转运。唛头:PARMIX/TORONTO/P.O.NO.585/NO.1-1000。凭保兑的不可撤销的即期信用证在装运日后15天内中国议付有效。

SALES CONTRACT

To: S/C NO.:WEI258

DATE:MAY 05,2015

We hereby confirm having sold to you the following goods on terms and conditions as stated below:

Commodity & Specifications	Quantity	Unit Price	Amount
TOTAL:			
TOTAL CONTRACT VALUE:			

SHIPPING MARK:

PACKING：

PORT OF SHIPMENT：

PORT OF DESTINATION：

TIME OF SHIPMENT：

TRANSSHIPMENT：

PARTIAL SHIPMENT：

TERMS OF PAYMENT：

INSURANCE：

Signed by:

THE SELLER: THE BUYER:

二、信用证分析表填制

THE HONG KONG AND SHANGHAI BANKING CORPORATION

INCORPORATED IN HONG KONG WITH LIMITED LIABILITY

SHANGHAI OFFICE:185 YUANMINGYUAN ROAD,

P.R.CHINA SHANGHAI 20002

香港上海汇丰银行有限公司

上海分行:中国上海

圆明园路185号

邮政编码:20002

OUR REF. EXP DC 007545

ASAS OMBEI ONATARDIIYANN OAA OANOE THOIT

DATE:23 MAY,2010

WE ADVISE HAVING RECEIVED THE FOLLOWING TELETRANSMISSION DATED 22 MAY 2010 FROM THE HONG KONG AND SHANGHAI BANKING CORP.,DOWNING STREET,PENANG:ISSUE OF AN IRREVOCABLE DOCUMENTARY CREDIT.

DOC. CREDIT NUMBER:PGHO00348DC

DATE OF ISSUE:21 MAY,2010

EXPIRY DATE AND PLACE:21 JULY,2010,CHINA

APPLICANT:

      SOO HUP SENG TRADING CO. ADN BHD.,

        165 1ST FLOOR,VICTORIA STREET,10300 PENANG MALAYSIA

BENEFICIARY:

      SHANDONG HOPE NATIVE PRODUCE I/E CORP.,

        62,GUANGXI ROAD,QINGDAO,CHINA

CCY/AMOUNT:HKD46,150.00

AVAILABLE:BY NEGOTIATION

DRAFTS:AT SIGHT FOR FULL INVOICE VALUE OF GOODS DRAWN ON OURSELVES

PARTIAL SHIPMENT:PROHIBITED

TRANSSHIPMENT:PERMITTED

SHIPMENT FROM ANY PORT IN CHINA TO PENANG LATEST 06 JULY/2010

GOODS:5 M/TONS SHANDONG BLACK DATES(H.S.CODE:578950000)HIGH QUALITY AT HKD9,230

      PER M/TON,CIF PENANG AS PER ORDER NO.SOO-6378 AND S/C NO.HP4578

DOCUMENTS:

+INVOICE IN TRIPLICATE INDICATING BREAKDOWN OF COST

+PACKING LIST IN ONE ORIGINAL AND THREE COPIES

+FULL SET ORIGINAL CLEAN ON BOARD BILL OF LADING MADE OUT TO SHIPPER'S ORDER

AND ENDORSED IN BLANK AND MARKED FREIGHT PREPAID AND NOTIFY APPLICANT AND ISSUING BANK

+MARINE INSURANCE POLICY OR CERTIFICATE FOR FULL CIF VALUE PLUS 10 PERCENT COVERING OCEAN MARINE CLAUSES ALL RISKS (INCLUDING WAREHOUSE TO WAREHOUSE CLAUSES) AND WAR RISK CLAUSES(1/1/1981) OF THE PEOPLE'S INSURANCE COMPANY OF CHINA

SPECIAL CONDITIONS：

1)WEIGHT LIST IN TRIPLICATE TO BE ISSUED BY THE SHANDONG/QINGDAO IMP. AND EXP. COMMODITY INSPECTION BUREAU OF THE PEOPLE'S REPUBLIC OF CHINA TO STATE THAT GOODS ARE PACKED IN 25KGS NET OR 26.2KGS PER CARTON REQUIRED

2)CERTIFICATE OF CHINESE ORIGIN IN TRIPLICATE ISSUED BY CHINA COUNCIL FOR THE PROMOTION OF INTERNATIONAL TRADE TO STATE THAT GOODS ARE OF SHANDONG/QINGDAO ORIGIN REQUIRED

3)ALL DOCUMENTS EXCEPT DRAFT(S) TO EVIDENCE THAT ALL PACKINGS BEAR SHIPPING MARKS：SHS/PENANG/1-UP

4)ALL DOCUMENTS EXCEPT DRAFT(S) TO EVIDENCE THAT PACKING IS DONE AS FOLLOWS： IN CARDBOARD CARTONS OF 25KGS NET OR 26.2KGS GROSS PER CARTON

5)ALL DOCUMENTS EXCEPT DRAFT(S) WITHOUT MENTIONING L/C NO., ALL DOCUMENTS INDICATING OUR BANK'S NAME

6)BENEFICIARY TO ADVISE OPENER BY TELEX/FAX ALL DETAILS OF SHIPMENT AND SUCH TELEX/FAX COPY TO ACCOMPANY DOCUMENTS

7)BENEFICIARY TO AIRMAIL DIRECT TO OPENER ONE SET OF NON-NEGOTIABLE DOCUMENTS IMMEDIATELY AFTER SHIPMENT AND A CERTIFICATE OF COMPLIANCE TO THIS EFFECT IS REQUIRED

8)PLUS MINUS 5 PERCENT ON BOTH QUANTITY AND AMOUNT ACCEPTABLE

9)A USD30.00(OR EQUIVALENT)FEE SHOULD BE DEDUCTED FROM THE REIMBURSEMENT CLAIM FOR EACH PRESENTATION OF DISCREPANT DOCUMENTS UNDER THIS DOCUMENTARY CREDIT NOT WITH STANDING ANY INSTRUCTIONS TO THE CONTRARY，THIS CHARGE SHALL BE FOR THE ACCOUNT OF THE BENEFICIARY

BANK TO BANK INFO.：

1)WE HEREBY ENGAGE WITH DRAWERS AND/OR BONA FIDE HOLDERS THAT DRAFTS DRAWN AND NEGOTIATED ON PRESENTATION,SO LONG AS THERE HAS BEEN STRICT COMPLIANCE WITH ALL TERMS AND CONDITIONS(INCLUDING SPECIAL CONDITIONS)OF THIS CREDIT,SAVE TO THE EXTENT THAT THE SAME HAVE BEEN AMENDED IN WRITING AND SIGNED ON OUR BEHALF.

2)DOCUMENTARY EVIDENCE WILL BE REQUIRED OF COMPLIANCE WITH ALL CONDITIONS OF THIS CREDIT. NOTE：WE CANNOT MAKE ANY ALTERATIONS TO THIS CREDIT WITHOUT THE OPENER'S AUTHORITY.SHOULD ANY OF ITS TERMS OF CONDITIONS BE UNCLEAR OR

UNACCEPTABLE,THE BENEFICIARY OF THIS CREDIT MUST CONTACT THE OPENER DIRECTLY. WE SHALL INSIST ON STRICT COMPLIANCE WITH ALL THE TERMS AND CONDITIONS OF THIS CREDIT UNLESS AND UNTIL THEY HAVE BEEN FORMALLY AMENDED IN WRITING SIGNED ON OUR BEHALF. THE BENEFICIARY OF THIS CREDIT IS NOT ENTITLED TO RELY ON COMMUNICATIONS OR DISCUSSIONS WITH US,THE ADVISING BANK OF THE OPENER AS IN ANY WAY AMENDING THIS CREDIT.

CHARGES:ALL BANKING CHARGES OUTSIDE MALAYSIA INCLUDING ADVISING,NEGOTIATING COMMISSION AND REIMBURSING BANK'S FEES ARE FOR APPLICANT'S ACCOUNT.

PERIOD OF PRESENTATION:DOCUMENTS TO BE PRESENTED WITHIN 15 DAYS AFTER THE ISSUANCE OF THE SHIPPING DOCUMENTS BUT WITHIN THE VALIDITY OF THE CREDIT.

CONFIRMATION:WITHOUT

DIRECTIONS TO ADVISING BANK:YOUR CHARGES ARE FOR APPLICANT'S ACCOUNT

DIRECTIONS TO NEGOTIATING BANK:

+THE AMOUNT OF EACH NEGOTIATION MUST BE ENDORSED BELOW

+DOCUMENTS MUST BE DESPATCHED BY REGISTERED AIRMAIL IN ONE COVER

REIMBURESEMENT INSTRUCTION:

ON RECEIPT OF DOCUMENTS CONFIRMING TO THE TERMS OF THIS DOCUMENTARY CREDIT,WE UNDERTAKE TO REIMBURSE YOU IN THE CURRENCY OF THIS DOCUMENTARY CREDIT IN ACCORDANCE WITH YOUR INSTRUCTIONS.NEGOTIATING BANK'S DISCOUNT AND/OR INTEREST,IF ANY,PRIOR TO REIMBURSEMENT BY US ARE FOR ACCOUNT OF BENEFICIARY.

THIS CREDIT IS SUBJECT TO UCP ICC PUB NO. 600 AND IS OPERATIVE CREDIT INSTRUMENT AND NO MAIL CONFIRMATION TO FOLLOW.

信用证号		合约号		受益人			
开证银行			开证申请人				
开证日期		兑付方式	起运口岸			目的地	
金额			可否转运			成交方式	
汇票付款人			可否分批				
汇票期限	见票____天期		装运期限			唛头	
			有效期				
			有效地点				

									提单日＿＿＿天内议付			＿＿＿天内寄单						
单证名称	提单	副本提单	商业发票	海关发票	装箱单	重量数量单	尺码单	保险单	产地证	普惠制产地证	贸促会产地证	出口许可证	装船通知书	投保通知	寄投保通知邮据	寄单证明	寄样证明	品质证明书
提交银行																		
提交客户																		

注：在"提交银行"或"提交客户"对应的栏目中填写应提交的单据份数，信用证要求提交的单据没有注明份数，默认为1份。

提单	抬头		保险	险种	
	通知				
运费支付方式（预付或到付）				投保加成率		赔款地点	

注：如果提供的信用证的内容没有涉及信用证分析表的某些栏目，该栏目为空。

三、国际贸易单证填制

请根据上述信用证和下列相关补充资料完成商业发票、装箱单、订舱委托书和汇票的缮制。

补充资料：

1. COMMODITY：SHANDONG BLACK DATES 山东黑枣

2. QUANTITY：5.25 M/T

3. PACKED IN CARDBOARD CARTONS OF 25KGS EACH

4. CONTAINER NO.：EISU2628205

5. GR. WT：5502KGS

6. MEASUREMENTS：13.419CBM

7. SHIPPING MARKS：SHS/PENANG/1-UP

8. SHIPPED PER M/V "VICTORIA" FROM QINGDAO TO PENANG ON JULY 5，2010　　B/L NO.：190

9. INVOICE NO.：HOPE24587　　DATE：JUNE 30，2010

10. FREIGHT：USD45/CBM　　一切险保险费率为0.8%，战争险费率为0.2%　　USD1=HKD7.83

SELLER				
	商业发票 COMMERCIAL INVOICE			
BUYER	INVOICE NO.		INVOICE DATE	
	L/C NO.		S/C DATE	
	S/C NO.		PRICE TERM	
	FROM		TO	
MARKS	DESCRIPTION OF GOODS	QUANTITY	UNIT PRICE	AMOUNT
	TOTAL:			

TOTAL AMOUNT IN WORDS:

_____

_____

SELLER						
	装箱单 PACKING LIST					
BUYER	NO.		DATE			
	S/C NO.		L/C NO.			
	FROM		TO			
	MARKS & NOS.					
C/NOS.	DESCRIPTION OF GOODS	NUMBERS & KIND OF PACKAGE	QUANTITY	G.W. （KGS）	N.W. （KGS）	MEAS. （CBM）

	TOTAL:				

TOTAL PACKAGES(IN WORDS):

_____

_____

Shipper:	订舱委托书

Consignee:	To: 开船日: 箱型、箱量:
Notify:	合同号:
	运费:
	Vessel/Voyage:

Port of Loading	Port of Discharge	Transshipment	Partial Shipment

Marks & Numbers	Description of Goods	No. of Packages	Gross Weight	Meas.

TOTAL NUMBERS OF CONTAINERS OR PACKAGES:

客户要求

□送货　　□产装　　□代理报关　　□代理报检　　□投保

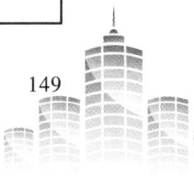

产装信息	产装地址及预计日期： 单位名称： 地址： 联系人： 电话：	订舱公司： 联系人： 电话： 传真：
特殊要求		

BILL OF EXCHANGE

凭
Drawn under _____

信用证　第　　　　号
L/C No. _____

日期
Dated _____ 支取 Payable with interest@

% per annum 按年息_____付款

号码
No. _____

汇票金额
Exchange for ░░░░░░░░

中国XX　　　年　　月　　日
China

见票
At _____

日后(本汇票之副本未付)付交
sight of this FIRST of Exchange(Second of Exchange

金额

being unpaid）Pay to the order of _____

the sum of

░░░░░░░░░░░░░░░░░░░░░░░░░░░░░░░░░░

款已收讫
Value received
此致
To:

_____

_____

_____

signature

第五节 外贸技能综合练习(五)

一、合同填制

请根据所提供的背景材料将下列合同填写完整。

2014 年 6 月 15 日，出口商 ZHEJIANG LONGXING BEARINGS COMPANY 总经理杨海平与进口商 GERMANY MASTER MACHINERY INC.代表总裁 PAUL 先生签订一份合同。合同编号为 LX-MM13012，交易货物为深沟球轴承(DEEP GROOVE BALL BEARINGS)，型号为 CX001，数量为 20000PCS，单价每个 1.30 美元，贸易术语为 CIF 德国汉堡，允许分批装运，不允许转运，在 2014 年 12 月装运。货物以木箱包装，每箱装 50 个，保险由卖方办理，保险金额为发票金额的 110%，根据中国人民保险公司海洋货物运输条款投保一切险混杂玷污险。结算方式为不可撤销可转让信用证，在开证行指定的付款行处 30 天延期付款。

ZHEJIANG LONGXING BEARINGS COMPANY

SALES CONTRACT

TO:GERMANY MASTER MACHINERY INC.　　　　　　S/C NO.:_____

　　　　　　　　　　　　　　　　　　　　　　　　DATE:_____

We hereby confirm having sold to you the following goods on terms and conditions as stated below:

Commodity & Specifications	Quantity	Unit Price	Amount
TOTAL CONTRACT VALUE:			

PACKING:TO BE PACKED IN _____ OF _____ EACH,TOTAL_____

PORT OF SHIPMENT:NINGBO,CHINA

PORT OF DESTINATION:_____

TIME OF SHIPMENT:TO BE EFFECTED _____

TRANSSHIPMENT:_____

PARTIAL SHIPMENT:_____

TERMS OF PAYMENT:THE BUYER SHALL OPEN THROUGH A BANK ACCEPTABLE TO THE SELLER

　　　　　　　　　AN _____ LETTER OF CREDIT TO REACH THE SELLER 30 DAYS

　　　　　　　　　BEFORE SHIPMENT,AVAILABLE BY _____ AT _____ IN PAYING

　　　　　　　　　BANK DESIGNATED BY ISSUING BANK

INSURANCE:TO BE COVERED BY THE SELLER FOR _____AGAINST _____

_____ AS PER _____ OF THE PEOPLE'S INSURANCE COMPANY OF CHINA DATED 01/01/1981

Signed by:

THE SELLER: THE BUYER:

二、信用证分析表填制

DOCUMENTARY LETTER OF CREDIT

APPLICATION HEADER:BANK OF CHINA,ATHENS,GREECE

USER HEADER:BANK OF CHINA,HANGZHOU

SEQUENCE OF TOTAL	27:1/1
FORM OF DOC. CREDIT	40A:IRREVOCABLE
DOC. CREDIT NUMBER	20:LC-AG-0086
DATE OF ISSUE	31C:130115
EXPIRY	31D:DATE:130720 PLACE:CHINA
APPLICANT	50:JJ BROTHER TRADING COMPANY
	VAS GEORGIOUA-5 10564 ATHENS,GREECE
BENEFICIARY	59:ZHEJIANG STATIONERY GROUP
	NO.1329,WANSHA ROAD,HANGZHOU,CHINA
AMOUNT	32B:CURRENCY USD AMOUNT 22,000.00
AVAILABLE WITH	41D:ADVISING BANK BY NEGOTIATION
DRAFTS AT	42C:SIGHT
DRAWEE	42D:ISSUING BANK
PARTIAL SHIPMENT	43P:ALLOWED
TRANSSHIPMENT	43T:ALLOWED
LOADING IN CHARGE	44A:NINGBO,CHINA
FOR TRANSPORT TO	44B:ATHENS,GREECE
LATEST DATE OF SHIP.	44C:130630
DESCRIPT. OF GOODS	45A:400 GROSS OF PENS AS PER S/C NO. ZSG-JJ-1326
	FOB SHANGHAI AT EUR55.00 PER GROSS
DOCUMENTS REQUIRED	46A:

+ SIGNED COMMERCIAL INVOICE IN TWO ORIGINAL AND FIVE COPIES

+ PACKING LIST INDICATING SIZES IN TWO ORIGINAL AND THREE COPIES

+ FULL SET OF CLEAN ON BOARD OCEAN BILL OF LADING ISSUED TO ORDER OF SHIPPER AND ENDORSED IN BLANK,MARKED FREIGHT PREPAID NOTIFY APPLICANT

+ INSURANCE POLICY IN DUPLICATE BLANK ENDORSED COVERING ALL RISKS AND WAR RISK FOR 110% OF THE INVOICE VALUE. CLAIMS, IF ANY, PAYALBE AT DESTINATION IN THE CURRENCY OF THE DRAFT

+G.S.P CERTIFICATE OF ORIGIN FORM A ISSUED BY CIQ

+CERTIFICATE OF BENEFICIARY STATING THAT FIVE SHIPPING SAMPLES MUST BE SENT TO APPLICANT BEFORE SHIPMENT BY COURIER

+ BENEFICIARY'S FAX COPY OF SHIPPING ADVICE TO APPLICANT AFTER SHIPMENT ADVISING L/C NO., SHIPMENT DATE, VESSEL NAME, TOTAL QUANTITY AND WEIGHT OF GOODS

ADDITIONAL COND.	47A:

+A DISCREPANCY HANDLING FEE OF USD50.00 AND THE RELATIVE TELEX COST WILL BE DEDUCTED FROM THE PROCEEDS NO MATTER THE BANKING CHARGES ARE FOR WHOEVER ACCOUNT

+ DISCREPANT DOCUMENTS WILL BE REJECTED BUT IF INSTRUCTIONS FOR THEIR RETURN ARE NOT RECEIVED BY THE TIME. THE APPLICANT HAS ACCEPTED AND PAID FOR THEM, THEY MAY BE RELEASED TO APPLICANT. IN SUCH EVENT BENEFICIARY/NEGOTIATING BANK SHALL HAVE NO CLAIM AGAINST ISSUING BANK

+TOLERANCE OF 5 PERCENT MORE OR LESS ON QUANTITY OF THE GOODS AND AMOUNT IS ACCEPTABLE

+SHPPING MARKS: JJ/ATHENS, GREECE/MADE IN CHINA/NO.1-UP

DETAILS OF CHARGES	71B: ALL BANKING CHARGES OUTSIDE GREECE ARE FOR THE BENEFICIARY'S ACCOUNT
PRESENTATION PERIOD	48: DOCUMENTS MUST BE PREDENTED WITHIN 10 DAYS FROM THE DATE OF SHIPMENT, BUT WITHIN THE VALIDITY OF THE L/C
CONFIRMATION	49: WITHOUT
INSTRUCTIONS	72: THIS CREDIT IS SUBJECT TO THE UNIFORM CUSTOMS AND PRACTICE FOR DOCUMENTARY CREDIT ICC, PUBLICATION NO.666

信用证号		合约号			受益人		
开证银行				开证申请人			
开证日期		兑付方式		起运口岸		目的地	
金额			可否转运			成交方式	
汇票付款人			可否分批				
汇票期限	见票＿＿＿天期			装运期限		唛头	
				有效期			
				有效地点			
				提单日＿＿＿天内议付		＿＿＿天内寄单	

单证名称	提单	副本提单	商业发票	海关发票	装箱单	重量数量单	尺码单	保险单	产地证	普惠制产地证	贸促会产地证	出口许可证	装船通知书	投保通知	寄投保通知邮据	寄单证明	寄样证明	品质证明书
提交银行																		
提交客户																		

注:在"提交银行"或"提交客户"对应的栏目中填写应提交的单据份数,信用证要求提交的单据没有注明份数,默认为1份。

提单	抬头		保险	险种		
	通知					
运费支付方式(预付或到付)				投保加成率		赔款地点

注:如果提供的信用证的内容没有涉及信用证分析表的某些栏目,该栏目为空。

三、国际贸易单证填制

请根据下列信用证信息和补充资料完成商业发票、装箱单和汇票的缮制。

DOCUMENTARY LETTER OF CREDIT

APPLICATION HEADER:AMERICAN BANK

SEATTLE,USA

USER HEADER:BANK OF CHINA,HANGZHOU BRANCH

SEQUENCE OF TOTAL	27:1/1
FORM OF DOC. CREDIT	40A:IRREVOCABLE
DOC. CREDIT NUMBER	20:LC-AB-91
DATE OF ISSUE	31C:130512
APPLICABLE RULES	40E:UCP LATEST VERSION
EXPIRY	31D:DATE:130920 PLACE:CHINA
APPLICANT	50:K-NOON TRADING COMPANY
	2212 GEORGE AVENUE,SEATTLE,USA
BENEFICIARY	59:ZHEJIANG TENGHUI IMP. & EXP. CO.,LTD.,
	NO.4712,WENER ROAD,HANGZHOU,CHINA
AMOUNT	32B:CURRENCY USD AMOUNT 92,000.00
AVAILABLE WITH	41D:ICBC,HANGZHOU BY NEGOTIATION
DRAFTS AT	42C:45 DAYS FROM THE DATE OF B/L FOR 100 PCT OF INVOICE VALUE
DRAWEE	42D:AMERICAN BANK,NY,USA
PARTIAL SHIPMENT	43P:NOT ALLOWED
TRANSSHIPMENT	43T:ALLOWED
LOADING IN CHARGE	44A:SHANGHAI,CHINA
FOR TRANSPORT TO	44B:SEATTLE,USA
LATEST DATE OF SHIP.	44C:130905
DESCRIPT. OF GOODS	45A:8000 DOZEN TEA TOWELS AT USD11.50/DOZ CFR SEATTLE, USA
DOCUMENTS REQUIRED	46A:

+SIGNED COMMERCIAL INVOICE IN FIVE COPIES INDICATING FOB VALUE, BEARING THE FOLLOWING CLAUSE:WE CERTIFY THAT THE CONTENTS OF THIS INVOICE ARE TRUE AND CORRECT

+ORIGINAL PACKING LIST IN FOUR COPIES INDICATING QUANTITY / GROSS AND NET WEIGHT OF EACH AND TOTAL CARTON, CERTIFYING THAT EACH TEA TOWEL CARRIES A "MADE IN CHINA" LABEL

+FULL SET OF CLEAN ON BOARD OCEAN BILL OF LADING MADE OUT TO THE ORDER OF AMERICAN BANK,SEATTLE, USA,MARKED FREIGHT PREPAID AND NOTIFYING SKY TRADING COMPANY

ADDITIONAL COND.	47A:

+ALL DOCUMENTS MUST INDICATE B/L NO.

+EACH CARTON MUST INDICATE THE DESIGN NUMBER, COLOR, QUANTITY, SIZE AND INVOICE AND PACKING LIST TO CERTIFY THE SAME

+SHIPMENT MUST BE EFFECTED BY A REGULAR LINE VESSEL AND B/L TO CERTIFY THE SAME

+THE GOODS WILL BE PACKED IN STANDARD EXPORT STRONG CARTONS AND PACKING LIST TO CERTIFY THE SAME

PRESENTATION PERIOD   48:DOCUMENTS MUST BE PREDENTED WITHIN 15 DAYS AFTER SHIPMENT DATE,BUT WITHIN THE VALIDITY OF THE L/C

CONFIRMATION   49:WITHOUT

DETAILS OF CHARGES   71B: ALL BANKING CHARGES OUTSIDE USA ARE FOR THE BENEFICIARY'S ACCOUNT

INSTRUCTIONS   78:

+A DISCREPANT DOCUMENTS FEE OF USD60.00 WILL BE DEDUCTED FROM PROCEEDS IF DOCUMENTS WITH DISCREPANCIES ARE ACCEPTED

+UPON RECEIPT OF ALL DOCUMENTS AND DRAFT IN CONFORMITY WITH PROCEEDS TO THE BANK DESIGNATED BY YOU

补充资料

1. 合同号:13ZTH-KN03　DATE:130425

2. 法人代表:楼学军

3. 发票号码:ZTH13-06

4. 发票日期:2013年8月18日

5. 装运日期:2013年8月27日

6. 提单号码:JX0012

7. 货运代理:宁波外运/岑辉

8. 中转港:香港

9. 运费:1200美元

10. 唛头:K-NOON/SEATTLE,USA/ CHINA/NO.1-800

11. 包装:PACKED IN STANDARD EXPORT CARTONS OF 10 DOZEN EACH

12. G.W:@17.00KGS　　　N.W:@15.00KGS

13. MEASUREMENT:@45cm×42cm×40cm

SELLER	商业发票 COMMERCIAL INVOICE			
BUYER	INVOICE NO.		INVOICE DATE	
	L/C NO.		S/C DATE	
	S/C NO.		PRICE TERM	
	FROM		TO	
MARKS	DESCRIPTION OF GOODS	QUANTITY	UNIT PRICE	AMOUNT
	TOTAL:			

TOTAL AMOUNT IN WORDS:

SELLER	装箱单 PACKING LIST	
BUYER	NO.	DATE
	S/C NO.	L/C NO.
	FROM	TO
	MARKS & NOS.	

C/NOS.	DESCRIPTION OF GOODS	NUMBERS & KIND OF PACKAGE	QUANTITY	G.W.（KGS）	N.W.（KGS）	MEAS.（CBM）

	TOTAL:				

TOTAL PACKAGES(IN WORDS):

_____

_____

BILL OF EXCHANGE

凭
Drawn under _____

信用证　第　　　号
L/C No. _____

日期
Dated _____ 支取 Payable with interest@　　　% per annum 按年息_____付款

号码　　　　　汇票金额
No. _____ Exchange for ▩▩▩▩▩▩

中国XX　　年　　月　　日
China

见票　　　　　日后(本汇票之副本未付)付交
At _____ sight of this FIRST of Exchange(Second of Exchange

金额

being unpaid) Pay to the order of _____ the sum of

款已收讫
Value received

此致
To:

_____

_____

signature

第六节　外贸技能综合练习(六)

一、合同填制

请根据所提供的背景材料将下列合同填写完整。

2019年4月5号,进口商SAMSUNG CORPORATION,SAMSUNG-PLAZA BUILDING 263,SEOHYEON-DONG,BUNDANG-GU,BUSAN,KOREA,TEL:82-2-2145-2500,FAX:82-2-2145-2596与出口商ZHEJIANG ALISON IMP. & EXP. CO.,LTD.,C-719,WORLD TRADE CENTRE OFFICE BUILDING,122 SHUGUANG ROAD,HANGZHOU,CHINA,TEL:0086-571-87631686,FAX:0086-571-87950611就9004级与3234级红枣(RED DATES)进行磋商谈判,分别按单价9.37欧元与9.27欧元进口204M/T和198M/T,双方约定运输由卖方负责,保险由买方负责。货物每0.2公吨装入一个标准的出口纸箱中。运输标志应该包括SAMSUNG,S/C NO.,GRADE NO.,PORT OF DESTINATION AND CARTON NO.。装运时间为收到定金后的20天内,从中国上海海运往韩国釜山,允许转运和分批装运。双方按保兑不可撤销信用证结算,付款时间为提单日后60天。次日双方在上海按上述条件签订编号为SMST/24116的出口合同。

SALES CONTRACT

TO:　　　　　　　　　　　　　　　　　　　　　　　　S/C NO:

　　　　　　　　　　　　　　　　　　　　　　　　　　DATE:

We hereby confirm having sold to you the following goods on terms and conditions as stated below:

Commodity & Specifications	Quantity	Unit Price	Amount
TOTAL:			

TOTAL CONTRACT VALUE: (16)

SHIPPING MARK:

PACKING:

PORT OF SHIPMENT:

PORT OF DESTINATION:

TIME OF SHIPMENT:

TRANSSHIPMENT:

PARTIAL SHIPMENT:

TERMS OF PAYMENT:BY _____ AT _____

INSURANCE:

Signed by:

THE SELLER:　　　　　　　　　　　THE BUYER:

二、信用证分析表填制

SEQUENCE OF TOTAL	*27:1/1
FORM OF DOC. CREDIT	*40A:IRREVOCABLE
DOC. CREDIT NUMBER	*20:0011LC123756
DATE OF ISSUE	31 C:190320
EXPIRY	*31D:DATE:190515 PLACE:CHINA
APPLICANT	*50:NEO GENERAL TRADING CO.,
	P.O. BOX 99552,RIYADH 22766,KSA
BENEFICIARY	*59:DESUN TRADING CO.,LTD.,
	NO.85 GUANJIAQIAO,NANJING 210005,CHINA
AMOUNT	*32B:CURRENCY USD AMOUNT 13,260.00
AVAILABLE WITH	*41D:BANK OF CHINA,NINGBO BRANCH BY NEGOTIATION
DRAFTS AT	42C:SIGHT
DRAWEE	42A:ALRAJHI BANKING AND INVESTMENT
	(HEAD OFFICE)
PARTIAL SHIPMENT	43P:NOT ALLOWED
TRANSSHIPMENT	43T:NOT ALLOWED
LOADING ON BRD/IN CHARGE	44A:CHINA MAIN PORT
DESTINATION PROT	44B:DAMMAM PORT,SAUDI ARABIA
LATEST SHIPMENT	44C:190430
GOODS DESCRIPT.	45A:

1700 CARTONS ROSE BRAND, CANNED MUSHROOM PIECES & STEMS 24 TINS × 425 GRAMS(NET WEIGHT) AT USD7.80 PER CARTON

CIF DAMMAM

DOCUMENTS REQUIRED   46A:

+SIGNED COMMERCIAL INVOICE IN TRIPLICATE ORIGINAL AND MUST SHOW BREAK DOWN OF THE AMOUNT AS FOLLOWS:FOB VALUE,FREIGHT CHARGES AND TOTAL AMOUNT C AND F

+FULL SET CLEAN ON BOARD BILL OF LADING MADE OUT TO THE ORDER OF ALRAJHI BANKING AND INVESTMENT CORP., MARKED FREIGHT PREPAID AND NOTIFY APPLICANT, INDICATING THE FULL NAME, ADDRESS AND TEL NO. OF THE CARRYING VESSEL'S AGENT AT THE PORT OF DISCHARGE

+ INSURANCE POLICY / CERTIFICATE MADE OUT FOR INVOICE VALUE PLUS 20% AND COVERING ALL RISKS AND WAR RISK AS PER C.I.C. DATED 1/1/1981

+ PACKING LIST IN ONE ORIGINAL PLUS 5 COPIES, ALL OF WHICH MUST BE MANUALLY SIGNED

+ INSPECTION (QUALITY) CERTIFICATE FROM C. I. Q. STATING GOODS ARE FIT FOR HUMAN BEING.

+ CERTIFICATE OF ORIGIN DULY CERTIFIED BY C.C.P. I.T. STATING THE NAME OF THE MANUFACTURERS OF PRODUCERS AND THAT GOODS EXPORTED ARE WHOLLY OF CHINESE ORIGIN

+ SHIPPING ADVICE INDICATE THAT THE PRODUCTION DATE OF THE GOODS NOT TO BE EARLIER THAN HALF MONTH AT TIME OF SHIPMENT

ADDITIONAL CONDITION   47A:

+ SHIPMENT TO BE EFFECTED BY CONTAINER AND BY REGULARE LINE

+ A DISCREPANCY FEE OF USD50.00 WILL BE IMPOSED ON EACH SET OF DOCUMENTS PRESENTED FOR NEGOTIATION UNDER THIS L/C WITH DISCREPANCY. THE FEE WILL BE DEDUCTED FROM THE BILL AMOUNT

+ SHIPPING MARK:N/M

CHARGES*   71B: ALL CHARGES AND COMMISSIONS OUTSIDE KSA ON BENEFICIARIE'S ACCOUNT INCLUDING REIMBURSING, BANK COMMISSION, DISCREPANCY FEE (IF ANY) AND COURIER CHARGES

CONFIRMAT INSTR.   *49: WITHOUT

ADVISING BANK   53A: ALRAJHI BANKING AND INVESTMENT CORP. RIYADH (HEAD OFFICE)

INS. PAYING BANK   78:

DOCUMENTS TO BE DESPATCHED IN ONE LOT BY COURIER. ALL CORRESPONDENCE TO BE SENT TO ALRAJHI BANKING AND INVESTMENT COPRORATION RIYADH (HEAD OFFICE)

信用证号		合约号	CD512-7	受益人				
开证银行			开证申请人					
开证日期		兑付方式	起运口岸			目的地		
金额			可否转运			成交方式		
汇票付款人			可否分批					
汇票期限	见票____天期		装运期限			唛头		
			有效期					
			有效地点					
			提单日____天内议付		____天内寄单			

单证名称（26）	提单	副本提单	商业发票	海关发票	装箱单	重量数量单	尺码单	保险单	产地证	普惠制产地证	贸促会产地证	出口许可证	装船通知书	投保通知	寄投保通知邮据	寄单证明	寄样证明	品质证明书
提交银行																		
提交客户																		

注：在"提交银行"或"提交客户"对应的栏目中填写应提交的单据份数，信用证要求提交的单据没有注明份数，默认为1份。

提单	抬头			保险	险种		
	通知						
运费支付方式（预付或到付）					投保加成率		赔款地点

三、国际贸易单证填制

请根据上述信用证和下列相关补充资料完成商业发票和订舱委托书的缮制。

补充资料

INVOICE NO.:GF/8-95　　　　　　　　　　INVOICE DATE:2019-03-28

S/C DATE:2019-03-17

出口商单证员小章委托上海货代有限公司的晓峰办理本批蘑菇罐头(H.S.:62451301476)的运输和保险事项。其中纸箱的单位重量为0.78千克,单位体积为24cm×25cm×22cm;罐头的单位重量为0.05千克,运费计算标准为W/M,每运费吨计收USD8.68,中国人民保险公司战争险和一切险的保险费率分别为0.8%。

货物于2019年4月28日装于"DONGFENG.V342"船从中国宁波驶离。

出口商的授权签字人为:代敏

SELLER	商业发票 COMMERCIAL INVOICE				
BUYER	INVOICE NO.			INVOICE DATE	
	L/C NO.			S/C DATE	
	S/C NO.			PRICE TERM	
	FROM			TO	
MARKS	DESCRIPTION OF GOODS	QUANTITY		UNIT PRICE	AMOUNT
	TOTAL:				
TOTAL AMOUNT IN WORDS:					

Shipper:			订舱委托书		
Consignee:			To: 开船日： 箱型、箱量：		
Notify:			合同号：		
			运费：		
			Vessel/Voyage:		
Port of Loading	Port of Discharge		Transshipment	Partial Shipment	
Marks & Numbers	Description of Goods		No. of Packages	Gross Weight	Meas.

TOTAL NUMBERS OF CONTAINERS OR PACKAGES：

客户要求
□送货　　　　□产装　　　　□代理报关　　　　□代理报检　　　　□投保

产装信息	产装地址及预计日期： 单位名称： 地址： 联系人： 电话：	(39)订舱公司： 联系人： 电话： 传真：
特殊要求		

第二章专项练习参考答案

第一节　外贸合同的填制

练习一

NANTONG VICTORY TRADING CO.,LTD.

NO.234,GONGNONG ROAD,NANTONG,CHINA

SALES CONTRACT

TO:THE GOLDEN LION TRADING CO.,LTD.   S/C NO.NTSL4445

DATE:SEPT. 23,2018

We hereby confirm having sold to you the following goods on terms and conditions as stated below:

Commodity & Specifications	Quantity	Unit Price	Amount
		CIFC3 SINGAPORE	
ART NO. GWAS01	24,000PCS	USD88.00/PC	USD2,112,000.00
ART NO. GWAS02	12,800PCS	USD92.50/PC	USD1,184,000.00
TOTAL:	36,800PCS		USD3,296,000.00
TOTAL CONTRACT VALUE: SAY U.S.DOLLARS THREE MILLION TWO HUNDRED AND NINETY-SIX THOUSAND ONLY.			

SHIPPING MARK:N/M

PACKING:ART NO.GWAS01 ARE PACKED IN CARTONS OF 24PCS EACH,ART NO. GWAS02 ARE PACKED IN CARTONS OF 16PCS EACH

SHIPMENT:FROM SHANGHAI,CHINA TO SINGAPORE. THE GOODS TO BE DELIVERED TO THE CONTAINER YARD AND LEAVE THEM TO MULTIMODAL TRANSPORT OPERATOR IN DECEMBER 2018. THE GOODS SHALL BE DELIVERED TO THE DESTINATION BY THE USUAL WAY AND ROUTE. TRANSSHIPMENT AND PARTIAL SHIPMENT ALLOWED

TERMS OF PAYMENT:BY SIGHT L/C, TO REACH THE SELLER BEFORE THE MIDDLE OF OCTOBER

INSURANCE:TO BE EFFECTED BY THE SELLER FOR 110% OF THE INVOICE VALUE COVERING ICC (A) ONLY

Signed by:

THE SELLER:NANTONG VICTORY

          TRADING CO.,LTD

          XXX

THE BUYER:THE GOLDEN LION

          TRADING CO.,LTD

          XXX

练习二

TIANJIN MORNING STAR CORPORATION

16TH FLOOR,DRAGON MANSION,1008 LIYANG ROAD, TIANJIN,CHINA

SALES CONTRACT

TO:CANADIAN K. & LIFDON DISTRIBUTORS

    RM.1008-1011,OFFICE TOWER,CONVENTION PLAZA

    1 HARBOUR ROAD,VANCOUVER CANADA

S/C NO.TJCHX050212

DATE:SEPT. 02,2018

We hereby confirm having sold to you the following goods on terms and conditions as stated below:

Commodity & Specifications	Quantity	Unit Price	Amount
VOLLEYBALL		CIF VANCOUVER	
ART. NO. GBW32	2,000PCS	USD2.15/PC	USD4,300.00
ART. NO. GBW322	2,000PCS	USD2.60/PC	USD5,200.00
ART. NO. ERVS	3,000PCS	USD1.45/PC	USD4,350.00
TOTAL:	7,000PCS		USD13,850.00
TOTAL CONTRACT VALUE: SAY U.S.DOLLARS THIRTEEN THOUSAND EIGHT HUNDRED AND FIFTY ONLY.			

SHIPPING MARK:AS STATED IN THE L/C

PACKING:IN CARTONS OF 50PCS EACH,TOTAL 140 CARTONS

PORT OF SHIPMENT:TIANJIN,CHINA

PORT OF DESTINATION:VANCOUVER,CANADA

TIME OF SHIPMENT:IN NOVEMBER,2018

TRANSSHIPMENT:ALLOWED

PARTIAL SHIPMENT:ALLOWED

TERMS OF PAYMENT:20% OF THE INVOICE VALUE AS DOWN PAYMENT PAYABLE BY T/T,THE BALANCE OF 80% OF THE INVOICE VALUE PAYABLE BY IRREVOCABLE L/C AT SIGHT

INSURANCE:TO BE COVERED BY THE SELLER FOR 120% OF THE INVOICE VALUE COVERING ICC(A) AND INSTITUTE WAR RIAKS ONLY

INSPECTION:BY THE PRODUCER

Signed by:

THE SELLER:TIANJIN MORNING

STAR CORPORATION

XXX

THE BUYER:CANADA K. &

LIFDON DISTRIBUTORS

XXX

练习三

TIFERT TRADING CO.,LTD.

SALES CONTRACT

TO:GENERAL TRADING COMPANY,JAPAN

S/C NO.TJ101211

DATE:SEPT. 11,2018

We hereby confirm having sold to you the following goods on terms and conditions as stated below:

Commodity & Specifications	Quantity	Unit Price	Amount
		CIF OSAKA	
"DOVE" BRAND PRINTED SHIRTING	67,200YARDS	YEN3.00/YARD	YEN210,600.00
TOTAL:	67,200YARDS		YEN210,600.00
TOTAL CONTRACT VALUE: SAY JAPANESE YEN TWO HUNDRED AND TEN THOUSAND SIX HUNDRED ONLY.			

SHIPPING MARK:N/M

PACKING:NO PACKING

PORT OF SHIPMENT:ANY CHINESE PORT

PORT OF DESTINATION:OSAKA,JAPAN

TIME OF SHIPMENT:BEFORE DEC.04,2018

TRANSSHIPMENT:ALLOWED

PARTIAL SHIPMENT:ALLOWED

TERMS OF PAYMENT:BY AN IRREVOCABLE L/C AT SIGHT,TO REACH THE SELLER BEFORE ONE-MONTH PRECEDING THE DATE OF SHIPMENT AND AFTER THE ABOVE DATE,TO BE VALID FOR NEGOTIATION IN CHINA WITHIN 15 DAYS

INSURANCE:TO BE COVERED BY THE SELLER FOR 110% OF INVOICE VALUE COVERING ALL RISKS AND WAR RISK AS PER PICC DATED 01/01/1981

Signed by:

THE SELLER:TIFERT TRADING CO.,LTD   THE BUYER:GENERAL TRADING COMPANY,JAPAN

XXX   XXX

练习四

BEIJING LIGHT INDUSTRIAL PRODUCTS IMP. & EXP. CORP.

SALES CONTRACT

TO:BOSTON TRADE CO.,LTD.

S/C NO.5454

DATE:JAN. 18,2009

We hereby confirm having sold to you the following goods on terms and conditions as stated below:

Commodity & Specifications	Quantity	Unit Price	Amount
FOUNTAIN PENS		CFR BOSTON	
MODEL NO. LC001	1,000DOZEN	USD19.00/DOZEN	USD19,000.00
TOTAL:	1,000DOZEN		USD19,000.00
TOTAL CONTRACT VALUE: SAY U.S.DOLLARS NINETEEN THOUSAND ONLY.			

SHIPPING MARK:N/M

PACKING:PACKED IN BOXES OF ONE DOZEN EACH,AND 20 BOXES TO A CARTON.

PORT OF SHIPMENT:TIANJIN,CHINA

PORT OF DESTINATION:BOSTON,USA

TIME OF SHIPMENT:DURING MARCH/APRIL,2009

TRANSSHIPMENT:ALLOWED

PARTIAL SHIPMENT:ALLOWED

TERMS OF PAYMENT:TO BE MADE BY CONFIRMED,IRREVOCABLE L/C PAYABLE BY DRAFT AT
    SIGHT

INSURANCE:TO BE COVERED BY THE BUYER

Signed by:

THE SELLER:BEIJING LIGHT   THE BUYER:BOSTON TRADE CO.,LTD.

    INDUSTRIAL PRODUCTS IMP. & EXP. CORP.

    XXX   XXX

练习五

JIANGSU INTERNATIONAL IMP. & EXP. CORP.,LTD.

80 ZHONGSHAN ROAD,NANJING,CHINA

FAX:86-025-12345678   TEL:86-025-1234567

SALES CONTRACT

TO:SHEMSY NEGOCE ID CORP.   S/C NO.08CAN-1108

  75 ROUTE 96570 DARDILLY,FRANCE   DATE:NOV. 08,2018

   FAX:33-56-34567891   TEL:33-56-123456789

We hereby confirm having sold to you the following goods on terms and conditions as stated below:

Commodity & Specifications	Quantity	Unit Price	Amount
LEATHER BAG		FOB C5% SHANGHAI	
THE GOODS ARE AS PER BUYER'S ORDER NO. FE022G			
ITEM NO. SL100	1,000PCS	USD2.00/PC	USD2,000.00
ITEM NO. SG120	2,000PCS	USD1.50/PC	USD3,000.00
ITEM NO. SF200	3,000PCS	USD3.00/PC	USD9,000.00
TOTAL:	6,000PCS		USD14,000.00
TOTAL CONTRACT VALUE: SAY U.S.DOLLARS FOURTEEN THOUSAND ONLY.			

SHIPPING MARK:AS PER BUYER'S DEMAND

PACKING:AS PER BUYER'S DEMAND

PORT OF SHIPMENT:SHANGHAI,CHINA

PORT OF DESTINATION:PORT REQUIRED BY THE BUYER

TIME OF SHIPMENT:TO BE MADE WITHIN 45 DAYS BY SEA AFTER 30% BY T/T AS THE DEPOSIT

TRANSSHIPMENT:ALLOWED

PARTIAL SHIPMENT:ALLOWED

TERMS OF PAYMENT:30% BY T/T AS DEPOSIT,70% BY D/P AT 30 DAYS AFTER SIGHT

INSURANCE:TO BE COVERED BY THE BUYER

Signed by:

THE SELLER:JIANGSU INTERNATIONAL   THE BUYER:SHEMSY NEGOCE

     IMP. & EXP. CORP.,LTD.   ID CORP.

     XXX   XXX

练习六

TIFERT TRADING CO.,LTD.

86,ZHUJIANG ROAD,TIANJIN,CHINA

SALES CONTRACT

TO:ASTAK FOOD,INC.   S/C NO.TJ101211

5-18 ISUKI-CHOHAKI,TOKYO,JAPAN   DATE:NOV. 08,2018

We hereby confirm having sold to you the following goods on terms and conditions as stated below:

Commodity & Specifications	Quantity	Unit Price	Amount
CHINESE RICE F.A.Q. 2018		CIF OSAKA	
BROKEN GRAINS(MAX.)20%	200M/T	USD360.00 PER M/T	USD720,000.00
ADMIXTURE(MAX.)0.2%			
MOISTURE(MAX.)10%			
TOTAL:	200M/T		USD720,000.00
TOTAL CONTRACT VALUE: SAY U.S.DOLLARS SEVEN HUNDRED AND TWENTY THOUSAND ONLY.			

REMARKS:WITH 5% MORE OR LESS BOTH IN AMOUNT AND QUANTITY AT THE SELLER'S OPTION

SHIPPING MARK:N/M

PACKING:50KGS TO ONE GUNNY BAG,TOTAL 40,000 BAGS.

PORT OF SHIPMENT:TIANJIN,CHINA

PORT OF DESTINATION:TOKYO,JAPAN

TIME OF SHIPMENT:TO BE EFFECTED DURING DECEMBER 2018.

TRANSSHIPMENT:ALLOWED

PARTIAL SHIPMENT:ALLOWED

TERMS OF PAYMENT:THE BUYER SHALL OPEN AN L/C AT SIGHT,TO REACH THE SELLER BE-
FORE NOVEMBER 25,2018.AND TO BE VALID FOR NEGOTIATION IN JA-
PAN WITHIN 15 DAYS AFTER THE DATE OF SHIPMENT.

INSURANCE:TO BE COVERED BY THE SELLER FOR 110% OF INVOICE VALUE AGAINST ALL
RISKS AS PER AND SUBJECT TO OCEAN MARINE CARGO CLAUSES OF PICC DATED
01/01/1981.

Signed by:

THE SELLER:TIFERT TRADING CO.,LTD.   THE BUYER:ASTAK FOOD,INS.

XXX   XXX

第二节　信用证分析表的填制

练习一

信用证号	R027-20160416	合约号		DF2016022	受益人	NINGBO DONGSHAN VEGETABLES CO.,LTD., NO. 211 ZHONGSHAN ROAD, NINGBO,CHINA,315228		
开证银行	BANK OF CHINA,SYDNEY,AUSTRALIA				开证申请人	SYDNEY INTERNATIONAL TRADE CO. 155/6 WEST STREET,SYDNEY,AUSTRALIA		
开证日期	JUN. 23,2016	兑付方式	L/C BY NEGOTIATION		起运口岸	NINGBO,CHINA	目的地	SYDNEY, AUSTRALIA
金额	USD19,600.00				可否转运	ALLOWED	成交方式	CIF SYDNEY
汇票付款人	BANK OF CHINA,SYDNEY,AUSTRALIA				可否分批	PROHIBITED		
汇票期限	见票____***____天期				装运期限	SEPT. 20,2016	唛头	SYDNEY NO.1-1000
					有效期	OCT. 05,2016		
					有效地点	COUNTERS OF NEGOTIATING BANK		
					提单日___15___天内议付			

单证名称	提单	副本提单	商业发票	海关发票	装箱单	重量数量单	尺码单	保险单	产地证	普惠制产地证	贸促会产地证	出口许可证	装船通知书	投保通知	寄投保通知邮据	寄单证明	寄样证明	品质证明书
提交银行	3		3		3				2		2		1					
提交客户									1				1					

注:在"提交银行"或"提交客户"对应的栏目中填写应提交的单据份数,信用证要求提交的单据没有注明份数,默认为1份。

提单	抬头	TO ORDER	保险	险种	ALL RISKS AND WAR RISK AS PER C.I.C. DATED 01/01/1981
	通知	SYDNEY INTERNATIONAL TRADE CO. 155/6 WEST STREET,SYDNEY,AUSTRALIA			
运费支付方式(预付或到付)		FREIGHT PREPAID	投保加成率	10%	赔款地点 SYDNEY, AUSTRALIA

注:如果提供的信用证的内容没有涉及信用证分析表的某些栏目,该栏目为空。

练习二

信用证号	DOC-812-353	合约号		SL08121	受益人		SHANGHAI LUCKY PLASTIC IMP. AND EXP. CO.,LTD., 22/F JINMAO TOWER, SHANGHAI,CHINA
开证银行	STATE BANK OF INDIA,NEW DELHI				开证申请人		RAM PLASTICS CO.,LTD., 201 HAUK ROAD,MALVIYA NAGAR NEW DELHI, INDIA
开证日期	DEC. 23,2017	付款方式		L/C BY NEGOTIATION	起运口岸	SHANGHAI, CHINA	目的地	NHAVA SHEVA, INDIA
金额	USD18,600.00			可否转运	ALLOWED	成交方式	CIF NHAVA SHEVA
汇票付款人	STATE BANK OF INDIA,NEW DELHI			可否分批	ALLOWED		
汇票期限	见票___***___天			装运期限	FEB. 28,2018	唛头	RAM/ SL081218N. SHEVA/ NO. 1-100
				有效期	MAR. 15,2018		
				有效地点	CHINA		
				提单日___15___天内议付			

单证名称	提单	副本提单	商业发票	海关发票	装箱单	重量数量单	尺码单	保险单	产地证	普惠制产地证	贸促会产地证	出口许可证	装船通知书	投保通知	寄投保通知邮据	寄单证明	寄样证明	品质证明书
提交银行	3		3		2			2	2							1		
提交客户		1	1		1			1	1									

注:在"提交银行"或"提交客户"对应的栏目中填写应提交的单据份数,信用证要求提交的单据没有注明份数,默认为1份。

提单	抬头	TO ORDER OF SHIPPER(+受益人名称、地址)	保险	险种	INSTITUTE CARGO CLAUSE(A)AS PER I.C.C. DATED 01/01/1982		
	通知	RAM PLASTICS CO.,LTD., 201 HAUK ROAD,MALVIYA NAGAR NEW DELHI,INDIA					
运费支付方式		FREIGHT PREPAID		投保加成	110%	赔款地点	NHAVA SHEVA, INDIA

练习三

信用证号	211LC200116	合约号	02EC301302	受益人	ZHEJIANG BAIMEI GARMENTS IMP. & EXP. CO.,LTD., JINAN MANSION 306 HONGDA ROAD,XIAOSHAN DISTRICT,HANGZHOU,ZHEJIANG,CHINA		
开证银行	BANK OF CHINA,BARCELONA BRANCH			开证申请人	HOP TONG HAI(PIE) LTD., BLK15,NORTH BRIPDE ROAD #04-9370 BARCELONA SPAIN 100032,FAX:2953397		
开证日期	FEB. 18,2017	兑付方式	L/C BY NEGOTIATION	起运口岸	CHIAN MAIN PORT,CHINA	目的地	BARCELONA PORT,SPAIN WITH TRANSSHIPMENT AT SINGAPORE
金额	USD37,850.00+/-10%			可否转运	ALLOWED	成交方式	CFRC3 BARCELONA AS PER INCOTERMS 2010
汇票付款人	BANK OF CHINA,BARCELONA BRANCH			可否分批	ALLOWED		
汇票期限	见票__120__天期			装运期限	APR. 05,2017	唛头	C.T.H. BARCELONA NO.1-UP
				有效期	APR. 15,2017		
				有效地点	CHINA		
				提单日__10__天内议付			

单证名称	提单	副本提单	商业发票	海关发票	装箱单	重量数量单	尺码单	保险单	产地证	普惠制产地证	贸促会产地证	出口许可证	装船通知书	投保通知	寄投保通知邮据	寄单证明	寄样证明	品质证明书
提交银行	3		3	1				2	1				1				1	
提交客户		1	1	1				1	1				1					

注:在"提交银行"或"提交客户"对应的栏目中填写应提交的单据份数,信用证要求提交的单据没有注明份数,默认为1份。

提单	抬头	TO ORDER		保险	险种	ALL RISKS AND WAR RISK OF C.I.C. OF PICC(1/1/1981), WAREHOUSE TO WAREHOUSE		
	通知	HOP TONG HAI(PIE) LTD., BLK15,NORTH BRIPED ROAD #04-9370 BARCELONA SPAIN 100032, FAX:2953397						
运费支付方式(预付或到付)		FREIGHT PREPAID			投保加成率	10%	赔款地点	BARCELONA PORT,SPAIN

练习四

信用证号	17-LC-205	合约号	SSYG17086	受益人	SHANGHAI SHENGYANG GROUP, NO. 1150 SHAOXING ROAD, SHANGHAI,CHINA		
开证银行	HABIB BANK LTD.,DUBAI			开证申请人	EASTERN CITY TRADING INC., P.O.BOX NO. 8901,DUBAI,U.A.E.		
开证日期	APR. 01,2017	兑付方式	L/C BY NEGOTIATION	起运口岸	ANY CHINESE PORT	目的地	DUBAI,U.A.E.
金额	USD24,800.00+/-5%			可否转运	NOT ALLOWED	成交方式	CIF DUBAI, U.A.E.
汇票付款人	HABIB BANK LTD.,DUBAI			可否分批	ALLOWED		
汇票期限	见票___45___天期			装运期限	MAY 02,2017	唛头	EASTERN NO.01TH DUBAI,U.A.E. NO.1-UP
				有效期	MAY 17,2017		
				有效地点	CHINA		
				提单日___15___天内议付			

单证名称（25）	提单	副本提单	商业发票	海关发票	装箱单	重量数量单	尺码单	保险单	产地证	普惠制产地证	贸促会产地证	出口许可证	装船通知书	投保通知	寄投保通知邮据	寄单证明	寄样证明	品质证明书
提交银行	2		5		4			2	3								1	4
提交客户	1		1															

注:在"提交银行"或"提交客户"对应的栏目中填写应提交的单据份数,信用证要求提交的单据没有注明份数,默认为1份。

提单	抬头	TO ORDER OF SHIPPER(+受益人名称、地址)	保险	险种	ALL RISKS AND WAR RISK		
	通知	EASTERN CITY TRADING INC., P.O.BOX NO. 8901,DUBAI,U.A.E. HABIB BANK LTD.,DUBAI					
运费支付方式(预付或到付)		FREIGHT PREPAID		投保加成率	20%	赔款地点	DUBAI

练习五

信用证号	G/FO-7752807		合约号	99JA7031KL		受益人	DONGYUE KNITWEARS AND HOME TEXTILES IMPORT AND EXPORT CORPORATION 197 ZHONGSHAN ROAD,NINGBO, CHINA		
开证银行	SUMITOMO BANK LTD.,OSAKA					开证申请人	TOSHU CORPORATION OSALM12-36,KYUTARO-MACHI 4-CHOME CHUO-KU,OSAKA 561-8177,JAPAN		
开证日期	FEB. 23,2017		付款方式	L/C BY NEGOTIATION		起运口岸	NINGBO, CHINA	目的地	YOKOHAMA, OSAKA
金额	USD201,780.00					可否转运	PROHIBITED	成交方式	CIF YOKOHAMA, OSAKA
汇票付款人	SUMITOMO BANK LTD.,OSAKA					可否分批	ALLOWED		
汇票期限	见票___×××___天					装运期限	JUN. 10,2017		
						有效期	JUN. 10,2017	唛头	
						有效地点	NINGBO, CHINA		
						提单日__10__天内议付	_____天内寄单		

单证名称	提单	副本提单	商业发票	海关发票	装箱单	重量数量单	尺码单	保险单	产地证	普惠制产地证	贸促会产地证	出口许可证	装船通知书	投保通知	寄投保通知邮据	寄单证明	寄样证明	品质证明书
提交银行	2		5		3			2		2			1			1		
提交客户	1									1								

注:在"提交银行"或"提交客户"对应的栏目中填写应提交的单据份数,信用证要求提交的单据没有注明份数,默认为1份。

提单	抬头	TO ORDER	保险	险种	INSTITUTE WAR CLAUSE INSTITUTE CARGO CLAUSES(ALL RISKS),INSTITUTE S.R.C.C. CLAUSES
	通知	TOSHU CORPORATION OSALM12-36,KYUTARO-MACHI 4-CHOME CHUO-KU,OSAKA 561-8177, JAPAN SUMITOMO BANK LTD.,OSAKA			

运费支付方式	FREIGHT PREPAID	投保加成	120%	赔款地点	JAPAN

第三节　商业发票的填制

练习一

SELLER NINGBO INT PRODUCTS CO., NO.115 DONGFENG ROAD, NINGBO,CHINA	商业发票 COMMERCIAL INVOICE			
BUYER DRF INTERNATIONAL FOOD CO., 26 TORIMI—CHO NISHI-PU NAGOYA 546,JAPAN	INVOICE NO. NP180620		INVOICE DATE JUNE 20,2018	
	L/C NO. 9426		S/C DATE MAY 01,2018	
	S/C NO. NP180501		PRICE TERM CIF NAGOYA	
	FROM NINGBO		TO NAGOYA	
MARKS	DESCRIPTION OF GOODS	QUANTITY	UNIT PRICE	AMOUNT
NO MARKS	FRESH BAMBOO SHOOTS FRESH ASPARAGUS	20M/T 30M/T	CIF NAGOYA USD1,080.00PER M/T USD1,600.00PER M/T	USD21,600.00 USD48,000.00
	TOTAL:	50M/T		USD69,600.00
TOTAL AMOUNT IN WORDS:SAY U.S.DOLLARS SIXTY-NINE THOUSAND SIX HUNDRED ONLY.				
			NINGBO INT PRODUCTS CO. ***	

练习二

SELLER ZHEJIANG YUANDONG CO.,LTD., NO.1121,YAN'AN ROAD, HANGZHOU,CHINA	商业发票 COMMERCIAL INVOICE			
BUYER ABC TRADING CO.,LTD.	INVOICE NO. BPCH13-23		INVOICE DATE JUNE 05,2018	
	L/C NO. LC-21683		S/C DATE APR. 23,2018	
	S/C NO. BP13-2594		PRICE TERM CIFC2% LONDON	
	FROM SHANGHAI,CHINA		TO LONDON,UK	
MARKS	DESCRIPTION OF GOODS	QUANTITY	UNIT PRICE	AMOUNT

续表

DFG BP13-2594 LONDON NO.1-123	100% COTTON LADIES' DRESS AS PER S/C NO. BP13-2594 SPECIFICATION LD-501 SH-401	3,350PCS 2,800PCS	CIFC2% LONDON USD14.55/PC USD20.35/PC	USD48,742.50 USD56,980.00
	TOTAL:	6,150PCS	LESS C2% FREIGHT CHARGES PREMIUM CIF NET VALUE	USD105,722.50 USD2,114.45 USD2,000.00 USD1,800.00 USD99,808.05

TOTAL AMOUNT IN WORDS:SAY U.S.DOLLARS ONE HUNDRED AND FIVE THOUSAND SEVEN HUNDRED AND TWENTY-TWO AND CENTS FIFTY ONLY.

ZHEJIANG YUANDONG CO.,LTD.

李宏

练习三

SELLER SHANGHAI FOREIGN TRADE CORP., SHANGHAI,CHINA	商业发票 COMMERCIAL INVOICE			
BUYER ABC COMPANY	INVOICE NO. SHE 02/1845		INVOICE DATE NOV. 26,2018	
	L/C NO. 0011LC123756		S/C DATE OCT. 25,2018	
	S/C NO. S/C00112233		PRICE TERM CFRC5% BANGKOK	
	FROM SHANGHAI,CHINA		TO BANGKOK,THAILAND	
MARKS	DESCRIPTION OF GOODS	QUANTITY	UNIT PRICE	AMOUNT
N/M	ISONIAZID BP98	2,000KGS	CFRC5% BANGKOK USD9.00 PER KG	USD18,000.00
	TOTAL:	2,000KGS	LESS C5% FREIGHT CHARGES FOB VALUE	USD18,000.00 USD900.00 USD160.00 USD16,940.00

TOTAL AMOUNT IN WORDS:SAY U.S.DOLLARS EIGHTEEN THOUSAND ONLY.

B/L NUMBER:SCOISG7564

SHANGHAI FOREIGN TRADE CORP.

张丽(手签)

练习四

SELLER SHANGHAI GARMENTS IMP. AND EXP. CO., LTD., 309 SUZHOU ROAD NORTH, SHANGHAI,CHINA	商业发票 COMMERCIAL INVOICE			

BUYER POWER PLAY INC. 2ND FLOOR,NO. 137E,33ROAD STREET, LOS ANGELES, CA. 90011 U.S.A.	INVOICE NO. 11SG09-301		INVOICE DATE AUG. 07,2018	
	L/C NO. 309M116905		S/C DATE JUNE 25,2018	
	S/C NO. PS11E06F025		PRICE TERM CFR LONG BEACH INCOTERMS 2010	
	FROM SHANGHAI,CHINA		TO LONG BEACH CA,USA	

MARKS	DESCRIPTION OF GOODS	QUANTITY	UNIT PRICE	AMOUNT
POWER PLAY PS11E06F025 LONG BEACH NO.1-280 MADE IN CHINA	MEN'S SHIRTS AND PANTS ITEM NO.7001 ITEM NO.7002 ITEM NO.7003	 2,160SETS 780SETS 420SETS	CFR LONG BEACH INCOTERMS 2010 USD19.35/SET USD20.35/SET USD18.80/SET	 USD41,796.00 USD15,873.00 USD7,896.00
	TOTAL:	3,360SETS		USD65,565.00

TOTAL AMOUNT IN WORDS:SAY U.S.DOLLARS SIXTY-FIVE THOUSAND FIVE HUNDRED AND SIXTY-FIVE ONLY.

WE HEREBY CERTIFY THAT THE QUALITY COLOR SIZE AND STYLE ON EACH
ITEM ARE AS PER S/C NO.PS11E06F025 DATED 180625.

SHANGHAI GARMENTS IMP. AND EXP. CO.,LTD.

李晓雨

练习五

SELLER GREAT WALL TRADING CO.,LTD., RM201,HUASHENG BUILDING, NINGBO,P.R.CHINA	商业发票 COMMERCIAL INVOICE	
BUYER F.T.C. CO., AKEKSANTERINK AUTO P. O. BOX 9,FINLAND	INVOICE NO. GW2005M06-2	INVOICE DATE MAY 22,2018
	L/C NO. LRT9802457	S/C DATE APR. 22,2018
	S/C NO. GW2005M06	PRICE TERM CIFC5% HELSINKI
	FROM NINGBO	TO HELSINKI

MARKS	DESCRIPTION OF GOODS	QUANTITY	UNIT PRICE	AMOUNT
ROYAL 05AR225031 JEDDAH C/N:1-460	P.P INJECTION CASES ZL0322+BC05 P. P INJECTION CASES ZL0319+BC01	230SETS 230SETS	CIFC5% HELSINKI USD42.00/SET USD41.00/SET	USD9,660.00 USD9,430.00
	TOTAL:	460SETS	LESS C5% CIF VALUE	USD19,090.00 USD954.50 USD18,135.50

TOTAL AMOUNT IN WORDS:SAY U.S.DOLLARS EIGHTEEN THOUSAND ONE HUNDRED AND THIRTY-FIVE AND CENTS FIFTY ONLY.

GREAT WALL TRADING CO.,LTD.
***

第四节　装箱单的填制

练习一

SELLER					

SELLER
ZHEJIANG BAIMEI GARMENTS IMP. & EXP. CO.,LTD.,
JINAN MANSION 762 HONGDA ROAD,
XIAOSHAN DISTRICT,HANGZHOU,ZHEJIANG,CHINA
A/C NO:85324136-00213

装箱单
PACKING LIST

NO. ANC20170018	DATE MAR.25,2019
S/C NO. 02EC301302	L/C NO. 5248FG5210
FROM NINGBO,CHINA	TO BARCELONA PORT,SPAIN VIA SINGAPORE

BUYER
HOP TONG HAI LTD.,BLK15,SOUTH BRIPDE ROAD,
#04-9370 BARCELONA SPAIN 100032,FAX:459802

MARKS & NOS.
C.T.H./BARCELONA/NO.:1-25

C/NOS.	DESCRIPTION OF GOODS	NUMBERS & KIND OF PACKAGES	QUANTITY	G.W. (KGS)	N.W. (KGS)	MEAS. (CBM)
C/NO. 1-10	80% COTTON OVERALLS	10CTNS	@30DOZ 300DOZ	@552.00KGS 5,520.00KGS	@504.00KGS 5,040.00KGS	@2.400CBM 24.000CBM
C/NO. 11-20	80% COTTON SHIRTS	10CTNS	@120DOZ 1,200DOZ	@198.00KGS 1,980.00KGS	@186.00KGS 1,860.00KGS	@1.920CBM 19.200CBM
C/NO. 21-25	80% COTTON SINGLETS AS PER S/C NO. 02EC301302 DATED 23-01-2019	5CTNS	@20DOZ 100DOZ	@496.00KGS 248.00KGS	@48.00KGS 240.00KGS	@0.840CBM 4.200CBM
	TOTAL:	25CTNS	1,600DOZ	7,748.00KGS	7,140.00KGS	47.400CBM

续表

TOTAL PACKAGES(IN WORDS):SAY TWENTY-FIVE CARTONS ONLY.

WE HEREBY CERTIFY THAT EACH PACKAGE IS MARKED THE SHIPPING MARK:C.T.H/BARCELONA/NO.1-25.
ISSUING BANK'S DATE:FEB.18,2019
ISSUING BANK'S NAME:BANK OF CHINA,BARCELONA BRANCH
SHIPMENT HAS BEEN EFFECTED BY 1×20' FCL CONTAINER LOAD

ZHEJIANG BAIMEI GARMENTS IMP. & EXP. CO.,LTD.
金胜利

练习二

SELLER SHANGHAI ZHEN YUAN IMP. AND EXP. CO.,LTD., RM 302-305,700 JIANGUODONG RD.,SHANGHAI, CHINA	装箱单 PACKING LIST				
	NO. ZYIE1702		DATE AUG. 20,2019		
	S/C NO. 17SHSS199		L/C NO. 1920/742		
BUYER STRONG SAN PAOLO DI, TORINO S.P.A.	FROM SHANGHAI,CHINA		TO PALERMO,ITALY		
	MARKS & NOS. SEMPREVIVO 5330703199 PAI ERMO C/NO.1-450				

C/NOS.	DESCRIPTION OF GOODS	NUMBERS & KIND OF PACKAGES	QUANTITIY	G.W.（KGS）	N.W.（KGS）	MEAS.（CBM）
C/NO. 1-150	SPORTS MUG ART. NO.DL-001A	150CTNS	@24PCS 3,600PCS	@12.00KGS 1,800.00KGS	@10.00KGS 1,500.00KGS	@0.030CBM 4.200CBM
C/NO. 151-300	ART. NO.DL-002A	150CTNS	@24PCS 3,600PCS	@15.00KGS 2,250.00KGS	@13.00KGS 1,950.00KGS	@0.0504CBM 7.560CBM
C/NO. 301-350	ART. NO.YQB-A315	500CTNS	@40PCS 2,000PCS	@17.00KGS 850.00KGS	@16.00KGS 800.00KGS	@0.0693CBM 3.465CBM
C/NO. 351-450	ART. NO.YQB-A500 AS PER SALES CONTRACT NO.17SHSS199 DATED 10-JULY-19	100CTNS	@40PCS 4,000PCS	@19.00KGS 1,900.00KGS	@15.00KGS 1,500.00KGS	@0.075CBM 7.500CBM
	TOTAL:	450CTNS	13,200PCS	6,800.00KGS	5,750.00KGS	23.025CBM

TOTAL PACKAGES(IN WORDS):SAY FOUR HUNDRED AND FIFTY CARTONS ONLY.

NAME OF ISSUING BNAK:ISTITUTO BANCARIO SAN PAOLO DI,TORINO S.P.A.,PALERMO
PACKING:ALL GOODS ARE PACKED IN CARDBOARD CARTON

SHANGHAI ZHEN YUAN IMP. AND EXP. CO.,LTD.
王晓

练习三

SELLER	NINGBO HUAFENG FOOD CO.,LTD., NO.215 JIEFANF ROAD,NINGBO,CHINA		装箱单 PACKING LIST		

<table>
<tr><td colspan="2" rowspan="3">SELLER
NINGBO HUAFENG FOOD CO.,LTD.,
NO.215 JIEFANF ROAD,NINGBO,CHINA</td><td colspan="4" align="center">装箱单
PACKING LIST</td></tr>
</table>

SELLER NINGBO HUAFENG FOOD CO.,LTD., NO.215 JIEFANF ROAD,NINGBO,CHINA			**装箱单 PACKING LIST**		
BUYER DAIHATSU TRADE CORPORATION 17-6,NISHIOGU,ARAWAKAN,TOKYO,JAPAN			NO. HF192026		DATE JULY 10,2019
			S/C NO. HD012		L/C NO. H486-20194730
			FROM NINGBO,CHINA		TO TOKYO,JAPAN
			MARKS & NOS. DAIHATSU/MADE IN CHINA/NO.1-2000		

C/NOS.	DESCRIPTION OF GOODS	NUMBERS & KIND OF PACKAGES	QUANTITY	G.W.（KGS)	N.W.（KGS)	MEAS.（CBM)
NO.1-2000	FROZEN SOYBEANS	2,000CTNS	@10KGS 20,000KGS	@11.00KGS 22,000.00KGS	@10.00KGS 20,000.00KGS	@0.0294CBM 58.800CBM
	TOTAL:	2,000CTNS	20,000KGS	22,000.00KGS	20,000.00KGS	58.800CBM

TOTAL PACKAGES(IN WORDS):SAY TWO THOUSAND CARTONS ONLY.

GOODS ARE PACKED IN SEAWORTHY CARTONS.

NINGBO HUAFENG FOOD CO.,LTD.

王冰

练习四

SELLER SHANGHAI GARDEN PRODUCTS IMP. AND EXP. CO.,LTD. 27 ZHONGSHAN DONGYI ROAD,SHANGHAI,CHINA			装箱单 PACKING LIST		
BUYER LAIKI PERAGORA ORPHANIDES LTD., 020 STRATIGOU TIMAGIA AVE., 6046,LARNAKA, CYPRUS			NO. 19SGHTRY3023		DATE FEB. 09,2019
			S/C NO. E03FD121		L/C NO. FG26/19/358
			FROM SHANGHAI PORT		TO LIMASSOL PORT
			MARKS & NOS. L.P.O.L. DC. NO. FG26/19/358 MADE IN CHINA NO.1-265		
C/NOS.	DESCRIPTION OF GOODS	NUMBERS & KIND OF PACKAGES	QUANTITY	G.W.（KGS)	N.W.（KGS)	MEAS.（CBM)

续表

C/NO. 1–145 C/NO. 146–265	LADIES' SHIRT LADIES' SKIRT	145CTNS 120CTNS	@4PCS 580PCS @6PCS 720PCS	@16.30KGS 2,363.50KGS @17.40KGS 2,088.00KGS	@12.80KGS 1,856.00KGS @15.60KGS 1,872.00KGS	@0.0168CBM 2.436CBM @0.0304CBM 3.648CBM
	TOTAL:	265CTNS	1,300PCS	4,451.50KGS	3,728.00KGS	6.084CBM

TOTAL PACKAGES (IN WORDS):SAY TWO HUANDRED AND SIXTY–FIVE CARTONS ONLY.

WE HEREBY CERTIFY THAT EACH PACKING UNIT BEARS AN INDELIBLE MARK INDICATING THE COUNTRY OF ORIGIN OF THE GOODS.
WE HEREBY CERTIFY THAT THE GOODS ARE OF CHINESE ORIGIN.
L/C DATE:JAN.01,2019

SHANGHAI GARDEN PRODUCTS IMP. AND EXP. CO.,LTD.
×××

练习五

SELLER ZHENGCHANG TRADING CO.,LTD., NO.168 XUESHI ROAD,HUZHOU,ZHEJIANG,CHINA	装箱单 PACKING LIST	
	NO. VGDET42KLJ	DATE JAN. 11,2019
	S/C NO. HZ0114	L/C NO. LC1JD624
BUYER ELEC TRADE CO. LTD., THE FIRST STREET,COLOMBO,SRI LANKA	FROM SHANGHAI,CHINA	TO COLOMBO,SRI LANKA
	MARKS & NOS. E.L.E. HZ0114 COLOMBO C/NO.1–160	

C/NOS.	DESCRIPTION OF GOODS	NUMBERS & KIND OF PACKAGES	QUANTITY	G.W. (KGS)	N.W. (KGS)	MEAS. (CBM)
C/NO. 1–50 C/NO. 51–110 C/NO. 111–160	TRAVELING BAGS ITEM NO.:PG6520 ITEM NO.:DG6359 ITEM NO.:TQ3523	60CTNS 50CTNS 50CTNS	@50PCS 3,000PCS 2,500PCS 2,500PCS	@10.95KGS 657.00KGS 547.50KGS 547.50KGS	@9.50KGS 570.00KGS 475.00KGS 475.00KGS	@0.018CBM 1.080CBM 0.900CBM 0.900CBM
	TOTAL:	160CTNS	8,000PCS	1,751.00KGS	1,520.00KGS	2.880CBM

TOTAL PACKAGES (IN WORDS):SAY ONE HUNDRED AND SIXTY CARTONS ONLY.

PACKING:1PC/BOX,50BOXES/CTN
ALL GOODS ARE SHIPPED IN 1×20' CONTAINER
WE HEREBY CERTIFY THAT GOODS ARE IN ACCORDANCE WITH CONTRACT NO. HZ0114.

ZHENGHANG TRADING CO.,LTD.
徐汇(手签)

第五节 订舱委托书的填制

练习一

Shipper: HANGZHOU ABC IMPORT & EXPORT LTD., NO. 40 BINGWEN ROAD, HANGZHOU, CHINA, 310053	订舱委托书	
Consignee: TO ORDER	To:杭州大地物流公司/小王 开船日:2010年10月15日 箱型、箱量:20'FCL*1	
Notify: AST NATIONAL TRADING COMPANY, CANADA	合同号:	
	运费: FREIGHT PREPAID	
	Vessel/Voyage: DONGFANG V.589	

Port of Loading SHANGHAI, CHINA	Port of Discharge MONTREAL	Transshipment ALLOWED	Partial Shipment ALLOWED	
Marks & Numbers	Description of Goods	No. of Packages	Gross Weight	Meas.
N/M	LEATHER COMPUTER CASES 皮质电脑套 8754211100	800CTNS	17600.00KGS	26.880CBM

TOTAL NUMBERS OF CONTAINERS OR PACKAGES:
SAY EIGHT HUNDRED CARTONS ONLY.

客户要求

☐ 送货　　☑ 产装　　☑ 代理报关　　☐ 代理报检　　☐ 投保

产装信息	产装地址及预计日期:杭州,2010年10月11日 单位名称:杭州ABC进出口公司 地址:浙江杭州市滨康路450号 联系人:吴森琦 电话:18767169488	订舱公司:杭州ABC进出口公司 联系人:吴森琦 电话:18767169488 传真:
特殊要求	1. 签全套3份正本清洁已装船海运提单 2. 提单上要注明L/C NO.:FD878/38DES	

练习二

Shipper: ZHEJIANG TEXTILES IMPORT & EXPORT TRADE CORPORATION,201 BAOCHU ROAD, HANGZHOU,CHINA		订舱委托书	
Consignee: TO THE ORDER OF SHIPPER		To:上海外运/小李 开船日:2014年7月1日 箱型、箱量:LCL 40CTNS	
Notify: TIVOLI PRODUCTS PLC COMPANY, NATIONAL AUSTRALIA BANK LIMITED,SYDNEY		合同号: 8612	
		运费: FREIGHT PREPAID	
		Vessel/Voyage: VICTORY V.123	

Port of Loading: SHANGHAI,CHINA	Port of Discharge: MELBOURNE, AUSTRALIA	Transshipment: NOT ALLOWED	Partial Shipment: ALLOWED
Marks & Numbers	Description of Goods	No. of Packages	Gross Weight	Meas.
NABLS NO.8612 MELBOURNE NO.1~40	KNITTED GARMENTS 针织衫 4785200010	40CTNS	1,040.00KGS	1.200CBM

TOTAL NUMBERS OF CONTAINERS OR PACKAGES:
SAY FORTY CARTONS ONLY.

客户要求

☑ 送货 ☐ 产装 ☑ 代理报关 ☑ 代理报检 ☐ 投保

产装 信息	产装地址及预计日期: 单位名称: 地址: 联系人: 电话:	订舱公司:ZHEJIANG TEXTILES IMPORT & EXPORT TRADE CORPORATION 联系人:李丹 电话:0571-88546000 传真:0571-88546500
特殊要求	签全套正本清洁已装船海运提单	

练习三

Shipper: SHANGHAI FOREIGN TRADE CORP., SHANGHAI,CHINA		订舱委托书	
Consignee: TO ORDER OF BANGKOK BANK PUBLIC COMPANY LIMITED,BANGKOK		To:金丰货代/小金 开船日:2000年11月29日 箱型、箱量:40'FCL*1	
Notify: MOUN CO. LTD., NO. 443,249 ROAD,BANGKOK THAILAND		合同号: S/C00112233	
		运费: FREIGHT PREPAID	
		Vessel/Voyage: JENNY V.03	
Port of Loading SHANGHAI,CHINA	Port of Discharge BANGKOK, THAILAND	Transshipment ALLOWED	Partial Shipment NOT ALLOWED
Marks & Numbers	Description of Goods	No. of Packages	Gross Weight	Meas.
N/M	ISONIAZID BP98 异烟肼 29333999	40 DRUMS	2,200.00KGS	50.000CBM

TOTAL NUMBERS OF CONTAINERS OR PACKAGES:
SAY FORTY DRUMS ONLY.

客户要求

☐ 送货　　☑ 产装　　☑ 代理报关　　☐ 代理报检　　☐ 投保

产装信息	产装地址及预计日期:上海,2000年11月27日 单位名称:上海对外贸易有限公司 地址:中国上海东一路387号 联系人:张丽 电话:021-88665768	订舱公司:上海对外贸易有限公司 联系人:张丽 电话:021-88665768 传真:021-88665769
特殊要求	1. 签全套三份正本清洁已装船海运提单和两份副本提单 2. 提单要注明L/C NUMBER 0011LC123756	

练习四

Shipper: NANJING GARMENTS IMP. AND EXP. CO.,LTD., NO. 301 ZHEN'ANTONG ROAD, NANJING,210002,CHINA		订舱委托书	
Consignee: TO ORDER OF SHIPPER		To:南京远洋货运公司/王一南 开船日:2017年12月10日 箱型、箱量:LCL 200CTNS	
Notify: M/S HALLSON TRADING, P. O. BOX NO. 2512 DUBAI U.A.E.		合同号: NG08-2578	
		运费: FREIGHT PREPAID	
		Vessel/Voyage: CMA CROWN V. 987	

Port of Loading NANJING,CHINA	Port of Discharge DUBAI U.A.E.	Transshipment ALLOWED	Partial Shipment ALLOWED
Marks & Numbers	Description of Goods	No. of Packages	Gross Weight	Meas.
HALLSON HT-2578 DUBAI NO. 1-200	MEN'S 2 PCS SET 男式两件套 6302.2900	200CTNS	4,400.00KGS	11.600CBM

TOTAL NUMBERS OF CONTAINERS OR PACKAGES:
SAY TWO HUNDRED CARTONS ONLY.

客户要求

☑ 送货　☐ 产装　☑ 代理报关　☐ 代理报检　☐ 投保

产装信息	产装地址及预计日期: 单位名称: 地址: 联系人: 电话:	订舱公司:NANJING GARMENTS IMP. AND EXP. CO.,LTD. 联系人: 电话: 传真:
特殊要求	1. 签全套正本清洁已装船海运提单 2. 提单上要注明L/C NUMBER LC-2008-1098 3. 提单上要注明THE NAME,ADDRESS,TEL. NO. OR FAX NO. OF THE CARRYING VESSEL'S AGENT 　　AT PORT OF DISCHARGE	

练习五

Shipper: SHANGHAI TOYSON IMPORT AND EXPORT CO., 27 ZHONGSHAN ROAD, E.1 CN-200002 SHANGHAI, CHINA			订舱委托书		
Consignee: TO ORDER			To:上海扬帆海运公司/小王 开船日:JUL. 25,2015 箱型、箱量:LCL 535CTNS		
Notify: SIS & BRO TRADING CO.,LTD.,8230 AADYYHOEJ			合同号: 4CA3068		
			运费: FREIGHT PREPAID		
			Vessel/Voyage: NAM KING, V.987		
Port of Loading SHANGHAI	Port of Discharge AARHUS		Transshipment ALLOWED	Partial Shipment PROHIBITED	
Marks & Numbers	Description of Goods	No. of Packages	Gross Weight	Meas.	
REV 240553 AARHUS DENMARK ART. NO. 2021 NO.1-290 JSL 857235 AARHUS DENMARK ART. NO. 2151 NO. 291-535	TOWELS 毛巾 61171000	535CTNS	14,445.00KGS	38.392CBM	
TOTAL NUMBERS OF CONTAINERS OR PACKAGES: SAY FIVE HUNDRED AND THIRTY-FIVE CARTONS ONLY.					
客户要求 ☑ 送货　☐ 产装　☑ 代理报关　☐ 代理报检　☐ 投保					
产装信息	产装地址及预计日期: 单位名称: 地址: 联系人: 电话:		订舱公司:SHANGHAI TOYSON IMPORT AND EXPORT CO. 联系人: 电话: 传真:		
特殊要求	签全套至少3份正本和1份副本已装船海运提单				

第六节　汇票的填制

练习一

BILL OF EXCHANGE

凭 Drawn under BANK OF CHINA,LONDON	信用证 第 号 L/C No. LC-17G021

日期
Dated MAR. 18,2017　　　　　支取 Payable with interest@　　　% per annum 按年息＿＿＿＿＿付款

号码 No. BP-BJ023	汇票金额 Exchange for USD190,800.00	中国XX　　年　月　日 Shanghai,China　JUNE 28, 2017

见票
At ***＿＿＿＿＿＿＿＿＿ 日后(本汇票之副本未付)付交
sight of this FIRST of Exchange(Second of Exchange 金额

being unpaid) Pay to the order of ＿＿＿BANK OF CHINA,SHANGHAI＿＿＿ the sum of

SAY U.S.DOLLARS ONE HUNDRED AND NINETY THOUSAND EIGHT HUNDRED ONLY.

款已收讫
Value received　　　CONTRACT NO.:GB1703
此致
To：BANK OF CHINA,LONDON

＿＿＿＿＿＿＿＿＿＿＿＿＿＿＿

＿＿＿＿＿＿＿＿＿＿＿＿＿＿＿　　SHANGHAI BAOJING COMPANY

＿＿＿＿＿＿＿＿＿＿＿＿＿＿＿　　　　蔡佩琪

练习二

BILL OF EXCHANGE

凭 Drawn under BANK OF CHINA,LONDON	信用证 第 号 L/C No. LC-17G021

日期
Dated MAR. 18,2017　　　　　支取 Payable with interest@　　　% per annum 按年息＿＿＿＿＿付款

号码 No. BP-BJ023	汇票金额 Exchange for EUR185,076.00	中国XX　　年　月　日 Shanghai,China　JUNE 28, 2017

见票
At ***＿＿＿＿＿＿＿＿＿ 日后(本汇票之副本未付)付交
sight of this FIRST of Exchange(Second of Exchange 金额

being unpaid) Pay to the order of ＿＿＿BANK OF CHINA,SHANGHAI＿＿＿ the sum of

SAY EURO ONE HUNDRED AND EIGHTY-FIVE THOUSAND AND SEVENTY-SIX ONLY.

款已收讫
Value received
此致
To：LONDON COMMERCIAL BANK,LONDON

＿＿＿＿＿＿＿＿＿＿＿＿＿＿＿

＿＿＿＿＿＿＿＿＿＿＿＿＿＿＿　　SHANGHAI BAOJING COMPANY

＿＿＿＿＿＿＿＿＿＿＿＿＿＿＿　　　　蔡佩琪

练习三

BILL OF EXCHANGE

凭
Drawn under BANK OF CHINA,LONDON   信用证 第   号
                                                     L/C No. LC-17G021

日期
Dated MAR. 18,2017   支取 Payable with interest@   % per annum 按年息_____付款

号码   汇票金额   中国XX   年   月   日
No. BP-BJ023   Exchange for USD20,977.45   Shanghai,China   JUNE 28, 2017

见票   日后(本汇票之副本未付)付交
At 60 DAYS FROM THE DATE OF   sight of this FIRST of Exchange(Second of Exchange
    INVOICE:MAY 15,2017
                                                                          金额
being unpaid) Pay to the order of _____BANK OF CHINA,SHANGHAI_____   the sum of

SAY U.S.DOLLARS TWENTY THOUSAND NINE HUNDRED AND SEVENTY-SEVEN AND CENTS FORTY-FIVE ONLY.

款已收讫
Value received
此致
To: BANK OF CHINA,LONDON

_____
_____   SHANGHAI BAOJING COMPANY
_____   蔡佩琪

练习四

BILL OF EXCHANGE

凭
Drawn under BANK OF CHINA,LONDON   信用证 第   号
                                                     L/C No. LC-17G021

日期
Dated MAR. 18,2017   支取 Payable with interest@   % per annum 按年息_____付款

号码   汇票金额   中国XX   年   月   日
No. BP-BJ023   Exchange for USD95,400.00   Shanghai,China   JUN.5TH,2017

见票   日后(本汇票之副本未付)付交
At 45 DAYS AFTER THE B/L DATE: sight of this FIRST of Exchange(Second of Exchange
    MAY 25TH,2017
                                                                          金额
being unpaid) Pay to the order of _____BANK OF CHINA,SHANGHAI_____   the sum of

SAY U.S.DOLLARS NINETY-FIVE THOUSAND FOUR HUNDRED ONLY.

款已收讫
Value received
此致
To: LONDON COMMERCIAL BANK,LONDON

_____
_____   SHANGHAI BAOJING COMPANY
_____   蔡佩琪

BILL OF EXCHANGE

凭
Drawn under BANK OF CHINA,LONDON   L/C No. LC-17G021

日期
Dated MAR. 18,2017   支取 Payable with interest@   % per annum 按年息_____ 付款

号码   汇票金额   中国XX   年   月   日
No. BP-BJ023   Exchange for USD95,400.00   Shanghai,China   JUN. 23,2017

见票   日后(本汇票之副本未付)付交
At 45 DAYS AFTER THE B/L DATE: sight of this FIRST of Exchange(Second of Exchange
    JUN. 15TH,2017   金额
being unpaid) Pay to the order of _____ BANK OF CHINA,SHANGHAI _____   the sum of

SAY U.S.DOLLARS NINETY-FIVE THOUSAND FOUR HUNDRED ONLY.

款已收讫
Value received
此致
To: LONDON COMMERCIAL BANK,LONDON

SHANGHAI BAOJING COMPANY
蔡佩琪

练习五

BILL OF EXCHANGE

凭
Drawn under BANK OF CHINA,LONDON   L/C No. LC-17G021

日期
Dated MAR. 18,2017   支取 Payable with interest@   % per annum 按年息_____ 付款

号码   汇票金额   中国XX   年   月   日
No. BP-BJ023   Exchange for USD133,560.00   Shanghai,China   JUNE 28, 2017

见票   日后(本汇票之副本未付)付交
At ***_____   sight of this FIRST of Exchange(Second of Exchange
                                                                                     金额
being unpaid) Pay to the order of _____ BANK OF CHINA,SHANGHAI _____   the sum of

SAY U.S.DOLLARS ONE HUNDRED AND THIRTY-THREE THOUSAND FIVE HUNDRED AND SIXTY ONLY.

款已收讫
Value received
此致
To: BANK OF CHINA,LONDON

SHANGHAI BAOJING COMPANY
蔡佩琪

BILL OF EXCHANGE

凭
Drawn under BANK OF CHINA,LONDON   L/C No. LC-17G021

日期
Dated MAR. 18,2017   支取 Payable with interest@   % per annum 按年息_____付款

号码   汇票金额   中国XX   年   月   日
No. BP-BJ023   Exchange for USD57,240.00   Shanghai,China   JUNE 28, 2017

见票   日后(本汇票之副本未付)付交
At 30 DAYS AFTER   sight of this FIRST of Exchange(Second of Exchange
                                                                        金额
being unpaid) Pay to the order of _____BANK OF CHINA,SHANGHAI_____   the sum of

SAY U.S.DOLLARS FIFTY-SEVEN THOUSAND TWO HUNDRED AND FORTY ONLY.

款已收讫
Value received
此致
To：BANK OF CHINA,LONDON

SHANGHAI BAOJING COMPANY
蔡佩琪

外贸技能综合练习答案（一）

一、合同填制

SALES CONTRACT

TO：LONDON DOLL IMPORT & EXPORT CO.,LTD.

S/C NO.：SH20151014

DATE：OCT. 14,2015

We hereby confirm having sold to you the following goods on terms and conditions as stated below：

Commodity & Specifications	Quantity	Unit Price	Amount
DOLL		FOB HONG KONG,CHINA	
STYLE NO. 05	1,000PCS	USD10.00/PC	USD10,000.00
STYLE NO. 06	2,000PCS	USD15.00/PC	USD30,000.00
STYLE NO. 08	2,000PCS	USD12.00/PC	USD24,000.00
TOTAL：	5,000PCS		USD64,000.00
TOTAL CONTRACT VALUE：SAY U.S. DOLLARS SIXTY-FOUR THOUSAND ONLY.			

SHIPPING MARK：

LONDON DOLL

SH20151014

LONDON,ENGLAND

NO.1-UP

PACKING：OUTER PACKING AS PER BUYER'S EXPORT STANDARD CARTONS,INNER PACKING AS PER SELLER'S GIFT BOXES,PACKAGE DESIGN AND CONTENTS SUPPLIED BY THE BUYER

PORT OF SHIPMENT：HONG KONG,CHINA

PORT OF DESTINATION：LONDON,ENGLAND

TIME OF SHIPMENT：DURING JULY,2016

TRANSSHIPMENT：ALLOWED

PARTIAL SHIPMENT:NOT ALLOWED

TERMS OF PAYMENT:20% BY T/T IN ADVANCE AS DOWN PAYMENT,THE REST BY T/T BE-
FORE SHIPMENT

INSURANCE:TO BE EFFECTED BY THE BUYER FOR 110% OF THE INVOICE VALUE COVER-
ING ALL RISKS AND WAR RISK

Signed by:

THE SELLER:香港洋娃娃进出口公司   THE BUYER:LONDON DOLL IMPORT & EXPORT CO.,LTD.
李琳   LUCY

二、信用证分析表填制

信用证号	KLMU1234	合约号	SUM356/19		受益人	ABC COMPANY,SHANGHAI, NO.11 CHANGCHUN ROAD, SHANGHAI,CHINA	
开证银行	NATIONAL COMMERCIAL BANK,JEDDAH			开证申请人	ALOSMNY INTERNATIONAL TRADE CO., 177 ALHRAM STREET SECOND FLOOR-G102A EGYPT,12111		
开证日期	JULY 28,2019	兑付方式	L/C BY NEGOTIATION	起运口岸	SHANGHAI,CHINA	目的地	SAID, EGYPT
金额	USD28,820.00			可否转运	NOT ALLOWED	成交方式	CFR JED DAH
汇票付款人	NATIONAL COMMERCIAL BANK,JEDDAH			可否分批	NOT ALLOWED		
汇票期限	见票___***___天期			装运期限	AUG.30,2019	唛头	
				有效期	SEPT. 15,2019		
				有效地点	CHINA		
				提单日___15___天内议付		___天内寄单	

单证名称	提单	副本提单	商业发票	海关发票	装箱单	重量数量单	尺码单	保险单	产地证	普惠制产地证	贸促会产地证	出口许可证	装船通知书	投保通知	寄投保通知邮据	寄单证明	寄样证明	品质证明书
提交银行	2		3		1											1		

续表

提交客户	1								1					

注:在"提交银行"或"提交客户"对应的栏目中填写应提交的单据份数,信用证要求提交的单据没有注明份数,默认为1份。

提单	抬头	TO ORDER	保险	险种	
	通知	ALOSMNY INTERNATIONAL TRADE CO., 177 ALHRAM STREET SECOND FLOOR-G102A EGYPT,12111			
运费支付方式(预付或到付)		FREIGHT PREPAID		投保加成率	赔款地点

三、国际贸易单证填制

SELLER	商业发票 COMMERCIAL INVOICE		
BUYER DEF CO.,LTD.	INVOICE NO.		INVOICE DATE JUL. 28,2019
	L/C NO. KLMU1234		S/C DATE JUN. 19,2019
	S/C NO. SUM356/19		PRICE TERM CFR JEDDAH
	FROM SHANGHAI,CHINA		TO SAID,EGYPT
MARKS	DESCRIPTION OF GOODS	QUANTITY	UNIT PRICE	AMOUNT

MARKS	DESCRIPTION OF GOODS	QUANTITY	UNIT PRICE	AMOUNT
A.I.T.C. SUM356/19 SAID C/NO.1-4400	MEILING BRAND CANNED ORANGE JAM,PACKED IN SEAWORTHY CARTONS.250 GRAM PER CAN,12 CANS IN A CARTON COUNTRY OF ORIGIN:P.R.CHINA	4,400CTNS	CFR JEDDAH USD6.55/CTN	USD28,820.00
	TOTAL:	4,400CTNS		USD28,820.00

TOTAL AMOUNT IN WORDS:SAY U.S. DOLLARS TWENTY-EIGHT THOUSAND EIGHT HUNDRED AND TWENTY ONLY.

WE HEREBY CERTIFY THAT THE COMMERCIAL INVOICE IS TURE AND CORRECT.

SELLER			装箱单 PACKING LIST		
BUYER DEF CO.,LTD.			INVOICE NO. 123QWE		DATE JUL. 28,2019
			S/C NO. SUM356/19		L/C NO. KLMU1234
			FROM SHANGHAI,CHINA		TO SAID,EGYPT
			MARKS & NOS. N/M		

C/NOS.	DESCRIPTION OF GOODS	NUMBERS & KIND OF PACKAGE	QUANTITIY	G.W. （KGS）	N.W. （KGS）	Meas. （CBM）
C/NO. 4400	MEILING BRAND CANNED ORANGE JAM PACKED IN SEAWORTHY CARTONS.250 GRAM PER CAN, 12 CANS IN A CARTON COUNTRY OF ORIGIN： P.R.CHINA PACKING CONDITIONS AS REQUIRED BY L/C	4,400CTNS	@12CANS 52,800CANS	@4.00KGS 17,600.00KGS	@3.00KGS 13,200.00 KGS	@0.024CBM 105.600CBM
	TOTAL:	4,400CTNS	52,800.00CANS	17,600.00KGS	13,200.00 KGS	105.600CBM

TOTAL PACKAGES(IN WORDS):(29)SAY FOUR THOUSAND FOUR HUNDRED CARTONS ONLY.

Shipper：ABC COMPANY,SHANGHAI NO.11 CHANGCHUN ROAD, SHANGHAI,CHINA		订舱委托书
Consignee： TO ORDER		To:德安物流/王明 开船日： 箱型、箱量:40'FCL×2
Notify： ALOSMNY INTERNATIONAL TRADE CO., 177 ALHRAM STREET SECOND FLOOR-G102A EGYPT,12111		合同号:SUM356/19 运费:FREIGHT PREPAID Vessel/Voyage:MOONRIVER V.987

Port of Loading	Port of Discharge	Transshipment	Partial Shipment
Marks & Numbers	Description of Goods	No. of Packages	Gross Weight	Meas.

A.I.T.C. SUM356/19 SAID C/NO.1-4400	CANNED ORANGE JAM 罐装橘子酱 2132233288	4,400CTNS	17,600.00KGS	105.600CBM

TOTAL NUMBERS OF CONTAINERS OR PACKAGES:SAY FOUR THOUSAND FOUR HUNDRED CARTONS ONLY.

客户要求

☐ 送货　　☑ 产装　　☑ 代理报关　　☐ 代理报检　　☐ 投保

产品信息	产装地址及预计日期: SHANGHAI　2019年8月25日 单位名称: ABC COMPANY,SHANGHAI 地址: NO.11 CHANGCHUN ROAD,SHANGHAI, CHINA 联系人:××× 电话:×××	订舱公司:ABC COMPANY,SHANGHAI 联系人:××× 电话:××× 传真:×××
特殊要求	签全套清洁已装船海运提单 提单上显示SHIPPING MARK: A.I.T.C. SUM356/19 SAID C/NO.1-4400	

BILL OF EXCHANGE

凭
Drawn under　NATIONAL COMMERCIAL BANK,JEDDAH

信用证　第　　　号
L/C No.　KLMU1234

日期
Dated　JUL. 28,2019　　　　　支取 Payable with interest@　　　% per annum 按年息　　　　付款

号码　　　　　　　　汇票金额　　　　　　　　　　　　中国XX　　年　　月　　日
No.　123QWE　　　Exchange for　USD28,820.00　　China　SEPT. 05,2019

见票
At　***　　　　　　　　　　　日后(本汇票之副本未付)付交
　　　　　　　　　　　　　　　sight of this FIRST of Exchange(Second of Exchange　　金额

being unpaid) Pay to the order of　　BANK OF CHINA,SHANGHAI BRANCH　　　　the sum of

SAY U.S. DOLLARS TWENTY-EIGHT THOUSAND EIGHT HUNDRED AND TWENTY ONLY.

款已收讫
Value received
此致
To:

NATIONAL COMMERCIAL BANK,JEDDAH

ABC COMPANY,SHANGHAI

signature 李丰

外贸技能综合练习答案(二)

一、合同填制

SALES CONTRACT

TO:ITOCHU CORPORATION, S/C NO.:AN120

OSAKA,JAPAN,OSACY SECTION DATE: JAN. 20,2019

We hereby confirm having sold to you the following goods on terms and conditions as stated below:

Commodity & Specifications	Quantity	Unit Price	Amount
100% PURE COTTON APRON		FOB OSAKA, JAPAN	
ART. NO. 49394(014428)	3,216PCS	USD1.00/PC	USD3,216.00
ART. NO. 49393(014428)	3,960PCS	USD1.00/PC	USD3,960.00
ART. NO. 55306(014429)	1,560PCS	USD1.25/PC	USD1,950.00
TOTAL:	8,736PCS		USD9,126.00
TOTAL CONTRACT VALUE: SAY U.S. DOLLARS NINE THOUSAND ONE HUNDRED AND TWENTY-SIX ONLY.			

SHIPPING MARK:ITOCHU/OSAKA/NO.1-728

PACKING:TO BE PACKED IN EXPORT CARTONS SUITABLE FOR LONG DISTANCE OCEAN TRANS-
PORTATION,ONE PIECE TO A PLEAST BAG,12 BAGS TO A CARTON,TOTAL 728 CARTONS.

PORT OF SHIPMENT:SHANGHAI,CHINA

PORT OF DESTINATION:OSAKA,JAPAN,VIA QINGDAO ONLY

TIME OF SHIPMENT:WITHIN 45 DAYS AFTER RECEIPT OF L/C,AND NOT LATER THAN MAY,
2019

TRANSSHIPMENT:ALLOWED

PARTIAL SHIPMENT:ALLOWED

TERMS OF PAYMENT:BY CONFIRMED IRREVOCABLE L/C TO BE AVAILABLE BY DRAFT AT
SIGHT,TO BE OPENED BY THE BUYER AND TO REACH THE SELLER BE-

FORE APR. 15, 2019. THE L/C TO BE VALID FOR NEGOTIATION UNTIL THE 15TH DAY AFTER THE SHIPMENT DATE. IN CASE OF LATE ARRIVAL OF THE L/C, THE SELLER SHALL NOT BE LIABLE FOR ANY DELAY IN SHIPMENT AND SHALL HAVE THE RIGHT TO RESCIND THE CONTRACT AND/OR CLAIM FOR DAMAGES

INSURANCE: TO BE EFFECTED BY THE BUYER FOR 120% OF CIF INVOCE VALUE COVERING ALL RISKS, WAR RISK AND STRIKES RISK AS PER C.I.C., THE EXTRA PREMIUM ARE FOR BUYER'S ACCOUNT

Signed by:

THE SELLER: SHANGHAI TEXTILES IMP. AND EXP. CORPORATION

　　　　陈彤

THE BUYER: ITOCHU CORPORATION

　　　　AC-KIE CHANG

二、信用证分析表填制

信用证号	ADK/32921/05	合约号	DLLI5739	受益人	DALIAN LIGHT INDUSTRIAL PRODUCTS IMPORT AND EXPORT CORPORATION, NO.23 FUGUI STREET ZHONGSHAN DISTRICT, DALIAN, CHINA		
开证银行	45071932 CIYIBANK N.A., NEW YORK			开证申请人	GRUEN FRED CO., LTD., 6270N PORT WASHINGTON ROAD, MILWAUKEE WI 53217 UNITED STATES		
开证日期	FEB. 20, 2019	兑付方式	L/C BY NEGOTIATION	起运口岸	CHINESE MAIN PORT	目的地	NEW YORK, USA
金额	USD276,331.00±10%			可否转运	PROHIBITED	成交方式	CIF NEW YORK, USA
汇票付款人	CIYIBANK N.A., NEW YORK			可否分批	PROHIBITED		
汇票期限	见票___***___天期			装运期限	MAR. 31, 2019	唛头	ROLISA/ LEIXOES/ 1-UP
				有效期	APR. 21, 2019		
				有效地点	CHINA		
				提单日__21__天内议付	___天内寄单		

单证名称	提单	副本提单	商业发票	海关发票	装箱单	重量数量单	尺码单	保险单	产地证	普惠制产地证	贸促会产地证	出口许可证	装船通知书	投保通知	寄投保通知邮据	寄单证明	寄样证明	品质证明书

提交银行	2	3	3		3	2	1		1			3
提交客户	1								1			

注:在"提交银行"或"提交客户"对应的栏目中填写应提交的单据份数,信用证要求提交的单据没有注明份数,默认为1份。

提单	抬头	TO THE ORDER OF CIYIBANK N.A.,NEW YORK	保险	险种	ALL RISKS,WAR RISK AND S.R.C.C.		
	通知	GRUEN FRED CO.,LTD.,6270N PORT WASHINGTON ROAD,MILWAUKEE WI 53217 UNITED STATES					
运费支付方式(预付或到付)		PREIGHT PREPAID		投保加成	120%	赔款地点	NEW YORK, USA

注:如果提供的信用证的内容没有涉及信用证分析表的某些栏目,该栏目为空。

三、国际贸易单证填制

SELLER DALIAN LIGHT INDUSTRIAL PRODUCTS IMPORT AND EXPORT CORPORATION,NO.23 FUGUI STREET ZHONGSHAN DISTRICT,DALIAN, CHINA	商业发票 COMMERCIAL INVOICE		
	INVOICE NO. DAL12345		INVOICE DATE MAR. 12,2019
	L/C NO. ADK/32921/05		S/C DATE FEB. 08,2019
BUYER ABC CO.	S/C NO. DLLI5739		PRICE TERM CIF NEW YORK,USA
	FROM DALIAN,CHINA		TO NEW YORK,USA
MARKS	DESCRIPTION OF GOODS	QUANTITY	UNIT PRICE	AMOUNT
ROLISA/ LEIXOES/ 1-164	ENERGY SAVING LAMPS 8 WATT 10 WATT 12 WATT	25,000PCS 27,000PCS 30,000PCS	CIF NEW YORK, USA USD2.45/PC USD2.98/PC USD3.65/PC	USD61,250.00 USD80,460.00 USD109,500.00
	TOTAL:	82,000PCS		USD251,210.00

TOTAL AMOUNT IN WORDS:
SAY U.S. DOLLARS TWO HUNDRED AND FIFTY-ONE THOUSAND TWO HUNDRED AND TEN ONLY.

B/L NO. JTX562/0003

DALIAN LIGHT INDUSTRIAL PRODUCTS IMPORT AND EXPORT CORPORATION

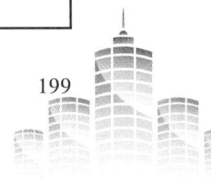

张莉

SELLER DALIAN LIGHT INDUSTRIAL PRODUCTS IMPORT AND EXPORT CORPORATION,NO.23 FUGUI STREET ZHONGSHAN DISTRICT,DALIAN,CHINA	装箱单 PACKING LIST		

	INVOICE NO. DAL12345		DATE MAR. 12,2019
	S/C NO. DLLI5739		L/C NO. ADK/32921/05
BUYER ABC CO.	FROM DALIAN,CHINA		TO NEW YORK,USA
	MARKS & NOS. ROLISA/ LEIXOES/ 1-164		

C/NOS.	DESCRIPTION OF GOODS	NUMBERS & KIND OF PACKAGE	QUANTITIY	G.W. (KGS)	N.W. (KGS)	Meas. (CBM)
C/NO.1-50 C/NO.51-104 C/NO.164	50CTNS 54CTNS 60CTNS	ENERGY SAVING LAMPS 8 WATT 10 WATT 12 WATT ONE PIECE TO A PAPER BOX,500PCS TO A CARTON,TOTAL 164 CARTONS. B/L NO:JTX562/0003	@500PCS 25,000PCS 27,000PCS 30,000PCS	@20.00KGS 1,000.00KGS 1,080.00KGS 1,200.00KGS	@19.00KGS 950.00KGS 1,026.00KGS 1,140.00KGS	@0.14076CBM 7.038CBM 7.601CBM 8.446CBM
TOTAL:	164CTNS		82,000 PCS	3,280.00 KGS	3,116.00 KGS	23.085CBM

TOTAL PACKAGES(IN WORDS):SAY ONE HUNDRED AND SIXTY-FOUR CARTONS ONLY.

DALIAN LIGHT INDUSTRIAL PRODUCTS IMPORT AND EXPORT CORPORATION

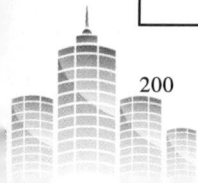

张莉

Shipper: DALIAN LIGHT INDUSTRIAL PRODUCTS IMPORT AND EXPORT CORPORATION,NO.23 FUGUI STREET ZHONGSHAN DISTRICT, DALIAN,CHINA		订舱委托书		
Consignee: TO THE ORDER OF CITIBANK N.A.,NEW YORK		To:委托汇通货/李云 开船日:2019年3月19日 箱型箱量:20FCL×1 CY/CY		
Notify: GRUEN FRED CO.,LTD., 6270N PORT WASHINGTON ROAD,MILWAUKEE WI 53217 UNITED STATES		合同号: DLLI5739		
		运费: FREIGHT　PREPAID		
		Vessel/Voyage: TIAN LI SHAN V.562E		
Port of Loading DALIAN,CHINA	Port of Discharge NEW YORK, USA	Transshipment PROHIBITED	Partial Shipment PROHIBITED	
Marks & Numbers	Description of Goods	No. of Packages	Gross Weight	Meas.
ROLISA/ LEIXOES/ 1-164	ENERGY SAVING LAMPS 8539319900 H.S.CODE:	164CTNS	3,280.00KGS	23.085CBM
TOTAL NUMBERS OF CONTAINERS OR PACKAGES: SAY ONE HUNDRED AND SIXTY-FOUR CARTONS ONLY.				

客户要求

☐ 送货　　☑ 产装　　☑ 代理报关　　☐ 代理报检　　☐ 投保

产品信息	产装地址及预计日期: DALIAN,2019年3月14日 单位名称:大连轻工业品进出口公司 地址:NO.23 FUGUI STREET ZHONGSHAN DISTRICT,DALIAN,CHINA 联系人:王琦 电话:×××	订舱公司:大连轻工业品进出口公司 联系人:王琦 电话:××× 传真:×××
特殊要求	签两份正本清洁已装船海运提单	

BILL OF EXCHANGE

凭
Drawn under CIYIBANK N.A.,NEW YORK   信用证 第   号
                                                                      L/C No. ADK/32921/05

日期
Dated FEB.20,2019   支取 Payable with interest@   % per annum 按年息_____ 付款

号码   汇票金额   中国XX   年   月   日
No. DAL12345   Exchange for USD200,968.00   Dalian China MAR. 21,2019

见票   日后(本汇票之副本未付)付交
At ***   sight of this FIRST of Exchange(Second of Exchange

                                                                      金额
being unpaid）Pay to the order of   DALIAN FINANCE,CORPRATION   the sum of

SAY U.S. DOLLARS TWO HUNDRED THOUSAND NINE HUNDRED AND SIXTY-EIGHT ONLY.

款已收讫   B/L NUMBER:JTX56210003
Value received
此致
To:

CIYIBANK N.A.,NEW YORK

                                        DALIAN LIGHT INDUSTRIAL PRODUCTS
                                        IMPORT AND EXPORT CORPORATION
                                                    张莉

外贸技能综合练习答案（三）

一、合同填制

SALES CONTRACT

TO:CROMBONGO TEXTILES CO.,LTD.　　　　　　S/C NO.:SH20151014

　　　　　　　　　　　　　　　　　　　　　　DATE:OCT. 14,2015

We hereby confirm having sold to you the following goods on terms and conditions as stated below:

Commodity & Specifications	Quantity	Unit Price	Amount
PRINTED SHIRTING		CIF　LAGOS	
(STYLE NO.)ART. NO. 82	1,000YARDS	USD0.40/YARD	USD400.00
(STYLE NO.)ART. NO. 72	1,000YARDS	USD0.45/YARD	USD450.00
(STYLE NO.)ART. NO. 84	2,000YARDS	USD0.50/YARD	USD1,000.00
TOTAL:	4,000YARDS		USD1,850.00
TOTAL CONTRACT VALUE: SAY U.S.DOLLARS ONE THOUSAND EIGHT HUNDRED AND FIFTY ONLY.			

SHIPPING MARK:AT THE SELLER'S OPTION

PACKING:IN ROLLS OF 100 YARDS EACH

PORT OF SHIPMENT:SHANGHAI,CHINA

PORT OF DESTINATION:LAGOS

TIME OF SHIPMENT:DURING JUL.,2015

TRANSSHIPMENT:ALLOWED

PARTIAL SHIPMENT:NOT ALLOWED

TERMS OF PAYMENT:BY CONFIRMED IRREVOCABLE L/C TO BE AVAILABLE BY DRAFT AT SIGHT AGAINST PRESENTATION OF SHIPPING DOCUMENTS

INSURANCE:TO BE EFFECTED BY THE SELLER FOR 110% OF THE INVOICE VALUE COVERING ALL RISKS AND WAR RISK

Signed by:

THE SELLER:SHANGHAI TEXTILES   THE BUYER:CROMBONGO TEX TILES

         IMP. & EXP. CORP.   CO.,LTD.

         王晶   MARY

二、信用证分析表填制

信用证号	XJF+5682135	合约号	OP45	受益人	JIAXING GUANGYUAN IMPORT & EXPORT CO.,LTD.,NO.563 YOUDIAN ROAD,JIAXING ZHEJIANG,CHINA		
开证银行	SPANIARD-BANK BERLIN,POTSDAM GERMANY			开证申请人	TGT IMPORT & EXPORT COMPANY POTSDAM GERMANY,WIESENHOF 12 POTSDAM BRANDENBURG GERMANY		
开证日期	FEB. 06,2014	兑付方式	L/C BY NEGOTIATION	起运口岸	ANY PORT IN CHINA	目的地	HAMBURG, GERMANY
金额	EUR495,620.00±5%			可否转运	NOT ALLOWED	成交方式	CFR HAMBURG
汇票付款人	SPANIARD-BANK BERLIN, POTSDAM GERMANY			可否分批	ALLOWED		
汇票期限	见票 30 DAYS AFTER THE DATE OF B/L 天期			装运期限	MAR. 15,2014	唛头	
				有效期	APR. 30,2014		
				有效地点	GHINA		
				提单日 15 天内议付	天内寄单		

单证名称	提单	副本提单	商业发票	海关发票	装箱单	重量数量单	尺码单	保险单	产地证	普惠制产地证	贸促会产地证	出口许可证	装船通知书	投保通知	寄投保通知邮据	寄单证明	寄样证明	品质证明书
提交银行	3		3		3								1			1		
提交客户			1		1								1					

注:在"提交银行"或"提交客户"对应的栏目中填写应提交的单据份数,信用证要求提交的单据没有注明份数,默认为1份。

提单	抬头	TO ORDER	保险	险种	
	通知	TGT IMPORT & EXPORT COMPANY POTSDAM GERMANY,WIESENHOF 12 POTSDAM BRANDENBURG GERMANY			
运费支付方式(预付或到付)		FREIGHT PREPAID		投保加成率	赔款地点

三、国际贸易单证填制

SELLER JIAXING GUANGYUAN IMPORT & EXPORT CO.,LTD., NO.563 YOUDIAN ROAD,JIAXING ZHEJIANG,CHINA	商业发票 COMMERCIAL INVOICE			
BUYER GFT IMPORT & EXPORT POTSDAM GERMANY	INVOICE NO. DIM/7-595		INVOICE DATE FEB. 16,2014	
	L/C NO. XJF+5682135		S/C DATE JAN. 29,2014	
	S/C NO. OP45		PRICE TERM CFR HAMBURG	
	FROM SHANGHAI,CHINA		TO HAMBURG,GERMANY	
MARKS	DESCRIPTION OF GOODS	QUANTITY	UNIT PRICE	AMOUNT
N/M	GOOD DAY BRAND TRAVELLING BAGS AS PER S/C NO.OP45 DD.140129 ART. QESW-12 ART. QESW-13	840PCS 630PCS	CFR HAMBURG EUR10.50/PC EUR12.70/PC	EUR8,820.00 EUR8,001.00
	TOTAL:	1,470PCS		EUR16,821.00

TOTAL AMOUNT IN WORDS:
SAY EUROS SIXTEEN THOUSAND EIGHT HUNDRED AND TWENTY-ONE ONLY.

COUNTRY OF ORIGIN:CHINA

JIAXING GUANGYUAN IMPORT & EXPORT CO.,LTD.
郑明敏（章）

BILL OF EXCHANGE

凭
Drawn under SPANIARD-BANK BERLIN,POTSDAM GERMANY　　　　　　　　　　L/C No. XJF+5682135

日期
Dated FEB.06,2014　　　　　支取 Payable with interest@　　　% per annum 按年息　　　　　付款

号码　　　　　　汇票金额　　　　　　　　　中国XX　　年　月　日
No. DIM/7-595　　Exchange for EUR16,821.00　　China SHANGHAI MAR. 11,2014

见票　　　　　　　日后(本汇票之副本未付)付交
At 30 DAYS AFTER THE DATE OF B/L sight of this FIRST of Exchange(Second of Exchange

金额
being unpaid）Pay to the order of　BANK OF CHINA,JIAXING BRANCH　　　the sum of

SAY EUROS SIXTEEN THOUSAND EIGHT HUNDRED AND TWENTY-ONE ONLY.

款已收讫　　　　　　B/L DATE:MAR. 01,2014
Value received　　　　COUNTRY OF ORIGIN:CHINA
此致
To:

SPANIARD-BANK BERLIN,POTSDAM GERMANY

JIAXING GUANGYUAN
IMPORT & EXPORT CO.,LTD.

郑明敏

外贸技能综合练习答案(四)

一、合同填制

SALES CONTRACT

To:PARMIX SPORTSWEAR INC.,   S/C NO.:WEI258

  591 EAST LAMEN STREET,TORONTO,CANADA   DATE:MAY 05,2015

We hereby confirm having sold to you the following goods on terms and conditions as stated below:

Commodity & Specifications	Quantity	Unit Price	Amount
		FOB SHANGHAI, CHINA	
50PCT NYLON/50PCT RAYON, WOVEN LADIES 2-PCE SUIT— JACKET L/S/FULLY LINED PANT W/BELT LOOPS STYLE 167C/168C	500SETS	USD10.00/SET	USD5,000.00
LADIES 2PCE ENSEMBLE— TAILORED WAISTCOAT/SKIRT, STYLE FULLY LINED 585A/169C	500SETS	USD8.00/SET	USD4,000.00
AS PER PURCHASE ORDER NO.585			
TOTAL:	1,000SETS		USD9,000.00
TOTAL CONTRACT VALUE: SAY U.S. DOLLARS NINE THOUSAND ONLY.			

SHIPPING MARK:PARMIX/TORONTO/P.O.NO.585/NO.1-1000

PACKING:TO BE EFFECTED IN HANGING PACKING

PORT OF SHIPMENT:SHANGHAI,CHINA

PORT OF DESTINATION:TORONTO,CANADA

TIME OF SHIPMENT:NOT LATER THAN THE END OF AUG.,2015

TRANSSHIPMENT:ALLOWED

PARTIAL SHIPMENT:NOT ALLOWED

TERMS OF PAYMENT: BY CONFIRMED IRREVOCABLE SIGHT L/C,TO BE VALID FOR NEGOTIA-

    TION IN CHINA UNTIL THE 15TH DAY AFTER THE SHIPMENT DATE

INSURANCE:TO BE EFFECTED BY THE BUYER

Signed by:

THE SELLER:NANJING LIHUA TEXTILES   THE BUYER:PARMIX SPORTSWEAR INC.

        MP. & EXP. CORP.

        XXX   XXX

二、信用证分析表填制

信用证号	PGHO00348DC	合约号	HP4578	受益人	SHANDONG HOPE NATIVE PRODUCE I/E CORP., 62,GUANGXI ROAD,QINGDAO,CHINA			
开证银行	THE HONG KONG AND SHANGHAI BANKING CORP., DOWNING STREET,PENANG			开证申请人	SOO HUP SENG TRADING CO. ADN BHD., 165 1ST FLOOR,VICTORIA STREET, 10300 PENANG MALAYSIA			
开证日期	MAY 21,2010	兑付方式	L/C BY NEGOTIATION	起运口岸	ANY PORT IN CHINA	目的地	PENANG	
金额	HKD46,150.00±5%			可否转运	PROHIBITED	成交方式	CIF PENANG	
汇票付款人	THE HONG KONG AND SHANGHAI BANKING CORPORATION			可否分批	PORBIDDEN			
汇票期限	见票____***____天期			装运期限	JULY 06,2010	唛头	SHS/ PENANG/ 1-UP	
				有效期	JULY 21,2010			
				有效地点	CHINA			
				提单日____15____天内议付				

单证名称	提单	副本提单	商业发票	海关发票	装箱单	重量数量单	尺码单	保险单	产地证	普惠制产地证	贸促会产地证	出口许可证	装船通知书	投保通知	寄投保通知邮据	寄单证明	寄样证明	品质证明书
提交银行	3		3		4			1			3		1			1		3
提交客户		1	1		1			1			1		1					1

注:在"提交银行"或"提交客户"对应的栏目中填写应提交的单据份数,信用证要求提交的单据没有注明份数,默认为1份。

提单	抬头	TO SHIPPER'S ORDER (SHANDONG HOPE NATIVE PRODUCE I/E CORP.,62,GUANGXI ROAD,QINGDAO, CHINA)	保险	险种	OCEAN MARINE CLAUSES ALL RISKS(INCLUDING WAREHOUSE TO WAREHOUSE CLAUSES) AND WAR RISK CLAUSES(1/1/1981) OF THE PEOPLE'S INSURANCE COMPANY OF CHINA		
	通知	SOO HUP SENG TRADING CO. ADN BHD., 165 1ST FLOOR,VICTORIA STREET, 10300 PENANG MALAYSIA THE HONG KONG AND SHANGHAI BANKING CORP.,DOWNING STREET, PENANG					
运费支付方式(预付或到付)		FREIGHT PREPAID		投保加成率	10%	赔款地点	PENANG

三、国际贸易单证填制

SELLER SHANDONG HOPE NATIVE PRODUCE I/E CORP.,62,GUANGXI ROAD,QINGDAO,CHINA	商业发票 COMMERCIAL INVOICE	

	INVOICE NO. HOPE24587	INVOICE DATE JUNE 30,2010
BUYER SOO HUP SENG TRADING CO. ADN BHD., 165 1ST FLOOR,VICTORIA STREET, 10300 PENANG MALAYSIA	L/C NO.	S/C DATE APR. 22,2015
	S/C NO. HP4578	PRICE TERM CIF PENANG
	FROM QINGDAO,CHINA	TO PENANG

MARKS	DESCRIPTION OF GOODS	QUANTITY	UNIT PRICE	AMOUNT
SHS/ PENANG/ 1-210	SHANDONG BLACK DATES HIGH QUALITY AS PER ORDER NO.SOO-6378 AND S/C NO. HP4578	5.25M/T	CIF PENANG HKD9,230.00 PER M/TON	HKD48,457.50
	TOTAL:	5.25M/T	FREIGHT CHARGES: PREMIUM: FOB VALUE:	HKD48,457.50 HKD4,728.18 HKD553.03 HKD43,176.29

TOTAL AMOUNT IN WORDS:
SAY HONG KONG DOLLARS FORTY-EIGHT THOUSAND FOUR HUNDRED AND FIFTY-SEVEN AND CENTS FIFTY ONLY.

WE HEREBY EVIDENCE THAT ALL PACKINGS
HAVE BEEN BEARED SHIPPING MARKS:SHS/PENANG/1-210.
WE HEREBY EVIDENCE THAT PACKING HAS BEEN DONE
AS FOLLOWS:
IN CARDBOARD CARTONS OF 25KGS NET OR 26.2KGS
GROSS PER CARTON.
ISSUING BANK'S NAME:THE HONG KONG AND SHANGHAI
BANKING CORP.

SHANDONG HOPE NATIVE PRODUCE I/E CORP.,
×××

SELLER SHANDONG HOPE NATIVE PRODUCE I/E CORP., 62,GUANGXI ROAD,QINGDAO,CHINA		装箱单 PACKING LIST	

BUYER SOO HUP SENG TRADING CO. ADN BHD., 165 1ST FLOOR,VICTORIA STREET, 10300 PENANG MALAYSIA	INVOICE NO. HOPE24587	DATE JUNE 30,2010
	S/C NO. HP4578	L/C NO.
	FROM QINGDAO,CHINA	TO PENANG
	MARKS & NOS. SHS/ PENANG/ 1-210	

C/NOS.	DESCRIPTION OF GOODS	NUMBERS & KIND OF PACKAGES	QUANTITY	G.W. （KGS）	N.W. （KGS）	MEAS. （CBM）
C/NO.1-210	SHANDONG BLACK DATES HIGH QUALITY AS PER ORDER NO.SOO-6378 AND S/C NO.HP4578 ISSUING BANK'S NAME:THE HONG KONG AND SHANGHAI BANKING CORP.	210CTNS	@25KGS 5,250KGS	@26.20KGS 5,502.00KGS	@25.00KGS 5,250.00KGS	@0.0639CBM 13.419CBM
	TOTAL:	210CTNS	5,250KGS	5,502.00KGS	5,250.00KGS	13.419CBM

TOTAL PACKAGES(IN WORDS):
SAY TWO HUNDRED AND TEN CARDBOARD CARTONS ONLY.

WE HEREBY EVIDENCE THAT ALL PACKINGS
HAVE BEEN BEARED SHIPPING MARKS:SHS/PENANG/1-UP.
WE HEREBY EVIDENCE THAT PACKING HAS BEEN DONE
AS FOLLOWS:
IN CARDBOARD CARTONS OF 25KGS NET OR 26.2KGS
GROSS PER CARTON.

SHANDONG HOPE NATIVE PRODUCE I/E CORP.

Shipper: SHANDONG HOPE NATIVE PRODUCE I/E CORP., 62,GUANGXI ROAD,QINGDAO,CHINA	订舱委托书	
Consignee： TO SHIPPER'S ORDER	To:汇通货代/李莉 开船日:JUL. 05,2010 箱型、箱量:20FCL×1	
Notify： SOO HUP SENG TRADING CO. ADN BHD., 165 1ST FLOOR,VICTORIA STREET, 10300 PENANG MALAYSIA THE HONG KONG AND SHANGHAI BANKING CORP.,DOWNING STREET,PENANG	合同号： HP4578	
	运费： FREIGHT PREPAID	
	Vessel/Voyage： Victoria V.113	

Port of Loading QINGDAO,CHINA	Port of Discharge PENANG	Transshipment PERMITTED	Partial Shipment PROHIBITED	
Marks & Numbers	Description of Goods	No. of Packages	Gross Weight	Meas.
SHS/ PENANG/ 1-210	SHANDONG BLACK DATES 山东黑枣 578950000	210CTNS	5,502.00KGS	13.419CBM

TOTAL NUMBERS OF CONTAINERS OR PACKAGES：
SAY TWO HUNDRED AND TEN CARDBOARD CARTONS ONLY.

客户要求

☐ 送货   ☑ 产装   ☑ 代理报关   ☐ 代理报检   ☐ 投保

产装信息	产装地址及预计日期： QINGDAO JUN. 31,2010 单位名称:SHANDONG HOPE NATIVE PRODUCE I/E CORP. 地址:62,GUANGXI ROAD,QINGDAO,CHINA 联系人:××× 电话:×××	订舱公司:SHANDONG HOPE NATIVE PRODUCE I/E CORP. 联系人:××× 电话:××× 传真:×××
特殊要求	签全套正本清洁已装船海运提单 提单上显示:WE HEREBY EVIDENCE THAT ALL PACKINGS HAVE BEEN BEARED SHIPPING MARKS:SHS/PENANG/1-120. 提单上显示:WE HEREBY EVIDENCE THAT PACKING HAS BEEN DONE AS FOLLOWS: IN CARDBOARD CARTONS OF 25KGS NET OR 26.2KGS GROSS PER CARTON. 提单上显示:ISSUING BANK'S NAME:THE HONG KONG AND SHANGHAI BANKING CORP.	

BILL OF EXCHANGE

凭
Drawn under THE HONG KONG AND SHANGHAI BANKING CORP., DOWNING
STREET, PENANG

信用证 第 号
L/C No. PGHO00348DC

日期
Dated MAY 21,2010   支取 Payable with interest@   % per annum 按年息_____ 付款

号码
No. HOPE24587   汇票金额
Exchange for HKD48,457.50   中国XX 年 月 日
QINGDAO China JUL.10,2010

见票
At ***_____   日后(本汇票之副本未付)付交
sight of this FIRST of Exchange(Second of Exchange

金额
being unpaid) Pay to the order of BANK OF CHINA,QINGDAO BRANCH   the sum of

SAY HONG KONG DOLLARS FORTY-EIGHT THOUSAND FOUR HUNDRED AND FIFTY-SEVEN AND CENTS FIFTY ONLY.

B/L DATE:MAR. 01,2014
COUNTRY OF ORIGIN:CHINA

款已收讫
Value received
此致
To:

THE HONG KONG AND SHANGHAI

BANKING CORP.,

DOWNING STREET,PENANG

SHANDONG HOPE NATIVE
PRODUCE I/E CORP.

× × ×

外贸技能综合练习答案（五）

一、合同填制

ZHEJIANG LONGXING BEARINGS COMPANY

SALES CONTRACT

TO:GERMANY MASTER MACHINERY INC.

S/C NO.:LX-MM13012

DATE:JUN. 15,2014

We hereby confirm having sold to you the following goods on terms and conditions as stated below:

Commodity & Specifications	Quantity	Unit Price	Amount
DEEP GROOVE BALL BEARINGS		CIF HAMBURG,GERMANY	
ART. NO. CX001	20,000PCS	USD1.30/PC	USD26,000.00
TOTAL:	20,000PCS		USD26,000.00
TOTAL CONTRACT VALUE:SAY U.S. DOLLARS TWENTY-SIX THOUSAND ONLY.			

PACKING:TO BE PACKED IN WOODEN CASES OF FIFTY PIECES EACH,TOTAL

　　　　 400 WOODEN CASES

PORT OF SHIPMENT:NINGBO,CHINA

PORT OF DESTINATION: HAMBURG,GERMANY

TIME OF SHIPMENT:TO BE EFFECTED DURING DEC.,2014

TRANSSHIPMENT: NOT ALLOWED

PARTIAL SHIPMENT: ALLOWED

TERMS OF PAYMENT:THE BUYER SHALL OPEN THROUGH A BANK ACCEPTABLE TO THE SELL-

　　　　　　 ER AN IRREVOCABLE AND TRANSFERABLE LETTER OF CREDIT TO

　　　　　　 REACH THE SELLER 30 DAYS BEFORE SHIPMENT, AVAILABLE BY DE-

<u>FERRED PAYMENT</u>   AT   <u>30 DAYS' SIGN</u>   IN PAYING BANK DESIGNATED
BY ISSUING BANK

INSURANCE:TO BE COVERED BY THE SELLER FOR <u>110% OF THE INVOICE VALUE</u> AGAINST

<u>ALL RISKS AND INTERMIXTURE AND CONTAMINATION RISKS</u> AS PER <u>O.M.C.C.</u>

OF THE PEOPLE'S INSURANCE COMPANY OF CHINA DATED 01/01/1981

Signed by:

THE SELLER:ZHEJIANG LONGXING   THE BUYER:GERMANY MASTER MACHINERY INC.

BEARINGS COMPAY

杨海平   PAUL

二、信用证分析表填制

信用证号	LC-AG-0086	合约号	ZSG-JJ-1326	受益人	ZHEJIANG STATIONERY GROUP NO.1329, WANSHA ROAD, HANGZHOU, CHINA		
开证银行	BANK OF CHINA,ATHENS,GREECE			开证申请人	JJ BROTHER TRADING COMPANY VAS GEORGIOUA-5 10564 ATHENS, GREECE		
开证日期	JAN. 15, 2013	兑付方式	L/C BY NEGOTIATION	起运口岸	NINGBO,CHINA	目的地	ATHENS, GREECE
金额	USD22,000.00			可否转运	ALLOWED	成交方式	FOB SHANGHAI
汇票付款人	BANK OF CHINA,ATHENS,GREECE			可否分批	ALLOWED		
汇票期限	见票___***___天期			装运期限	JUN. 30,2013	唛头	JJ/ ATHENS, GREECE/ MADE IN CHINA/ NO.1-UP
				有效期	JUL. 20,2013		
				有效地点	CHINA		
				提单日_10_天内议付	____天内寄单		

单证名称	提单	副本提单	商业发票	海关发票	装箱单	重量数量单	尺码单	保险单	产地证	普惠制产地证	贸促会产地证	出口许可证	装船通知书	投保通知	寄投保通知邮据	寄单证明	寄样证明	品质证明书

提交银行	3	7	5		2	1		1			1		
提交客户									1				

注:在"提交银行"或"提交客户"对应的栏目中填写应提交的单据份数,信用证要求提交的单据没有注明份数,默认为1份。

提单	抬头	TO ORDER OF SHIPPER (ZHEJIANG STATIONERY GROUP NO.1329,WANSHA ROAD,HANGZHOU,CHINA)	保险	险种	ALL RISKS AND WAR RISK		
	通知	JJ BROTHER TRADING COMPANY VAS GEORGIOUA-5 10564 ATHENS,GREECE					
运费支付方式(预付或到付)		FREIGHT PREPAID		投保加成	110%	赔款地点	ATHENS, GREECE

注:如果提供的信用证的内容没有涉及信用证分析表的某些栏目,该栏目为空。

三、国际贸易单证填制

SELLER ZHEJIANG TENGHUI IMP. & EXP. CO.,LTD., NO.4712, WENER ROAD, HANGZHOU,CHINA	商业发票 COMMERCIAL INVOICE		
BUYER K-NOON TRADING COMPANY 2212 GEORGE AVENUE, SEATTLE, USA	INVOICE NO. ZTH13-06	INVOICE DATE AUG. 18,2013	
	L/C NO. LC-AB-91	S/C DATE APR. 25,2013	
	S/C NO. 13ZTH-KN03	PRICE TERM CFR SEATTLE,USA	
	FROM SHANGHAI,CHINA	TO SEATTLE,USA VIA HONG KONG	

MARKS	DESCRIPTION OF GOODS	QUANTITY	UNIT PRICE	AMOUNT
K-NOON/ SEATTLE,USA/ CHINA/ NO.1-800	TEA TOWELS	8,000DOZEN	CFR EATTLE,USA USD11.50/DOZ	USD92,000.00
	TOTAL:	8,000DOZEN		USD92,000.00

TOTAL AMOUNT IN WORDS:SAY U.S. DOLLARS NINETY-TWO THOUSAND ONLY.

WE CERTIFY THAT THE CONTENTS OF THIS INVOICE ARE TRUE AND CORRECT.
WE HEREBY CERTIFY THAT EACH CARTON HAS BEEN INDICATED THE DESIGN NUMBER,COLOR,QUANTITY
AND SIZE.
FOB VALUE:USD90,800.00
B/L NUMBER:JX0012
ZHEJIANG TENGHUI IMP. & EXP. CO.,LTD.
楼学军

SELLER ZHEJIANG TENGHUI IMP.& EXP. CO.,LTD. NO.4712, WENER ROAD, HANGZHOU, CHINA	装箱单 PACKING LIST	

	INVOICE NO. CTH13-06	DATE AUG.18,2013
	S/C NO. 13ZTH-KN03	L/C NO. LC-AB-91
BUYER K-NOON TRADING COMPANY 2212 GEORGE AVENUE, SEATTLE, USA	FROM SHANGHAI, CHINA	TO SEATTLE, USA VIA HONGKONG
	MARKS & NOS. K-NOON SEATTLE,USA CHINA NO.1-800	

C/NOS.	DESCRIPTION OF GOODS	NUMBERS & KIND OF PACKAGE	QUANTITY	G.W. (KGS)	N.W. (KGS)	Meas. (CBM)
C/NO.1-800	800CTNS	TEA TOWELS	@10DOZEN 8,000DOZEN	@17.00KGS 13,600.00KGS	@15.00KGS 12,000.00KGS	@0.0756CBM 60.480CBM
TOTAL:	800CTNS		8,000DOZEN	13,600.00 KGS	12,000.00 KGS	60.480CBM

TOTAL PACKAGES(IN WORDS):
SAY EIGHT HUNDRED STANDARD EXPORT STRONG CARTONS ONLY.

WE HEREBY CERTIFY THAT EACH TEA TOWEL CARRIES A "MADE IN CHINA" LABEL.
B/L NUMBER:JX0012
WE HEREBY CERTIFY THAT EACH CARTON HAS BEEN INDICATED THE DESIGN NUMBER,COLOR,QUANTITY
AND SIZE.
WE HEREBY CERTIFY THAT THE GOODS ARE PACKED IN STANDRAD EXPORT CARTONS.
ZHEJIANG TENGHUI IMP. & EXP. CO.,LTD.
楼学军

BILL OF EXCHANGE

凭
Drawn under   AMERICAN BANK,SEATTLE,USA

信用证 第   号
L/C No.   LC-AB-91

日期
Dated   MAY 12,2013   支取 Payable with interest@   % per annum 按年息_____付款

号码   汇票金额
No.   ZTH13-06   Exchange for   USD92,000.00   中国XX   年   月   日
HANGZHOU China   SEPT. 05,2013

见票   日后(本汇票之副本未付)付交
At 45 DAYS FROM THE DATE OF B/L   sight of this FIRST of Exchange(Second of Exchange

金额
being unpaid) Pay to the order of   ICBC, HANGZHOU   the sum of

SAY U.S. DOLLARS NINETY-TWO THOUSAND ONLY.

款已收讫   B/L NO.:JX0012
Value received   B/L DATE:AUG.27,2013
此致
To:

AMERICAN BANK,NY,USA

ZHEJIANG TENGHUI IMP.
& EXP. CO.,LTD.

楼学军

外贸技能综合练习答案(六)

一、合同填制

ZHEJIANG ALISON IMP. & EXP. CO.,LTD.

C-719,WORLD TRADE CENTRE OFFICE BUILDING,

122 SHUGUANG ROAD,HANGZHOU,CHINA

TEL:0086-571-87631686,FAX:0086-571-87950611

SAES CONTRACT

TO:SAMSUNG CORPORATION,

SAMSUNG-PLAZA BUILDING 263,   S/C NO:SMST/24116

SEOHYEON-DONG,BUNDANG-GU,BUSAN,KOREA,   DATE:APR. 06,2019

TEL:82-2-2145-2500,FAX:82-2-2145-2596

We hereby confirm having sold to you the following goods on terms and conditions as stated below:

Commodity & Specifications	Quantity	Unit Price	Amount
		CFR BUSAN	
GRADE 9004 RED DATES	204M/T	EUR9.37PER M/T	EUR1,911.48
GRADE 3234 RED DATES	198M/T	EUR9.27PER M/T	EUR1,835.46
TOTAL:	402M/T		EUR3,746.94
TOTAL CONTRACT VALUE:SAY EUROS THREE THOUSAND SEVEN HUNDRED AND FORTY-SIX AND CENTS NINETY-FOUR ONLY.			

SHIPPING MARK:INCLUDING SUMSUNG,S/C NO.,GRADE NO.,PORT OF DESTINATION AND CARTON NO.

PACKING:0.2M/T TO A STANDARD EXPORT CARTON

PORT OF SHIPMENT:SHANGHAI,CHINA

PORT OF DESTINATION:BUSAN,KOREA

TIME OF SHIPMENT:WITHIN 60 DAYS AFTER RECEIPT OF DOWN PAYMENT

TRANSSHIPMENT:ALLOWED

PARTIAL SHIPMENT:ALLOWED

TERMS OF PAYMENT:BY CONFIRMED AND IRREVOCABLE L/C AT 60 DAYS AFTER B/L DATE signed by:

THE SELLER:ZHEJIANG ALISON IMP. & EXP. CO.,LTD. THE BUYER:SAMSUNG CORPORATION

        XXX   XXX

二、信用证分析表填制

信用证号	0011LC123756	合约号	CD512-7	受益人	DESUN TRADING CO., LTD., NO.85 GUANJIAQIAO, NANJING 210005, CHINA		
开证银行	ALRAJHI BANKING AND INVESTMENT (HEAD OFFICE)			开证申请人	NEO GENERAL TRADING CO., P.O. BOX 99552,RIYADH 22766, KSA		
开证日期	MAR. 20,2019	兑付方式	L/C BY NEGOTIATION	起运口岸	CHINA MAIN PORT	目的地	DAMMAM PORT, SAUDI ARABIA
金额	USD13,260.00			可否转运	NOT ALLOWED	成交方式	CIF DAMMAM
汇票付款人	RJHISARI ALRAJHI BANKING AND INVESTMENT CORPORATION RIYADH (HEAD OFFICE)			可否分批	NOT ALLOWED		
汇票期限	见票___×××___天期			装运期限	APR. 30,2019	唛头	N/M
				有效期	MAY 15,2019		
				有效地点	CHINA		
				提单日 21 天内议付	___天内寄单		

单证名称	提单	副本提单	商业发票	海关发票	装箱单	重量数量单	尺码单	保险单	产地证	普惠制产地证	贸促会产地证	出口许可证	装船通知书	投保通知	寄投保通知邮据	寄单证明	寄样证明	品质证明书	汇票
提交银行	3		3		6			1	1				1					1	2
提交客户																			

注:在"提交银行"或"提交客户"对应的栏目中填写应提交的单据份数,信用证要求提交的单据没有注明份数,默认为1份。

续表

提单	抬头	TO THE ORDER OF ALRAJHI BANKING AND INVESTMENT CORP.	保险	险种	ALL RISKS AND WAR RISK AS PER C.I.C. DATED 1/1/1981		
	通知	NEO GENERAL TRADING CO., P.O. BOX 99552,RIYADH 22766,KSA					
运费支付方式(预付或到付)		(22)FREIGHT PREPAID		投保加成率	20%	赔款地点	DAMMAM PORT, SAUDI ARABIA

注:如果提供的信用证的内容没有涉及信用证分析表的某些栏目,该栏目为空。

三、国际贸易单证填制

SELLER DESUN TRADING CO., LTD., NO.85 GUANJIAQIAO, NANJING 210005,CHINA	商业发票 COMMERCIAL INVOICE			
BUYER NEO GENERAL TRADING CO., P.O. BOX 99552,RIYADH 22766,KSA	INVOICE NO. GF/8-95		INVOICE DATE MAR. 28,2019	
	L/C NO. 0011LC123756		S/C DATE MAR. 17,2019	
	S/C NO. CD512-7		PRICE TERM CIF DAMMAM	
	FROM NINGBO CHINA		TO DAMMAM PORT, SAUDI ARABIA	
MARKS	DESCRIPTION OF GOODS	QUANTITY	UNIT PRICE	AMOUNT
N/M	ROSE BRAND, CANNED MUSHROOM PIECES & STEMS 24 TINS × 425 GRAMS (NET WEIGHT)	1,700CTNS	CIF DAMMAM USD7.80 PER CARTON	USD13,260.00
	TOTAL:	1,700CTNS		USD13,260.00

TOTAL AMOUNT IN WORDS:
(18)SAY U.S. DOLLARS THIRTEEN THOUSAND TWO HUNDRED AND SIXTY ONLY.
(19)FOB VALUE:USD12,810.63   FREIGHT CHARGS:USD194.78   CFR VALUE:USD13,005.41

DESUN TRADING CO., LTD.
代敏

Shipper: DESUN TRADING CO., LTD., NO.85 GUANJIAQIAO,NANJING 210005,CHINA	订舱委托书	
Consignee: TO THE ORDER OF ALRAJHI BANKING AND INVESTMENT CORP.	To:上海货代有限公司/晓峰 我司配载贵司货物如下: 开船日:APR. 28,2019 箱型、箱量:20FCL×1	
Notify: NEO GENERAL TRADING CO., P.O. BOX 99552,RIYADH 22766,KSA	合同号: CD512-7	
	运费: FREIGHT PREPAID	
	Vessel/Voyage: DONGFENG.V342	

Port of Loading NINGBO CHINA	Port of Discharge DAMMAM PORT, SAUDI ARABIA	Transshipment ALLOWED	Partial Shipment ALLOWED	
Marks & Numbers	Description of Goods	No. of Packages	Gross Weight	Meas.
N/M	ROSE BRAND, CANNED MUSHROOM 蘑菇罐头 62451301476	1,700CTNS	20,706.00 KGS	22.440CBM

TOTAL NUMBERS OF CONTAINERS OR PACKAGES:
SAY ONE THOUSAND AND SEVEN HUNDRED CARTONS ONLY.

客户要求

☐ 送货 ☑ 产装 ☑ 代理报关 ☐ 代理报检 ☑ 投保

产品 信息	产装地址及预计日期: NANJING,2019年4月23日 单位名称:DESUN TRADING CO.,LTD. 地址:NO.85 GUANJIAQIAO,NANJING 210005,CHINA 联系人:小章 电话:0086-25-4715004	订舱公司:DESUN TRADING CO.,LTD. 联系人:小章 电话:0086-25-4715004 传真:0086-25-4711363
特殊要求:	签全套清洁已装船海运提单 提单上显示:THE FULL NAME,ADDRESS AND TEL NO. OF THE CARRYING VESSEL'S AGENT AT THE PORT OF DISCHARGE.	